CRITICAL INSIGHTS

The Woman Warrior

by

Maxine Hong Kingston

CRITICAL INSIGHTS

The Woman Warrior

by

Maxine Hong Kingston

Editors

Linda Trinh Moser & Kathryn West

Missouri State University, Springfield

Bellarmine University, Louisville

SALEM PRESS

A Division of EBSCO Information Services, Inc.

Ipswich, Massachusetts

GREY HOUSE PUBLISHING

Publisher's Cataloging-In-Publication Data
(Prepared by The Donohue Group, Inc.)

Names: Moser, Linda Trinh, 1964- editor. | West, Kathryn, 1962- editor.
Title: The woman warrior / editors, Linda Trinh Moser & Kathryn West,
        Missouri State University, Springfield, Bellarmine University,
        Louisville.
Other Titles: Critical insights.
Description: [First edition]. | Ipswich, Massachusetts : Salem Press, a division
        of EBSCO Information Services, Inc. ; Amenia, NY : Grey
        House Publishing, [2016] | Includes bibliographical references
        and index.
Identifiers: ISBN 978-1-68217-394-7 (hardcover)
Subjects: LCSH: Kingston, Maxine Hong.Woman warrior. | Kingston, Maxine
        Hong--Criticism and interpretation. | Feminism in literature. |
        Women and literature--United States--History--20th century. |
        Transnationalism in literature. | Chinese Americans in literature.
Classification: LCC PS3561.I52 W653 2016 | DDC 813/.54--dc23

First Printing

Contents

Resources

About this Volume

Kathryn West

This volume on Maxine Hong Kingston's *The Woman Warrior: Memoirs of a Girlhood Among Ghosts* is being released in the year of the fortieth anniversary of its subject's publication. Although only forty years in the public view, similar to works such as Toni Morrison's *Beloved* (1987), Gabriel García Márquez's *One Hundred Years of Solitude* (1967; 1970 in English), Margaret Atwood's *The Handmaid's Tale* (1985), and John Updike's Rabbit Quartet (1960, 1971, 1981, 1990), *The Woman Warrior* is already considered a classic. In 2007, Jonathan Yardley, book critic for the *Washington Post,* declared that "*The Woman Warrior* is probably one of the most influential books now in print in this country—and certainly one of the most influential books with a valid claim to literary recognition." Garnering almost unprecedented attention on college and university campuses, multiple awards, continued recognition for its author, and critical attention around the world, *The Woman Warrior* continues to engage, delight, and sometimes perplex multiple audiences.

Here we offer a collection of essays designed to illuminate the major themes and stylistic features of *The Woman Warrior*, as well as to apprise readers of the debates and controversies surrounding Kingston's memoir. A key debate in discussions of *The Woman Warrior* has been and continues to be the question of genre. Questions regarding whether this *is* or *is not* memoir, autobiography, fact, truth, fiction, or fairytale—all debates generated in part by the decision publisher Alfred Knopf made to market the work as nonfiction—have been at the forefront of many considerations. Such questions are also pondered here, pushing into fresh territory through links to identity formation and communal versus individual understandings of Self. This volume also considers *The Woman Warrior* as a transnational text and offers explications of its importance to understandings of diaspora and cultural hybridity. Two essays offer comparative readings, one to Amy Tan's *The Joy Luck Club* and the other to Maya Angelou's *All God's Children Need Traveling Shoes*. A number of the essays make connections to Kingston's own later publications. Mother/daughter relationships and feminism, prominent in many discussions of this work, are also given fresh readings here.

Linda Trinh Moser's introduction traces the history and resonance of *The Woman Warrior* since its publication. This is followed by four Critical Contexts essays, providing contextual, historical, and comparative insights, as well as an overview of the critical reception of *The Woman Warrior*. Kathryn West's "Twentieth-Century China and US History, Meet Postmodern Sensibility" seeks out the historical references in the text and fleshes out the events to which they refer. While known for its play with mythical sources, *The Woman Warrior* is also peppered with references to Chinese and US history that resonate with the narrator's experiences. West's essay argues that Kingston's contemplation of these histories both create and are filtered through a postmodern understanding of the world in the narrator's consciousness.

The second context essay, Rickie-Ann Legleitner's "*The Woman Warrior*: An Examination of Genre, Representation, and Reception," surveys criticism on the text. After offering an overview of initial reviews, their tone, and the issues they raise, Legleitner highlights the recurring issues in the scholarship: genre, authenticity and ethnicity, identity, mother/daughter relationships, and feminism. She finds that in every category, critics see *The Woman Warrior* pushing boundaries, with some expressing skepticism for the practice and others finding it a virtue.

Linda Trinh Moser employs a transnational lens to read the fourth section of *The Woman Warrior*, "At the Western Palace." She notes that for Kingston (and her narrator), "cultural negotiation requires reimagining the shape and scope of nations, the cultures associated with them, and the boundaries between them." Moser reaches out to the Chinese myth, "Goddess Chang'e Ascends to the Moon," and to the US popular culture phenomenon of the "I Love Lucy" show to demonstrate that Kingston critiques gender and racial bias in both cultures. Heightening awareness and understanding of the concept of transnationalism, Moser's essay provides a path to several essays in Critical Readings that make reference to *The Woman Warrior* as a transnational text and to the turn in Asian American studies to transnational awareness.

In a continuation of the transnational concept through close reading, David Borman offers a comparative analysis of *The Woman Warrior* and Maya Angelou's *All God's Children Need Traveling Shoes*. Focusing on the respective narrators' attempts to establish a sense of connection to ancestors, he traces the complex paths each must take due to the complicated histories that took place between China and Chinese America, and Ghana and African America. He shows that each text both honors and problematizes the idea of the ancestor. In addition, Borman explores the dynamics of diaspora, a topic also taken up in Christopher Patterson's essay in this volume.

The first essays in the Critical Readings section feature explorations of identity, identity formation, mother/daughter relationships, language and life-writing, and the relationship among all those factors. These essays offer valuable insights on their own, but when read together offer a synergistic dialogue on these key concerns in *The Woman Warrior.*

Our Critical Readings section opens with Anne Rüggemeier, who interrogates the genres of autobiography and life-writing in "Kingston's *The Woman Warrior* in the Context of Life Writing Studies: An Exploration of Relational Selfhood." She addresses the long-standing debates over the "correct" generic designation for *The Woman Warrior* and argues that Kingston uses some of the traditional conventions of autobiography in order to question their very foundations. While the traditional autobiography narrates the development of an individual, Rüggemeier demonstrates that Kingston tells a story of a Self developing in relation to Others. There is an important shift from focus on the individual as individual to focus on an individual existing always as a part of, whether in agreement, reaction, or even opposition to, community. Rüggemeier extends her discussion to illustrate the presence of these same ideas in two of Kingston's later works, *China Men* and *I Love a Broad Margin to My Life*.

Lorna Martens, in "'The Words at My Back': Maxine Hong Kingston's *The Woman Warrior* and the Power of Discourse," explores issues of identity as well, but replaces Rüggemeier's focus on overall genre with attention to the roles of words, stories, talk-story, and writing. Reading each section of the work, Martens explicates Kingston's metaphors, such as tattooing, carving, eating, sitting, telling vs. secrecy, and the "song for a barbarian reed pipe," noting that the complexity of the metaphors increase over the course of the work, coming together in the end with a moving statement about the power of—and need for—discourse, much as the narrator's and her mother's voices come together to tell the final story. Martens reads *The Woman Warrior* as a dramatization of the complexities and the power of negotiating "two cultures, two languages, two sets of values, and two or more conflicting discourses."

Jeffrey Westover's "The Mother's Mark on the Daughter's Speech in *The Woman Warrior*" posits selfhood as fluid, an ongoing negotiation, and achieved socially in response to interactions with others (particularly Brave Orchid, Maxine's mother). He argues that there is a crucial connection between speech and the development of identity, and proceeds to explicate scenes in *The Woman Warrior* that feature the prohibition, incision, and inscription of words. Maxine negotiates her sense of identity through her own relationship to words as well as through the relationship with words and speech of the various female figures, historical and mythical, woven into the five sections. All these instances lead back to her mother, a virtuosic speaker and storyteller herself.

Susanna Hoeness-Krupsaw extends the discussion of Maxine's relationship to her mother to examine it in light of the critical trope of the mother/daughter plot. She reads *The Woman Warrior* alongside Amy Tan's *The Joy Luck Club* and its many mother/daughter relationships. Following an overview of the critical trajectory as it has engaged with the mother/daughter plot, Hoeness-Krupsaw demonstrates that these two texts maintain the necessity of both the daughter's voice and the mother's voice, rather than following past, oedipally-oriented models that insisted on the daughter's voice replacing that of the mother. Similarly, immigration becomes a metaphor for the need for cultural and familial bridges.

"Diaspora and its Others: *The Woman Warrior* and Southeast Asian Diasporic Literature" first discusses shifts in critical understandings and uses of the concept of diaspora and then makes a case for *The Woman Warrior* as a text that rejects a nostalgic view of the homeland and instead engages with the political and social issues present for Chinese people and Chinese Americans at the time of its composition. Christopher B. Patterson then turns to a reading of Lan Cao's *Monkey Bridge*, illustrating how it takes a position similar to *The Woman Warrior* but also satirizes Kingston's work to argue that American racism must be combatted on the way to establishing diasporic identity.

Alex Pinnon offers a shift in critical approach. Much attention to *The Woman Warrior* has focused on teasing out cultural influences. In contrast, "Creating Meaning and Self-Affirmation through Stories: Existentialism and *The Woman Warrior*" highlights a Western philosophical influence that traditionally foregrounds the importance of the individual. Examining each of the major female characters, Pinnon examines how their experiences and reactions can be read as engagements with the major tenets of existentialism, such as the meaning of freedom, free will, self-affirmation, and how to establish individual agency. Thus, in *The Woman Warrior* existentialist thought "also suggest[s] the capacity for humanity to effect positive change in the world."

Next, Nelly Mok explores in *The Woman Warrior* the workings of cultural hybridity, a position that necessitates constant mediation between differing cultural communities. Mok argues for cultural hybridity as requiring an always active engagement that can be taxing, but one that nevertheless holds enormous creative potential. She then illustrates how Kingston channels that creativity into mythopoesis, creating new myths from the interaction between the old versions and new, lived realities. She offers readings of "White Tigers" and "A Song for a Barbarian Reed Pipe" to illustrate Kingston's myth-making, arguing that Kingston's relationship to

Chinese culture may be Americanized in some aspects, but is still truthful.

Our final essay in the Critical Readings section, Elizabeth Rodrigues' "Truths and Tellings: *The Woman Warrior* and Kingston's Transformational Genres of the Real," revisits the controversy over "real" and "fake" versions of stories and realities in order to argue that the intangible may be just as real to a person's experience as the tangible, that 'story' and the 'real' are not opposing categories. Rodrigues reads *Tripmaster Monkey* and *The Fifth Book of Peace* to make the case that Kingston's writing career offers a "persistent critique of narrative forms that constrain the representation and imagination of difference." She sees Kingston as transforming the critique present in *The Woman Warrior* into a type of political action, offering powerful anti-war and anti-racist understandings of the real world.

The concluding section of this volume offers resources designed to provide quick access to facts about Kingston's life and writing. A chronology of Kingston's life is followed by a list of her publications, including books and essays and occasional pieces. A general bibliography then offers suggestions for further reading on Kingston and *The Woman Warrior*.

In keeping with the conventions of criticism on Kingston's work, essays refer to the author as Kingston and the narrator as Maxine; the shortened form of the title is *The Woman Warrior*, not *Woman Warrior*. The five sections of the work feature the narrator at different ages, although they do not proceed completely chronologically. In "No Name Woman," the adult narrator tells of a story her mother told her when she was entering puberty and her reflections on that story over time. In "White Tigers," the adult narrator tells of the fantasy she wove about Fa Mu Lan from the many songs and stories her mother recounted and then recounts her struggles to align the female power in those stories with the misogynistic sayings she has heard growing up in her city's Chinatown. "Shaman" largely recounts Maxine's mother's experiences as a young adult in China, attending medical school, followed by a section describing Maxine's later relationship with her mother, visiting home as an adult. Maxine the narrator is an adult in "At the Western Palace," spinning the story of what happens when Brave Orchid's sister comes to America (both sisters are elderly at this point), out of a sentence her brother told her sister who then passed it along to her: "I drove Mom and Second Aunt to Los Angeles to see Aunt's husband who's got the other wife" (163). In the final section, "A Song for a Barbarian Reed Pipe," the narrator recounts incidents from her life at various ages, centering on her struggles with speech and communication.

Works Cited

Yardley, Jonathan. "'Woman Warrior,' A Memoir That Shook the Genre." *The Washington Post*. The Washington Post Company, 19 June 2007. Web. 1 June 2016. <http://www.washingtonpost.com/wp-dyn/content/article/2007/06/18/AR2007061801713.html>.

THE BOOK
AND
AUTHOR

On Maxine Hong Kingston's *The Woman Warrior*

Linda Trinh Moser

Since its publication forty years ago, Maxine Hong Kingston's *The Woman Warrior: Memoirs of a Girlhood Among Ghosts* has become a widely read and much discussed and debated work that has generated a large body of scholarship devoted to its interpretation. When *The Woman Warrior* appeared, two important social movements were gaining ground and attracting increasingly more public attention: multiculturalism and feminism. Kingston's work voiced the concerns of both. At the time, very few American readers were familiar with the cultural details and traditions evoked in its pages nor were they accustomed to Kingston's representation of an American identity strongly rooted in Chinese traditions, which she would, years after publication, specify as "a transplanted oral culture, of the Say Yup (Cantonese) immigrants in California" (Lim, Preface x).

 The Woman Warrior is Kingston's first and still most successful book. She composed it while teaching English and language arts in Honolulu, Hawai'i. Based on her mother's "talk-story," *The Woman Warrior* weaves together elements of auto/biography, fiction, history, and myth and is divided into five sections, each featuring a female figure based on a family member or from myth. The first section, "No Name Woman," depicts the events leading to the suicide of the narrator's paternal aunt who becomes pregnant out of wedlock and gives birth to an illegitimate child. The second, "White Tigers," adapts the story of Fa Mu Lan, a legendary Chinese female warrior, and describes her specialized training and experiences on the battlefield. This section also imagines the famed woman warrior's marriage, childbirth, and devotion to her parents. "Shaman," the third section, follows Brave Orchid, the narrator's mother, from China, where she studies and practices medicine, to Stockton, California, where she raises six children and helps to run a family business.

Her sister, Moon Orchid, is the subject of the fourth section, "At the Western Palace," which depicts her experiences after she crosses the Pacific Ocean from Hong Kong in pursuit of a husband from whom she has been separated for thirty years. The last section, "A Song for a Barbarian Reed Pipe," details the narrator's childhood experiences before closing with a story about the early third century Chinese poet Ts'ai Yen, which combines the voices of the narrator and her mother.

Initial Acclaim and Criticism

The Woman Warrior received the National Book Critics Circle Award for best work of general nonfiction in 1976 after having been favorably reviewed by multiple media organizations. In the pages of *Newsweek*, for example, Walter Clemons proclaimed it "a book of fierce clarity and originality" (109). Paul Gray of *Time* described it as "astonishingly accomplished," praising it for "giv[ing]. . . voice" to "a generation of embarrassed silence." The book also found a fan in John Leonard of the *New York Times* who found it to be "dizzying, elemental" and "one of the best I've read for years" (69). Since then, Kingston's work has been a fixture in classrooms on many college campuses. A commonly held perception is that *The Woman Warrior* is "the book by a living author most widely taught in American universities and colleges" (Scalise), as noted by then-US poet laureate Robert Hass on the occasion of Kingston's receiving the National Humanities Medal in 1997 from President Bill Clinton. This observation had been made earlier by Bill Moyers, who reported that *The Woman Warrior* and Kingston's second work, *China Men*, are "among the most widely taught books by a living American author on college campuses today" (Kingston, "Maxine Hong Kingston on Memory"). Although Kingston is not featured on the list of "the 100 Most-Read Female Writers in College Classes," the result of a recent *Time* magazine survey of "1.1 million college syllabi collected by the *Open Syllabus Project*" (Johnson), *The Woman Warrior* has clearly been established as part of the academic literary canon and is taught across multiple disciplines. A 1991 Modern Language Association survey revealed that it:

> is taught in a wide range of courses, from lower-division courses for majors and nonmajors to upper-division electives and graduate seminars," and across "a number of departments, chiefly those of English literature, American culture and thought, women's studies, and ethnic studies." (Lim, *Approaches* 8)

Another common pedagogical use of *The Woman Warrior* is serving as a model in composition and creative writing courses. Its extensive appearance in classrooms has led Laura Hyun Yi Kang to describe Kingston as one of the "disciplinary brand names as Chaucer, Milton, and Shakespeare" (30).

The positive reception by the press and teachers is echoed by scholars in the field of literary studies who take note of the work's popularity and its primacy in the field of Asian American literature. King-kok Cheung proclaims *The Woman Warrior* to be "the first Asian American work to receive astounding national acclaim" ("Reviewing" 10). Elaine H. Kim describes it as "a crucible for Asian American issues" and notes it "has achieved status as an American literary classic; a top profit-maker for its publishers [and] standard text in American literature courses across the country" (79). The work continues to generate a large scholarly output today. A recent search (June 2016) of the MLA Bibliographic Database, using the search terms, "The Woman Warrior" as the primary subject and "Kingston" as the secondary, resulted in 271 items, including fifteen dissertations. This is twice as many as a similar search conducted by Sau-ling Cynthia Wong in 1999 using the same database; it "yielded 132 items under 'The Woman Warrior.'" Wong's earlier search also identified 185 under a separate search using "'Kingston'" (12, n. 2).

Despite these accolades and praise from the mainstream press and literary scholars, *The Woman Warrior* has also received a great deal of negative criticism. One debate centers on the issue of "authenticity" in Kingston's representation of Chinese and Chinese American culture, particularly her adaptations of the story of Fa Mu Lan and Ngak Fei (Yue Fei) depicted in "White Tigers." This debate has been well documented by Cheung (*Articulate Silences*), Ling ("Dialogic Dilemma"), and Wong ("Autobiography"); in this volume, see Legleitner, "*The Woman Warrior*: An Examination of Genre, Representation, and Reception." The negative criticism, predominately from the Asian American community, is iterated in three general ways: "this writer is a traitor to the community and to the cause; she's not telling the story right or she's telling the wrong one. . . she's falling into stereotypes and catering to base appetites for the exotic and the barbaric" (Ling 153). In addition, while critics appreciate the imaginative aspects of Kingston's stories, they take issue with what is believed to be a claim for representation of all Chinese and Chinese Americans. "As fiction, these stories are creatively written," Katheryn M. Fong writes in an open letter to Kingston, "The problem is that non-Chinese are reading your fiction as true accounts. . . . Your one experience, your one story, becomes the definitive description of all of us" (67). Although Kingston is well aware of the negative criticism directed at her and her work, she has not engaged in debating individual detractors. And in the works published after *The Woman Warrior*, she continues to engage her experimentation with genre and to highlight a subjective representation of Chinese American culture and identity.

Issues and Themes

When interpreting *The Woman Warrior,* readers must take to heart Lim's admonition that *The Woman Warrior* "is not. . . . the definitive Asian American text in the canon of American literature," nor is it "the only work needed for students and teachers to understand the Asian contribution to American civilization" ("Preface" ix). Furthermore, readers cannot—and should not—avoid questions related to cultural representation, an issue that overlaps and intersects with a range of themes engaged by Kingston. The debate over *The Woman Warrior* includes a fair amount of discussion about its genre. Kingston's detractors take issue with the categorization of the work as nonfiction. The cover of the original 1977 edition announced it to be "[t]he best book of nonfiction published in 1976," while the back cover described its classification as "autobiography." For the

1989 edition, the classification on the back cover was changed to "nonfiction/literature." Traditional autobiography is a chronological recounting that focuses on the factual details of a writer's entire life. A quick glance at *The Woman Warrior* reveals that it does not conform to this description. Rather than describing a year-by-year sequence of the narrator's life—from birth to adulthood—the narrator focuses on the experiences of five female characters, one of whom (Fa Mu Lan) is based on legend rather than on a figure in the historical record. The narrator is furthermore never identified by name (although most scholars use the accepted convention of referring to her as "Maxine").

The work's subtitle, "Memoirs of a Girlhood Among Ghosts," announces Kingston's obvious intention to deviate from traditional autobiography, a detail to be reckoned with in any interpretation of the work. Memoir, although a type of autobiographical writing, displays key differences. First, memoir generally covers a narrower span of time. In addition, rather than relaying objective facts and a chronological rendering of one person's life, memoir relies much more on the writer's subjective experiences. Fact is not the only foundation of *The Woman Warrior*. Even the female figures who have counterparts in the historical record and family history are rendered through the imagination of the narrator. Kingston's version of Ts'ai Yen, for example, is a "matter of selective focus" (Wong, "Kingston's Handling" 33), which highlights immigration and cultural fusion, two themes important to Kingston's representation of Chinese American identity. By making explicit her reliance on memories, imagination, and emotions throughout *The Woman Warrior*, Kingston suggests that stories, fantasy, and subjective experience are as much a part of reality as objective fact.

Kingston's use of literary technique in her memoir made a profound impact on the genre of memoir, changing its status as "a relatively minor genre in American literature," associated with "an older person's—an older man's—genre" (Yardley). The infusion of fantasy and myth suggests the influence of postmodernist fiction, especially in *The Woman Warrior*'s nonlinear presentation of events, blurring of fact and fiction, and emphasis on intertextuality, especially in the narrator's attempt to understand and represent her identity through her mother's talk-story. Kingston undercuts the literary aspects of her work by citing practical reasons for her obfuscation of fact. "I was thinking," she claims, "that if immigration authorities read my books they could not find evidence to deport my parents" (Alegre &Weich). Practical reasons notwithstanding, Kingston continually uses techniques associated with another postmodern hallmark: metafiction (imaginative writing whose central focus is the creation of fiction). The narrator undercuts, questions, and highlights her own elaborations in each of the five sections, emphasizing the idea that she is talking-story rather than relaying fact based on an objective reality. For example, soon after offering an image of her paternal aunt as "a wild woman" seeking to fulfill her desire in an extramarital affair, the narrator takes it back: "Imagining her free with sex doesn't fit, though. I don't know any women like that, or men either" (8). Kingston calls attention to the blurring of fiction and nonfiction in other ways. The rendering of Brave Orchid and her sister, Moon Orchid, while based on Kingston's mother and aunt, are strategically linked to "Fa Mu Lan, whose given name, Mu Lan, if translated literally character by character, would be Sylvan Orchid" (Wong, "Kingston's Handling" 32). The association of the legendary female warrior with the three female figures signals the narrator's manipulation of the representation of her family members. It also signals her interest in acknowledging in positive terms the lives of women and immigrants.

By focusing on female life stories and giving voice to concerns associated with women, *The Woman Warrior* echoes a larger body of literature giving support to feminism and the women's movement. In particular, through her reconstruction and consideration of the lives of other Chinese women before her, the narrator begins to undermine and revise the negative messages associated with her gender. She exposes sexist traditional practices from traditional China to contemporary America. In her reconstruction of China of the past, women are subjected to rape, slavery, and infanticide. In the Chinese immigrant community in Stockton, California, misogyny is part of everyday conversation and casual talk-story.

The narrator grows up trying to resist a barrage of sexist maxims and sayings: "Feeding girls is feeding cowbirds"; "There's no profit in raising girls. Better to raise geese than girls"; "When you raise girls, you're raising children for strangers" (46); and "When fishing for treasures in the flood, be careful not to pull in girls" (52). The denigration of girls and women is not, however, relegated to the past or to Chinese culture. *The Woman Warrior*'s narrator suggests correlations between practices related to female standards of beauty in China and the US. The practice of foot-binding, which leaves women physically disabled, is founded on the same kind of pressure to be attractive that the narrator feels "to turn [her]self American-feminine, or no dates" (47). This also can be damaging in physical and psychological terms. The narrator's strategy against the negative messages takes many forms. One is to embody characteristics that are deemed negative female attributes. In an attempt to appear not "marriageable" (190), for example, the narrator exhibits an inability to perform the basic domestic tasks traditionally (in China and the US) defined as women's work. "I dropped dishes," the narrator reveals, "I picked my nose while I was cooking and serving. My clothes were wrinkled even though [my family] owned a laundry" (190).

In addition to her reverse strategy, the narrator combats negative images through her consideration and reconstruction of Chinese culture. Seeing a gap she can take advantage of in the contradictory messages about girls and women, the narrator strategically reworks Chinese myth and talk-story to uncover models of female strength and ingenuity. Fa Mu Lan battles and wins against tyrants. Brave Orchid challenges social norms in China, where she earns a medical degree, and in the US, where she establishes a family despite prejudice against Chinese immigrants. Even the no name woman, whose story depicts her victimization, enacts revenge on her persecutors by contaminating the village well, "drowning herself in the drinking water" (16). Originating her "American" life story in Chinese culture is significant and reflects a rejection of racism in addition to sexism while also promoting an understanding of

American identity that Kingston has had since childhood, "the idea that you don't have to be white to be an American" (Martin).

China Men: Companion Volume to The Woman Warrior

Although *The Woman Warrior* is often read as a stand-alone work, it was conceived as one part of a larger work that would include *China Men*. "To best appreciate *The Woman Warrior*," Kingston asserts, "you do need to read *China Men*" ("Personal Statement," 23). Published separately in 1980, it was awarded the National Book Award for nonfiction in 1981 and exhibits the same thematic interests and narrative strategies as *The Woman Warrior*. Kingston shares that the connection between the works began from their inception, revealing, "I wrote much of those two books at the same time. I once meant for them to be one large book" ("Personal Statement" 24). Like *The Woman Warrior*, *China Men* wanders from a strict chronology and extends the exploration of family members begun by the narrator in the earlier work. The narrator centers it not on her mother but on her father, as she traces the experiences of her male relatives from her "[v]ery great grandfathers" in China (*China Men* 47) and great grandfathers, immigrants who harvested sugar cane in Hawai'i and lay track for the first transcontinental railroad, to a brother who served in the Vietnam War. Referring to them as "Men Warriors," Alfred S. Wang draws a strong connection between Kingston's female and male relatives, the latter whom he describes as "defiant of being outlawed, emasculated, even silenced, [and] were claiming forthright their shares of the American dream" (19).

Like its predecessor, *China Men* opens with the narrator's attempt to reconstruct a story that has been repressed. Her father is unwilling to speak about his life in China and immigration to the US. She tells him: "You say with the few words and the silence: No stories. No past. No China" (14). Resisting not only his silence, but also the "silence" imposed on Chinese immigrants by mainstream accounts of American history, the narrator deploys a mixture of family stories, myth, fantasy, legal writings, and memoir to conjure a version of her father's immigration to the US. She comes up with five, some legal, others not. The work implicates social discrimination against Chinese male immigrants as the reason for the father's silence. To make her point, Kingston includes a long list of anti-Chinese exclusion laws from 1968 to 1978 in the middle of the work, again merging historical detail with family lore. The difficulties and racism imposed on Chinese immigrants who make the US their permanent home suggest why she would eventually downplay illegal methods of entering the country and insist that he came, "a legal way" (53).

In addition to protesting the racist practices used against her relatives and other male immigrants, Kingston's use of Chinese myth in *China Men* also includes strong objections to patriarchy, continuing this theme from her first book. In "On Discovery," Kingston adapts details from the Chinese classic, "Flowers in the Mirror," to draw out the unfair and racist treatment in the US of the immigrant generation from China. In Kingston's version, Tang Ao is captured after "discovering" the "Land of Women," reputed to be located in North America, where he is captured and "forced" to take the role of a woman in service to the queen. Kingston's version renders his transformation as torture: he undergoes ear-piercing, foot-binding, depilatory procedures, and the objective gaze of the opposite sex who comment about him: "She's pretty, don't you agree?" (10). Implicit in the gender role reversal is criticism of the oppression of women. In addition, it draws out a motif that runs throughout *China Men*: the socially enforced emasculation of Chinese immigrants. By paralleling the experiences of Chinese male immigrants to that of women under patriarchy, Kingston demonstrates the similarities between racism and sexism: they both depend upon the subjugation of another.

Thematic Connections to Kingston's Other Works

Apparent in *The Woman Warrior* are Kingston's activism and her interest in social justice issues, especially those related to gender and race. These interests resonate throughout her other works as does her exploration of identity and its relationship to family, culture, and nation. In addition, Kingston's later works continue to challenge traditional distinctions between fiction and nonfiction, myth and history, and personal and communal stories. An examination of her later work expands and enriches readers' understanding of the experiment in form and theme she initiated in *The Woman Warrior.*

Tripmaster Monkey: His Fake Book (1989), Kingston's first novel, continues her exploration of Chinese American experience but without the forays into family history and the memoir genre. Although Kingston has cited autobiographical connections—for example, her own experiments as a "tripmaster," someone "who suggests trips for [people taking recreational drugs] and who guides them and keeps them from flipping out" (Schroeder 204) —the work is clearly fiction. In creating her protagonist, Kingston also draws from both Eastern and Western traditions. Wittman is the Monkey King, the mythical figure famous for helping to bring Buddhist scriptures to China. Like the Monkey King, Wittman brings "foreign" writing westward to the US. The name Wittman Ah Sing also pays homage to poet Walt Whitman and "Song of Myself." To enact his namesake's project ("I Celebrate myself, and sing myself"), Wittman has to bridge the cultures that influence his identity. This is, of course, the project the narrator of *The Woman Warrior* has undertaken. In an interview Kingston says: "I feel that I have had to translate a whole Eastern culture and bring it to the West, then bring the two cultures together seamlessly. That is how one makes the Asian American culture" (Alegre & Weich). The interplay of Chinese and Western sources and experiences, a hallmark of *The Woman Warrior*, is also a way to challenge those who refuse to see fifth-generation Wittman as American.

For the book following *Tripmaster Monkey*, Kingston's intention had been to write another novel, tentatively called *The Fourth Book of Peace*, continuing the story of Wittman's life. She had decided upon "fiction, because Peace is supposed, imagined, divined, dreamed" (*Fifth Book* 61). But in 1991, while attending a funeral ceremony honoring her father, the manuscript, "156 good pages" (1), was destroyed by a firestorm that ravaged the Oakland-Berkeley Hills along with her home and other possessions. Emerging from the ashes is *The Fifth Book of Peace* (2003). Like *The Woman Warrior*, it blurs the boundaries between memory and fiction as

Kingston attends to her grief and losses—psychological, physical, and spiritual. In "Fire," the first of four sections, Kingston meditates on narrative form, revealing: "After the fire, I could not re-enter fiction," which she had come to associate with "the selfish first person, author, narrator, protagonist, one" (61-62). Thus, for *The Fifth Book of Peace*, Kingston (who corresponds more overtly to her book persona than to those in her first published works) searches for a new form inspired by "a community of like minds. The Book of Peace, to be reconstructed, needs community" (62).

The process of healing that emerges resembles the narrative strategies she employed in *The Woman Warrior*. In "Paper," the second section, Kingston looks to Chinese legend for inspiration as she did in her first book. As she describes and searches for three legendary "Lost Books of Peace," reported also to have been "lost in deliberate fires" (44), she comes to understand writing as a way to build community and enact social change. Kingston puts this understanding into practice by establishing a writing workshop for veterans and survivors of war. This project, described in the fourth section, "Earth," also has its antecedents in *The Woman Warrior*. The latter's thematic interest in finding voice correlates with Kingston's desire to help others speak out in writing. The fiction, essays, and poems written by workshop participants appear in *Veterans of War, Veterans of Peace* (2006), edited by Kingston.

Kingston, too, finds her ability to speak out for peace by participating in a 2003 Washington, DC-based protest against the war in Iraq. She describes this and her subsequent arrest and imprisonment with fellow writers Terry Tempest Williams and Alice Walker in her "Epilogue." The descriptions of Kingston's activism notably appear after "Water," the third section, which presents the recreated manuscript lost to fire. Here, she is able to do what she could not just after the fire: "re-enter fiction." "Water" picks up the story of Wittman Ah Sing, who is now older and living with his wife and son in Hawai'i where he has escaped the draft. Waging peace, he establishes a sanctuary for American servicemen seeking to escape the war in Vietnam. In a testament to the power of imaginative writing to change the world, Kingston orders the sections of *The Fifth*

Book of Peace so that imagination—embodied by the reconstructed novel—precedes action. Without the power to dream, improvise, or imagine, there can be no peace according to Kingston: "The reasons for peace, the definitions of peace, the very idea of peace have to be invented, and invented again" (402).

Revisiting Fa Mu Lan

Kingston's two most recent works, *To Be the Poet* (2002) and *I Love a Broad Margin to My Life* (2011) include details that extend the story of Fa Mu Lan told in *The Woman Warrior*. These works, like Kingston's first, signal the importance of Fa Mu Lan as a source of inspiration and as a central figure in her life story while also employing the kind of genre-mixing she began early in her career with *The Woman Warrior*. *To Be the Poet* surprisingly adds poetry to her prose in a playful exploration of the process of creating meaning through art. In this work, based on her William E. Massey Sr. Lecture in the History of American Civilization at Harvard University, Kingston draws from the tradition of auto/biographical writing by offering details from her life: descriptions of quotidian events, brief mentions of friends, thoughts about her late parents, and descriptions of her travels. She also shares some examples of her attempts to write verse in the section, "Spring Harvest," which includes a revision of Fa Mu Lan, rendered as Fa Mook Lan (a spelling that replicates the oral tradition in its rendering of how the name is spoken): "Sparing her dear father / the wretched life of a soldier / she disguises herself as a man, / and goes in his stead to war" (108-9). In *The Woman Warrior*, Fa Mu Lan never reveals herself to be a woman to the army she leads; however in this version, she dresses in "pretty silks," adorns herself with flowers and makeup, before announcing to her men: "I was the general who led you" (110). In revealing her undisguised self, she encourages them to "come home from war." Kingston describes a strong connection between the revision, the new emphasis on pacifism, and choice of genre as she ends *To Be the Poet*: "If I hadn't put myself into a poetic state, I wouldn't have thought to end this way. I went through a poetry door and came out of the war story" (110-111).

Kingston also felt free to make changes to her earlier version of Fa Mu Lan in *I Love a Broad Margin to My Life* (2011), which also employs the strategy of combining fact and fiction while erasing the boundaries between them. In one example, she allows the protagonist of *China Men*, Wittman Ah Sing, to narrate an actual trip to China made by Kingston. In another updated version of Fa Mu Lan (rendered again as "Fa Mook Lan"), Kingston presents her as a victim of "P.T.S.D," explaining that "her soldier's heart broke / and she fell upon her sword" (211). This version is more overt in expressing Kingston's peace activism by drawing a connection between the woman warrior's experience to the reality experienced by war veterans. "This month, / May 2009, more American soldiers died by / their own hand than killed by Iraqis and Al Qaeda," Kingston reveals in verse, "So far this year, 62 suicides, / more than half of them National Guard; / 138 in 2008" (211). Kingston also revisits a scene from the "No Name Woman" section of *The Woman Warrior* in her description of a trip to the well where "[her] aunt killed herself, and she killed the baby" (169). But rather than reinforce the historical veracity of the earlier story, she surprisingly undercuts it in her observation that "[her] aunt / with the baby couldn't possibly have jumped into / a well this shallow, and drowned" (169).

At the risk of undermining her authority or upsetting and changing meanings established by her stories, Kingston continues in all her writing the process of questioning and revision employed in each section of *The Woman Warrior*. In this way, she resists the assumption that an ethnic American writer should serve as a guide whose sole purpose is to provide historical fact and anthropological information for her readers. About her original depiction of Fa Mu Lan, Kingston has said: "There are omissions that I'm sorry I didn't think of until long after I'd finished *The Woman Warrior*. I don't know why I didn't write down such obvious, important details" ("Personal Statement" 25). By actively insisting on improvisation and imagination and by seeking new ways to combine different modes of writing based in both fact and fiction, Kingston allows the possibility for her stories to remain relevant. She also paves the way for future versions of Fa Mu Lan and other women and men warriors. Through imagination, Kingston and her stories will adapt to any context: social, historical, and cultural.

Works Cited

Alegre, Miel & Dave Weich. "Maxine Hong Kingston After the Fire." Interview with Maxine Hong Kingston. *PowellsBooks.Blog*. Powells. com, 10 October 2006. Web. 15 May 2016. <http://www.powells. com/post/interviews/maxine-hong-kingston-after-the-fire>. Print.

Cheung, King-kok. *Articulate Silences: Hisaye Yamamoto, Maxine Hong Kingston, Joy Kogawa*. Ithaca, NY: Cornell UP, 1993. Print.

_____. "Reviewing Asian American Literary Studies." *An Interethnic Companion to Asian American Literature*. Ed. King-kok Cheung. Cambridge, UK: Cambridge UP, 1997. 1-36. Print.

Clemons, Walter. "East Meets West: *The Woman Warrior: Memoirs of a Girlhood Among Ghosts*." *Newsweek* (11 Oct.1976): 109. Print.

Fong, Katheryn M. "A Open Letter / Review." *Bulletin of Concerned Asian American Scholars* 9.4 (1977): 67-69. Print.

Gray, Paul. "Book of Changes." Review of *The Woman Warrior*. *Time*. Time Inc., 6 Dec. 1976. Web. 1 June 2016.<http://content.time.com/ time/magazine/article/0,9171,911897,00.html>. Print.

Johnson, David. "These Are the 100 Most-Read Female Writers in College Classes." *Time*. Time Inc., 25 Feb. 2016. Web. 1 June 2016.<http:// time.com/4234719/college-textbooks-female-writers/>. Print.

Kang, Laura Hyun Yi. *Compositional Subjects: Enfiguring Asian/ American Women*. Durham, NC: Duke UP, 2002. Print.

Kim, Elaine H. "Such Opposite Creatures": Men and Women in Asian American Literature. *Michigan Quarterly Review* 29.1 (Winter 1990): 68-93. Print.

Kingston, Maxine Hong. *China Men*. 1980. New York: Vintage/Random, 1989. Print.

_____. *The Fifth Book of Peace*. New York: Knopf, 2003. Print.

_____. *I Love a Broad Margin to My Life*. New York: Vintage/ Random, 2011. Print.

_____. *To Be the Poet*. The William E. Massey Sr. Lectures in the History of American Civilization. Cambridge: Harvard UP, 2002. Print.

_____. *Tripmaster Monkey: His Fake Book*. New York: Knopf, 1989. Print.

_____. "Personal Statement." Lim, *Approaches*. 23-25. Print.

Leonard, John. "In Defiance for 2 Worlds." *New York Times*. Travel Section (17 Sept.1976): 69. Print.

Lim, Shirley Geok-lin. *Approaches to Teaching Kingston's* The Woman Warrior. New York: Modern Language Association, 1991.

_____. "Preface to the Volume." Lim, *Approaches*, ix-xi.

Ling, Amy. "Maxine Hong Kingston and the Dialogic Dilemma of Asian American Writers." *Ideas of Home: Literature of Asian Migration*. Ed. Geoffrey Kain. East Lansing: Michigan State UP. 141-56.

Martin, Michel. "Maxine Hong Kingston Takes Pride in Mixed Heritage." Interview with Maxine Hong Kingston. *Tell Me More*. NPR, 4 Jul. 2007. Web. 1 June 2016. <http://www.npr.org/templates/story/story.php?storyId=11732740>.

Moyers, Bill. "Maxine Hong Kingston on Memory, Meditation and Magic (Part One)." *Moyers & Company*. Public Square Media, Inc., 25 Feb. 1990. Web. 1 June 2016. <http://billmoyers.com/content/maxine-hong-kingston-part-1/>.

Scalise, Kathleen. "The Humanities Medal For Kingston." *Berkeleyan*. The Regents of the University of California, 1 Oct. 1997. Web. 1 June 2016. <http://www.berkeley.edu/news/berkeleyan/1997/1001/kingston.html>.

Schroeder, Eric. "As Truthful as Possible: An Interview with Maxine Hong Kingston." *Conversations with Maxine Hong Kingston*. Ed. Paul Skenazy & Tera Martin. Jackson: UP of Mississippi, 1998. 215-228. Print.

Wang, Alfred S. "Maxine Hong Kingston's Reclaiming of America: The Birthright of the Chinese American Male." *South Dakota Review* 26.1 (1988): 18-29.

Wong, Sau-Ling C. "Autobiography as Guided Chinatown Tour? Maxine Hong Kingston's *The Woman Warrior* and the Chinese American Autobiography Controversy." *Multicultural Lives Autobiography: American Lives*. Ed. James Robert Payne. Knoxville: U of Tennessee P, 1992. 248-279. Rpt. in Wong, *Maxine Hong Kingston's* The Woman Warrior, 29-53.

_____. "Kingston's Handling of Traditional Chinese Sources." Lim, *Approaches*, 26-36.

_____. *Maxine Hong Kingston's* The Woman Warrior: *A Casebook.* New York and Oxford: Oxford UP, 1999.

_____. "Necessity and Extravagance in Maxine Hong Kingston's *Woman Warrior*: Art and the Ethnic Experience." *MELUS* 15.1 (1988): 3-26.

Yardley, Jonathan. "'Woman Warrior,' A Memoir That Shook the Genre." *The Washington Post.* The Washington Post Company, 19 June 2007. Web. 1 June 2016. <http://www.washingtonpost.com/wp-dyn/content/article/2007/06/18/AR2007061801713.html>.

Maxine Hong Kingston: A Biography_____

Kathryn West

In keeping, perhaps, with the fear of deportation on the part of many immigrants to the US and perhaps out of a family delight in spinning many different versions of a story, the 'facts' about Maxine Hong Kingston's parents' early lives exist in multiple versions in different sources. We know that Tom Hong and Ying Lan Chew originated in Sun Woi, in western Guangdong (Canton), China, speaking the Say Yup dialect that Kingston herself would speak exclusively until being sent to school at about five years of age. Tom (who, in the US, took that name as a tribute to Thomas Edison, whom he admired) received extensive training as a scholar in China, learning in great depth the Chinese classics. He worked as a teacher and scholar in their village. The couple had two children, but in 1924, Tom traveled to North America with other male relatives, working odd jobs until he was able to buy into a laundry in New York City with three other Chinese men. While he was there, their two young children in China died and Ying Lan decided to attend To Keung School of Medicine and Midwifery, where she became a doctor trained in Chinese and Western practices. She served as a doctor in her own and surrounding villages, including during a time as a refugee from the disruptions caused by the Japanese invasion of 1931; she served as a medic, treating people in caves, during the war. In 1939, she was able to join her husband in New York, coming into the US via Angel Island in California, then traveling across country by train. One story claims that Tom had won her visa in a gambling game; another version says she bribed her way onto a ship bound for San Francisco just as World War II was about to escalate. As had her husband before her, Ying Lan discovered that there was no interest in the US in the scholarly and medical training received in China; both were forced into manual labor jobs. Within a year of Ying Lan's arrival, she was pregnant with Maxine, and Tom found himself cheated out of his interest in the laundry. Together they moved to California, where

Maxine Ting Ting Hong was born in Stockton, California, October 27, 1940. She is the eldest of six children born to the couple in America.

Tom first managed a gambling house in Stockton, but then the family operated the New Port Laundry for many years, where eventually Maxine and the rest of the children would put in many hours: "It was *awfully* hard work," Kingston reported to Susan Brownmiller (210). The laundry also became a gathering place for the Chinese community in Stockton, providing Kingston with the opportunity to hear the community's stories, memories, songs, and gossip (Simmons 6; Huntley 5). Outside the laundry, the south side of Stockton was a tough neighborhood: "It was no suburban, middle-class background," Diane Simmons reports from Kingston, noting that the painter Rupert Garcia, whose years at Edison High overlapped with Kingston's, called it "horrific" (Simmons 9). In a number of her essays and interviews, Kingston has discussed the fighting and racism she experienced there, including "dead slum people" (*WW* 51). And yet, she has also stressed the strong sense of community in the "Chinatown" of Stockton and the delight in celebrations, ceremonies, and play.

Like so many other contemporary ethnic American writers, Kingston has spoken of the crucial discovery of a voice speaking to and of her experiences. In her case, it was Jade Snow Wong's *Fifth Chinese Daughter* (1945), an autobiographical story of a Chinese American girl growing up in the 1930s. She has described her experience reading Louisa May Alcott's *Little Women* before that discovery, first reveling in her identification with the March sisters until she was "reading along . . . when I came across this funny-looking little Chinaman. It popped out of the book. I'd been pushed into my place. I was him, I wasn't those March girls" (Hoy 62).

On the other hand, reading *Fifth Chinese Daughter*, "saved my life." It gave her the opportunity:

> for the first time [to] see a person somewhat like myself in literature. I had been trying to write about people who were blonde, or a beautiful redhead on her horse, because those were the people who were in

the books. So I was lucky that at a young age I could see a Chinese American. (62)

Kingston has also spoken extensively of the influence on her thinking and writing of Walt Whitman, William Carlos Williams, and Virginia Woolf. In particular, she singles out Woolf's *Orlando* as a book she goes back to over and over, in appreciation of its gender bending and other boundary breaking.

The other looming influence Kingston has identified over and over in her writing and interviews is war. She was born in the middle of World War II, grew up hearing her mother's stories of the Japanese invasion of China, and then read letters from China relatives about the Communist Revolution and the Cultural Revolution. She describes air raid drills during the Korean War (1950–53), when she and other children wore dog tags, "so we'd be identified if we were killed" (Jaggi). Two of her brothers and one brother-in-law were drafted into the Vietnam War, while another brother went to Canada. Her reaction to these and later wars has been to try to figure out peace for herself and for others.

At fifteen, Kingston began her career as a writer with an essay entitled "I Am an American," winning her a five dollar prize from the Girl Scouts and publication in their *American Girl* magazine. After graduating from Stockton's Edison High School in 1958, Kingston entered the University of California, Berkeley, in 1958, with eleven scholarships, some of which were journalism scholarships that were also a result of her writing. She began as an engineering student, mostly to please her parents, but ended up changing to English, even though she describes feeling guilty about the choice, as it was something she loved and it was easy for her; she felt she had been socialized to believe work wasn't worthwhile unless it was difficult.

In 1962, after graduation from Berkeley, Kingston married Earll Kingston, an actor, on November 23. Their son, Joseph Lawrence Cheung Mei, was born in 1964. That same year, Kingston returned to UC Berkeley for a teaching certificate. During both stretches as a student at UC Berkeley, Kingston joined the Free Speech Movement (FSM), admired the "stream-of-consciousness monologues of the comedian Lenny Bruce" (Simmons 11), and marched for civil rights and against the Vietnam War. Kingston also participated in the drug culture of the times, especially psychedelics. At times she acted as "tripmaster," a person, Kingston describes, "who suggests trips for [those on acid] and who guides them and keeps them from flipping out. I feel that I myself was very good at doing that. . . . I wanted to make sure that they did not go to any dangerous places, make sure they went to beautiful places with flowers and music and birds" (Seshachari 18). Her third book, the novel *Tripmaster Monkey*, draws its title and some of its content from these experiences.

After stints teaching in Hayward, California, Earll and Maxine Kingston decided to move to Hawai'i as a way to "drop out" of the US participation in the Vietnam War and escape the increasingly violent drug culture. In Hawai'i, however, they discovered that in some respects, they had come even closer to the war: the islands were a holding space and medical post for soldiers going to, on leave, or returning from the Vietnam War. Earll and Maxine eventually founded a kind of sanctuary for soldiers who had gone AWOL. Neither Earll nor Maxine looked for jobs when they first arrived in Hawai'i, attempting to live the sixties ideal of divorcing themselves from mainstream lifestyles. Eventually, Maxine took a series of teaching jobs at high schools and vocational schools. She was at Mid-Pacific Institute in 1976, when *The Woman Warrior: Memoirs of a Girlhood Among Ghosts* was published. Earll acted in various productions on the islands and in television series, such as *Hawaii Five-0* and *Magnum, P.I.*

Despite being a first book from an unknown writer, *The Woman Warrior* quickly became a publishing sensation, thanks in large part to a *New York Times Magazine* review by John Leonard, who declared, "this week a remarkable book has been quietly published; it is one of the best I've read in years. . . . It is fierce intelligence, all sinew, prowling among the emotions" (Skandera-Trombley 77). *The Woman Warrior* then received the National Book Critics Circle Award for 1976 and has remained the subject of worldwide acclaim and interest, and some controversy, since. (For more on controversies, see in this volume the introduction by Linda Trinh Moser and Rickie-

Ann Legleitner's "*The Woman Warrior*: An Examination of Genre, Representation, and Reception.") In the immediate years after its publication, Kingston and *The Woman Warrior* received a National Education Association Award, the *Mademoiselle* Magazine Award (both 1977), the Anisfield-Wolf Race Relations Award (1978), and a ranking in the top ten of nonfiction works of the decade from *Time*. In 1980, Kingston received an even rarer honor, being named by a Buddhist sect a "Living Treasure of Hawai'i." She was thirty-nine at the time; most honorees have been past eighty.

When *The Woman Warrior* was published, Kingston was already 200 typed manuscript pages into her next book, *China Men*, which recounts through a mixture of myth, history, legend, and different versions of family stories, the lives of the men in her family. In numerous interviews, Kingston has said she originally envisioned the two books as one, and that they should most properly be read together. *China Men* received the National Book Award for nonfiction in 1980 and, the next year, the American Book Award. Kingston has continued to receive many, many awards and honors over the decades, including a Guggenheim Fellowship in 1982, the American Academy and Institute of Arts and Letters Award in Literature in 1990, and membership in the American Academy of Arts and Sciences in 1992, among many others.

In 1984, Kingston visited China for the first time, traveling in the company of seven other writers: Allen Ginsberg, Francine du Plessix Gray, William Least Heat-Moon, Toni Morrison, Harrison Salisbury, Leslie Marmon Silko, and Gary Snyder. The extended trip was sponsored by UCLA and the Chinese Writers' Association, with the group visiting, among other places, the home village of the Hongs. In a 1991 interview, Kingston describes "throughout China people would say, 'Welcome home,' or, 'It's nice that you've come back.' They knew that it was my first trip there, but still they referred to it as a return" (Perry 186). Interviewer Donna Perry notes that Harrison Salisbury has written that people had been lined up to see her, with everyone claiming to be a relative. She replies, "Oh, yes. All my relatives at the train station. God, it was so wonderful! That whole journey was a linguistic adventure, too, because we traveled from the north to the south, and the closer we got to my home village the more I could communicate" (186-87). Simmons has noted that the trip also gave Kingston a stronger sense of the importance of theater in Chinese life (29-30).

Later in 1984, Maxine and Earll moved to Los Angeles, while Joseph, who had developed a career as a musician, stayed in Hawai'i. After Kingston served as the M. Thelma McAndless Distinguished Professor in the Humanities at Eastern Michigan University in 1986, the Kingstons moved to the Rockridge district of Oakland, California, in 1987. A limited hand-printed edition of 200 copies of twelve short essays written during her time in Hawai'i was published as *Hawai'i One Summer*; it was reprinted by the University of Hawai'i as a paperback in 1998.

Kingston's first novel, *Tripmaster Monkey: His Fake Book*, was published in 1989 and received the PEN USA West Award. Although not quite as enthusiastically received as her first books, its postmodern play with protagonist Wittman Ah Sing (think Walt Whitman and *Song of Myself*), sixties hippie culture, and the Chinese myth of the Monkey King has garnered it a good deal of popular and scholarly attention. It received the John Dos Passos Prize for Literature. A year later, in 1990, Kingston is appointed Chancellor's Distinguished Professor of English at the University of California, Berkeley. That same year, a public television station, KQED in San Francisco, produced a television program about her life and art, *Maxine Hong Kingston: Talking Story*.

Kingston's father, Tom Hong, passed away in 1991. In the opening section of *The Fifth Book of Peace*, Kingston writes movingly of driving back to her Oakland home from his one-month memorial service to encounter what has come to be called the "Tunnel Fire," an Oakland Hills firestorm that destroys her home and personal belongings, including a book manuscript for a sequel to *Tripmaster Monkey*. In line with the Buddhist principles by which she lives, Kingston has never been overly invested in material things, but the loss of the manuscript created, for a time after the fire, an inability to write. She overcame that, however, in part through the outpouring of gifts and bits of audio and video of her reading from the work-in-progress sent by friends and fans (Huntley 19-20).

Through the process of her own healing from the trauma of the fire, Kingston began offering writing and healing workshops for veterans of the Vietnam War. When she received the Lila Wallace Reader's Digest Writing Award in 1992, she used the money to expand those workshops. She takes a leave of absence from teaching at UC Berkeley from 1993 to 1997, continuing her workshops and expanding to include veterans from other wars. A collection of the work is published in 2006 as *Veterans of War, Veterans of Peace*, by Koa Books. During this period, her essay writing and public speaking about peace and about Buddhism grew. For instance, she wrote and published work with Thich Nhat Hanh, a well-known Buddhist monk and writer, and at an April 1995 conference at the University of California, Davis, "Vietnam Legacies: Twenty Years Later," Kingston sponsored a reading of US and Vietnamese novelists and poets. In 1997, Kingston was awarded one of the highest US honors in civilian life, the National Humanities Medal, receiving it from President Bill Clinton. She reportedly delivered a message to him from Vietnam War veterans with whom she worked: "They said, 'Tell Bill Clinton we're proud of him; he was right and brave not to go to Vietnam'." He replied, "But I thought they felt I'm a son of a bitch" (Jaggi). As an example of her peace activism outside her workshops, in 2003, she—along with writers Alice Walker and Terry Tempest Williams and over twenty other women—was arrested at a protest outside the White House on International Women's Day, rallying against the Bush administration's plan to invade Iraq.

Kingston delivered the William E. Massey Sr. Lectures in the History of American Civilization at Harvard in 2000; in 2002, they were published as *To Be the Poet*, a combination of prose and poetry describing her desire to give up the former and become a poet, for "the poet's day will be moment upon moment of gladsomeness. Poets do whatever they like" (6). She followed it the next year with the "longbook" she had referred to in the lectures, *The Fifth Book of Peace*. Its four major sections, "Fire," "Paper," "Water," and "Earth," narrate her experiences driving back from the memorial ceremony for her father and discovering her house and manuscript burned, provide an explanation of the Chinese books of peace, reconstruct the sequel to *Tripmaster Monkey* that burned in the fire, and describe her work with veterans in her writing workshops. These publications were followed with more major awards, including the Lifetime Achievement Award from the Asian American Literary Awards in 2006 and the Medal for Distinguished Contribution to American Letters from the National Book Foundation.

Kingston returned to the memoir form in 2011's *I Love a Broad Margin to My Life*, but this time mostly in verse, and a musing on her adult life rather than her experiences with her parents and family. She remarked to Julian Guthrie that it could be her last book, as she has:

> been writing since I could write. Now I'm 70. It's wonderful and unexpected to have this freedom from the desire to write. Sometimes I think about how there was this little girl who decided my life for me. This little girl said, 'I'm going to be a writer.' That determined my fate. (Guthrie)

President Barack Obama awarded Maxine Hong Kingston the 2013 National Medal of Arts in July, 2014. She continues to live and write in Oakland.

Works Cited

"Bill Moyers Interview." *Bill Moyers Journal*. Public Affairs Television, 25 May 2007. Web. 11 Sept. 2016. <http://www.pbs.org/moyers/journal/05252007/transcript1.html>.

Brownmiller, Susan. "Susan Brownmiller Talks with Maxine Hong Kingston." *Mademoiselle* (March 1977): 148-49, 210-11, 214-26.

Grice, Helena. *Maxine Hong Kingston*. Manchester, UK: Manchester UP, 2006.

Guthrie, Julian. "Maxine Hong Kingston Embarks on a New Life Chapter." *SFGate*. Hearst Communications, Inc., 23 Jan. 2011. Web. 11 Sept. 2016. <http://www.sfgate.com/bayarea/article/Maxine-Hong-Kingston-embarks-on-new-life-chapter-2478664.php#photo-2041821>.

Hoy, Jody. "To Be Able to See the Tao." Skenazy & Martin, 47-66.

Huntley, E. D. *Maxine Hong Kingston: A Critical Companion.* Westport, Connecticut: Greenwood, 2001.

Jaggi, Maya. "The Warrior Skylark." *The Guardian.* Guardian News & Media Ltd., 13 December 2003. Web. 11 Sept. 2016. <https://www.theguardian.com/books/2003/dec/13/featuresreviews.guardianreview6>.

Kingston, Maxine Hong. *Hawai'i One Summer.* Honolulu: U of Hawai'i P, 1998.

_____. *To Be the Poet.* Cambridge, MA: Harvard UP, 2002.

Leonard, John. "In Defiance of 2 Worlds." *New York Times.* 17 Sept. 1976. *Critical Essays on Maxine Hong Kingston.* Ed. Laura E. Skandera-Trombley. New York: G.K. Hall, 1998. 77-78.

Perry, Donna. "Maxine Hong Kingston." Skenazy & Martin, 168-188.

Seshachari, Neila C. "An Interview with Maxine Hong Kingston." *Weber Studies* 12 (Winter 1995): 7-26.

Simmons, Diane. *Maxine Hong Kingston.* New York: Twayne, 1999.

Skenazy, Paul & Tera Martin, eds. *Conversations with Maxine Hong Kingston.* Jackson: UP of Mississippi, 1998.

Wong, Sau-ling Cynthia. *Maxine Hong Kingston's* The Woman Warrior: *A Casebook.* New York and Oxford: Oxford UP, 1999.

Conversation with Maxine Hong Kingston_____

Linda Trinh Moser

Maxine Hong Kingston graciously agreed to speak about her work and particularly about *The Woman Warrior*. She spoke to me via telephone on August 22, 2016 from her home in the Oakland Hills during a break from writing.

LTM: In the forty years since the publication of *The Woman Warrior*, what has surprised you the most about how readers have responded to it?
MHK: Oh, I don't know whether I think in terms of the responses being a surprise. What I do like very much is how long-lived this book is. That it's forty years old! Thank you for remembering that, too. I have noticed that other people and organizations are also noticing and wanting to celebrate its anniversary. You know, it's very gratifying for me—to know that a book could, that my book could, live for forty years. And it makes me believe that it might go on living forever. It's a little like Shakespeare's idea of immortality. The writing that lives forever.

LTM: When you were writing this book, did you imagine that it would take on the life that it did?
MHK: I felt that I was writing something completely new and different from anything that I had ever read. I thought that I would have difficulty getting it published. I made up my mind that if I could not find a publisher, I would just keep copies of the writing. I imagined that it would be published 100 years from now. It would be all right. Even then, I was already thinking of an audience—readers who would be there to read it long after I was gone. The book would still be there. I hoped it would be appreciated.

LTM: You've said that "[t]o best appreciate *The Woman Warrior*, you need to read *China Men*. Do you think your

later works also shed light on *The Woman Warrior*?

MHK: I think of *China Men* as being complementary to *The Woman Warrior* because I was writing them at the same time. I was writing the stories simultaneously. They divided up neatly into two books. You know, the same characters appear, and you find out what happens to people in a different situation, or when they are older. Everyman's Library has published the two books as one. They really do belong together.

Tripmaster Monkey is different from the other two books. It is a book that I wanted to write using a modern, slangy, American language. It's the language that my contemporaries and I use, but I couldn't use that language in *The Woman Warrior* and *China Men*. Writing those books, I felt that I was translating Chinese, or that I was writing English in a Chinese accent. After a decade of doing that, it was such fun and freedom to write *Tripmaster Monkey*.

LTM: In *The Fifth Book of Peace*, *To Be the Poet*, and *I Love a Broad Margin to My Life*, you revisit and continue the stories you started in *The Woman Warrior*. Fa Mu Lan makes appearances in all those works. Why does the character continue to be such a powerful figure for you?

MHK: Maybe for the same reason that she's a powerful figure in the world. Her story continues to be told, to grow, to be chanted in China. You have plays and movies about Fa Mu Lan also. When I told her story in *The Woman Warrior*, I told everything that I knew about her. I wrote her as a feminist. Feminism, very popular at the time, was in my consciousness. But then years later, I wanted to be more accurate about the way the story is actually told. I made mistakes in *The Woman Warrior*. For example, I left out that she was a weaver. That is so important because she's Penelope and Odysseus in one. I had to correct that.

Another thing: I told the story of Fa Mu Lan in prose. It's actually a chant. I wanted to get closer to the way that it was presented—to be more authentically true. So I wrote it as poetry, and I got as close as I could to the versions that are alive now. Her being a weaver is so important. The chant starts with the sound of weaving: *Jik jik jik. Jik* means to weave, to knit, to heal. I have the poem in *The Fifth Book of Peace* and *To Be the Poet*.

Years later, I read in a footnote in a scholar's work that Fa Mu Lan committed suicide. That is really bad news! I didn't know about that when writing *The Woman Warrior*. I was trying to write something inspirational, something uplifting, and we don't want to hear that she killed herself. In *I Love a Broad Margin to My Life*, I deal with that. She kills herself. What does it mean? By this time, I knew about PTSD, and so I could tell her story in a different way, to show that war can cause suicide. In the footnote that I read, her suicide was a feminist action. The scholar said that she was being summoned to marry the emperor. To escape that fate, she killed herself. But the way I made sense of it was that she had PTSD. It is interesting how the story has evolved and changed as I am thinking of it through a lifetime.

LTM: I imagine that your experiences writing with veterans of war and pacifism played a part in the evolution of your version as well. When I read that Fa Mu Lan committed suicide, I was angry and upset, stopped reading, and shut the book.

MHK: I did that too when I read the footnote about her suicide. I thought: This is not good knowledge to have. I don't want to know this. But I also thought: We have got to deal with this fact and make sense of it. We can't keep it a secret. You know what? Most people don't know about Fa Mu Lan's end, and I can see why. There is denial. But her war chant becomes an anti-war chant. I'm glad you have those feelings, although they are hard to have.

LTM: Can I ask about the village well? *Broad Margin* **includes a description of a trip to the well where the "No Name Woman" drowned herself and her newborn.**

MHK: That is another example of the early stories changing. They can be solved years later in another time in my life, in another book. That story started in the very first chapter of *The Woman Warrior*. Four books later, I visit the village. And an old woman offers me water from that very well. I took it as a reconciliation ceremony. That's just me, making a meaning up. She could have just been giving me water on a hot day. I felt creeped out by her at first and thought about it some more. Yeah, I thought, she and I are making ceremony.

LTM: In that work, you also undercut the story about the "No Name Woman" with the observation: that "your aunt / with the baby couldn't possibly have jumped into a well this shallow and drowned."
MHK: Yes. There are other ways of supposing. Maybe the wells have been modernized. There are pumps and filters that could've been added. And the well seems shallow.

The villagers did something to the old well. I believe the cursed events actually happened.

LTM: Accounts of the drafting of *The Woman Warrior* often note that it was written in Hawai'i. Did being away from the mainland allow you to write better about events in California and China?
MHK: I'm not sure because writing just comes to me all the time. I don't know the cause or whether it was just a coincidence that I was in Hawai'i that allowed that book to come.

Being in Hawai'i was more an influence on *China Men* than on *The Woman Warrior* because of my two great grandfathers. I had two great grandfathers, on both sides of my family, who were in Hawai'i. I lived in the land where they lived. Also, there's inspiration that comes out of the land, the *'āina*, in Hawai'i. Walt Whitman and William Carlos Williams feel that way, too. Walt Whitman would lie on the ground and let the poetry come through him. For me, there were also ancestors who helped the writing. Those books were coming to me at the same time. There could be that influence.

LTM: A lot of attention is paid to your use of Chinese sources in *The Woman Warrior*, but you also seem influenced by American writers like William Carlos

Williams and Walt Whitman. What other writers, traditions, or works were inspirational to you as you were writing *The Woman Warrior*?

MHK: I think a very obvious influence in that first chapter in *The Woman Warrior* was Nathaniel Hawthorne's *The Scarlet Letter*. We've got a little village in the middle of nowhere, and all these puritanical people making for tragedy. Everybody knows about the adulterous woman's secret, and they want to punish her. I think that is a description of "No Name Woman" and of *The Scarlet Letter*. As I was writing it, I was thinking of *The Scarlet Letter*.

Have you heard of Viet Thanh Nguyen and his new book *The Sympathizer*? We have done a couple of events together. He was one of my students! I just feel really good that he could write a book like this. Readers will be amazed at the kind of background that he gives to what happened in Vietnam. He writes both fiction and scholarly nonfiction. He was writing scholarly work, but all of a sudden, this fiction comes out. He follows up *The Sympathizer* with *Nothing Ever Dies*, which gives hope that true memory can lead to peace and reconciliation.

I am hoping that Viet is also influenced by William Carlos Williams. Williams described the terrible slaughter of Native Americans, then asks, "Do these things ever die?" The consequences of war go on and on. Viet answered, "Nothing ever dies." Wow! He was listening in class.

LTM: So much contemporary American fiction features an ancestor who is a bearer of culture and wisdom; however, those ancestral figures also have some fault or flaw that calls into question some of their wisdom, or shows how their own history has created something that shouldn't be carried forward. Brave Orchid seems to be a figure like this. Why is the process of learning to appreciate ancestors so difficult?

MHK: Maybe because the griot *is* a difficult character. In ancient cultures, people (and I'm learning that Africans and Latin Americans also) listened to their ancestors. But the West described these spiritual practices as "ancestor worship." That is a put-down. We're superstitious; we don't know about God. We're pagans. People come to America to forget the old country, forget the old ways, forget history. Most people know who their parents are and who their grandparents were. But that's about it. We have to go against our culture to find ancestors.

In *Finding Your Roots*, a television show that traces the ancestors of celebrities, Henry Louis Gates [Jr.] tells people who their great-grandparents are, and they get excited. We have a culture here in the West in which it is very hard to get in touch with the past and ancestors. Caring about ancestors is important not just for the present but for the future. American Indians have a tradition of ancestors, but they also have a tradition of descendants. You must ask, "How will my actions affect my descendants for seven generations?" You have to think that far ahead. In America, in the West, we've lost a lot by ignoring ancestors.

LTM: What do you want your descendants, your future readers, to get from *The Woman Warrior*?
MHK: I should hope the same things that we are getting from the book now. The book is about humanity, how to be a human being, and how to be humane. What is the human life, and how do we live it? We are also still troubled about immigration. We are talking about closing the border with little sympathy for refugees. The people I write about in *The Woman Warrior* are refugees. All these people crossing the border from Mexico are refugees, and they are fleeing conditions that we are partially responsible for. I would like people reading *The Woman Warrior* to learn how to know, how to look inside someone who is foreign, "Other," and to recognize humanity. I want readers to have compassion for someone who is not like themselves.

LTM: What are you writing now?
MHK: I'm writing my posthumous work. I won't publish what I am writing until one hundred years after I die. That gives me freedom. I don't have to worry about form, or book sales, or anything. I'm free

to write whatever I want. That is what I'm trying to do—to liberate my writing and my thinking.

CRITICAL
CONTEXTS

Twentieth-Century Chinese and US History, Meet Postmodern Sensibility_____

Kathryn West

History Can Be Such a Mystery

Maxine Hong Kingston's *The Woman Warrior: Memoirs of a Girlhood Among Ghosts* has generated a great deal of discussion about its braiding of Chinese myths and legends into her account of growing up female and Chinese American in Stockton, California, in the mid-twentieth century (for investigations of Kingston's use of myths and legends, see Cynthia Sau-Ling Wong and, in this volume, articles by Martens, Westover, and Mok). Critics have also given attention to the coming-of-age dimensions woven into the text. Less attention has been paid to her similar weaving in of historical events and figures from both US and Chinese history. Just as she blends the genres of memoir, autobiography, myth, and fantasy, Kingston blends references to US and Chinese history into her text to highlight additional dimensions of the environment in which Maxine grows up. This essay pays attention to the history in the text both to provide an understanding of the historical background of author and text, and to argue that contrasting histories contend in Maxine's growing consciousness to create a filter that is distinctly postmodern. In turn, this postmodern sensibility contributes to the shaping of her perceptions and sense of self, and leads to the postmodern textual tendencies and philosophical assumptions of *The Woman Warrior*—such as genre-blending, the instability of events and their interpretation, the mixing of high and popular cultural products, and nonlinear chronologies.

Kingston's *China Men*, published three years after *The Woman Warrior* and originally conceived of as a diptych or even combined text with *The Woman Warrior*, consists of stories focusing on the men in Kingston's family. Importantly though, *China Men* also features sections presented as straightforward history. For instance, appearing about halfway through China Men is a section entitled

"The Laws." It opens with a quotation from Article V of the Burlingame Treaty as epigraph:

> The United States of America and the Emperor of China cordially recognize the inherent and inalienable right of man to change his home and allegiance, and also the mutual advantage of the free migration and emigration of their citizens and subjects respectively from the one country to the other for purposes of curiosity, of trade, or as permanent residents. (*China Men* 152)

The text does not stop here, however, in its excerpt and representation of laws, acts, treaties, and court cases connected to Chinese immigration to the US and to the lives and rights of Chinese people living in the US. "The Laws" offers eight pages of such entries, each beginning with a date ranging from 1868 to 1978. The narrator (arguably, there is very little distance in this section between Kingston's voice and the voice of the narrator) comments throughout on these marks of the 'legal' relationship between the United States, China, and Chinese immigrants to the US. In one instance dated 1882, Kingston writes,

> Encouraged by fanatical lobbying from California, the U.S. Congress passed the first Chinese Exclusion Act. It banned the entrance of Chinese laborers, both skilled and unskilled, for ten years. Anyone unqualified for citizenship could not come in—and by the terms of the Nationality Act of 1870, Chinese were not qualified for citizenship. (154)

While one might argue that the narrator's voice is not objective in the use of adjectives such as "fanatical," the representation of the Chinese Exclusion Act is factual and a crucially significant part of Chinese American history. Another example, from 1924, describes the congressional immigration act that indicated "'Chinese women, wives, and prostitutes'" were specifically banned from entry to the US. The act goes on to state that "any American who married a Chinese woman lost his citizenship; any Chinese man who married an American woman caused her to lose her citizenship" (156).

Kingston does not explicitly point out the implications of this act, but they are quite clear: to allow women as well as men entry is to encourage the formation of families and communities. To forbid Chinese women is to discourage permanent settlement in the US. "The Laws" also points to several of the myriad instances in which US policy is clearly more prejudicial against people from China than those from Japan (until World War II), Korea, or other Asian countries, and is particularly so compared to policies toward those of European ancestry.

The Woman Warrior contains no such straightforward recounting of legal, political, or social history. However, the text is rife with carefully woven references to Chinese and American history, references that help illuminate the lives of Kingston's characters and her own motivations for presenting them as she does. The following section highlights the presence of social and political histories that served as the backdrop for Kingston's (and by extension, her narrator's) life as she was growing up. This essay then argues that being immersed in the social, cultural, and political histories of this period in China, the US, and immigrant Chinese experience creates a distinctly postmodern sensibility in Kingston. Responding to (as well as helping to create) the literary history of the period, Kingston filters her memoirs of the development of her psyche through a postmodern structure and sensibility.

The *Woman Warrior* and Twentieth-Century China and the US

While *The Woman Warrior* does not feature the direct reportorial-style history found in "The Laws" in *China Men*, throughout Kingston weaves dates, events, and references significant to Chinese and Chinese American lives. The first such date and reference appears on the first page of text and is delivered through Brave Orchid's voice:

> In 1924 just a few days after our village celebrated seventeen hurry-up weddings—to make sure that every young man who went 'out on the road' would responsibly come home—your father and his

brothers and your grandfather and his brothers and your aunt's new husband sailed for America, the Gold Mountain. (*WW* 3)

Chinese people first began referring to San Francisco and other western parts of the US as "Gold Mountain" in the mid-1800s, when gold was discovered in the Sierra Nevada Mountains. The term eventually came to refer to the US and parts of Canada in general; as it was for Europeans emigrating across the Atlantic, the US was seen by the Chinese, coming across the Pacific, as a land of opportunity.

Perhaps less well known to US readers is the significance of 1924 in Chinese and Chinese American history. As noted above in the passage from "The Laws," 1924 was the year of the immigration act that forbade almost all Chinese women from entering the US. In other words, the new wives described by Brave Orchid could not have legally accompanied their husbands. The year 1924 has additional historical significance: while the Nationalist Revolution in China is typically dated from 1925, Arthur Waldron, in *From War to Nationalism: China's Turning Point, 1924–1925*, describes the early and mid-1920s as a "dark age of chaos" in China (11), with several factions struggling to achieve power and the imposition of contrasting ideologies. Being conscripted into battle was a very real possibility for Chinese men, providing another impetus for making the voyage to the US. In "No Name Woman," Kingston's scene of the village attacking one of its own due to an unexplained pregnancy takes on added resonance, serving as a metonymy for and a microcosm of the growing civil war in many regions of the country.

The first reference to US popular culture history comes just a few pages later, with narrator Maxine listing two of the American movies her family saw as a New Year's Day tradition, and one of the few, or perhaps only, opportunities to watch American movies in a year: *Oh, You Beautiful Doll* (1949), starring June Haver, and a John Ford western, *She Wore a Yellow Ribbon* (also 1949), with John Wayne in the lead. The John Wayne film may be most relevant to ideas in *The Woman Warrior*, as he plays a cavalry captain on the verge of retirement who, on a mission to stop a possible attack by the Cheyenne and Arapaho, finds himself "encumbered by women who must be evacuated" from the fort in his charge. To be "encumbered by women" may have resonated with a young girl hearing "'There's no profit in raising girls. Better to raise geese than girls'" (46). The young girl struggling with whether to be "Chinese-feminine" or "American-feminine" may well have also noted, even if subconsciously, the trope of white women and the necessity that they be protected "against the horde" in *She Wore a Yellow Ribbon* (IMDb).

Also in "No Name Woman," Kingston refers to Chinese pride in "the ideal of five generations under one roof" (11). This contrasts with the 1950s emergent ideal in the US of the single family home; the first Levittown, a large suburban housing development marketed toward and affordable for returning WWII veterans, was begun in 1947, when Kingston was seven years old. In addition to contrasting living arrangements, Kingston examines as well the differing customs of politeness and manners and gender-role expectations and the dilemma this created for her growing up, whether to strive to be "American-feminine" or "Chinese-feminine." We can surmise that the several struggles she dramatizes later in the book regarding her difficulties with speech arise at least in part from a paralysis created by trying to choose between Chinese loud voices ("I have not been able to stop my mother's screams in public libraries or over telephones") and "speaking in an inaudible voice, I have tried to turn myself American-feminine" (11). Just as she asks explicitly about her various cultures, "What is [. . .] tradition and what is the movies?" (6), she implicitly asks which offers better roles for women—and finds more confusion. In "White Tigers," she hears from the chants about Fa Mu Lan that she can grow up to be a warrior, but the everyday comments from her family imply she will grow up to be the equivalent of a servant to her future husband's family. In "At the Western Palace," she notes that her Americanized uncle sees little wrong with deserting his Chinese wife and daughter (except for continuing financial support) and marrying a younger Chinese American woman. Startling to most readers are the misogynistic proverbs about females the narrator recounts hearing from Chinese relatives and the "emigrant villagers" as she was growing up, such as "Feeding girls is feeding cowbirds" (46). Yet Kingston is careful to upend any possible perceptions that women are completely disregarded in China and experience equality in the US.

The middle and longest section of *The Woman Warrior*, "Shaman," recounts the history of the narrator's mother at a medical school in Canton, China (To Keung School of Midwifery, or Hackett Medical School); Brave Orchid's diploma declares her "Proficiency in Midwifery, Pediatrics, Gynecology, 'Medecine,'[*sic*] 'Surgary,' [*sic*] Therapeutics, Ophthalmology, Bacteriology, Dermatology, Nursing, and Bandage" (57). "Shaman" continues with stories of Brave Orchid's subsequent years practicing medicine in her own and surrounding villages and living as a refugee from the Japanese war on China before coming to the US to join her husband. (Interestingly, one of the few references to male roles come in the form of photographs of Maxine's father at Coney Island; he wears "a new straw hat, cocked at a Fred Astaire angle. He steps out, dancing down the stairs, one foot forward, one back, a hand in his pocket" [60].) Brave Orchid is not recognized as a medical practitioner in the US and instead works in the family laundry with her husband and supplements that with migrant fieldwork. She tells Maxine, "You have no idea how much I have fallen coming to America" (77). Kingston turns again to moments from Chinese history to contextualize and contrast her mother's US experience: "The students at the To Keung School of Midwifery were new women, scientists who changed the rituals" (75). As a young woman during the Women's Liberation Movement of the 1960s and 1970s, Kingston was living through and experiencing the increased calls for equality and rights for women and the birth of women's studies programs in the academy. The Berkeley women's studies program was established in 1976; the first women's studies program at a US university was founded at San Diego State University in 1970. However, when musing about "Communist pictures showing a contented woman sitting on her bunk sewing," Maxine decides, "The woman looks very pleased. The [Communist] Revolution put an end to prostitution by giving women what they wanted: a job and a room of their own" (62).

The Communist Revolution was not popular with Maxine's parents; relatives in China were killed and had land taken by the Communists. Many ironies reside in the suggestion that the Communists provided women with what one of the pillars of Western feminism, Virginia Woolf, declared the ultimate goal. Through her exploration of such ironies in the Chinese-feminine vs. American-feminine dilemma, Kingston does not allow alert readers to attach a rigidity of gender roles to one place and a better or more progressive expectation in the other. Instead, she uses her social and cultural references about each place to demonstrate the importance of context. While readers may take the sexist comments from relatives that so infuriated Maxine to mean that attitudes toward women in China were corrosive, dangerous, and ill-conceived, in fact some things turn out better for women in China. Indeed, the US had its share of assumptions, expectations, and models that warp ideas about the worth of women and girls. Both traditions inform her perceptions of gender and women's roles in both negative and positive ways.

Key figures in twentieth-century China's political history feature several times over the course of *The Woman Warrior*. Sun Yat-Sen (1866–1925), who led a nationalist movement in China, is a hero to Maxine's parents and the other emigrant Chinese in her community; he remains so to those of widely disparate political beliefs in China and Taiwan. He serves especially as a touchstone to Maxine's mother because of his professional background: he was "Doctor Sun Yat-sen, who was a western surgeon before he became a revolutionary" (63). Sun Yat-Sen had practiced as a surgeon in the West before returning to China as a leader of the nationalist movement and an instrumental figure in the overthrow of the Qing dynasty, the last of the imperial dynasties in China. Although Sun Yat-Sen briefly served as "provisional president" of the People's Republic of China, he died before being able to consolidate power. His picture hangs on the wall of young Maxine's Chinese school. Studies of Sun Yat-Sen published almost forty years apart highlight the cult of personality that grew up around him (see Bergère; Sharman). A cult of personality grew up around Chiang Kai-Shek as well; his picture also hangs in the Chinese school. The political heir to Sun

Yat-Sen, he oversaw a number of purges of Communists in China and took an authoritarian stance as a leader. After being driven off the mainland of China, he established himself in Taiwan and ruled there until his death, while Chairman Mao ruled the mainland as a Communist power (Taylor).

Mao Tse-Tung, or Mao Zedong, the Communist leader of China from 1949 to his death in 1976, crops up in a number of references in *The Woman Warrior*. His political policies and social programs are responsible for the "confusing" news from China and the "letters [that] made my parents, who are rocks, cry. My father screamed in his sleep. My mother wept and crumpled up the letters. She set fire to them page by page in the ashtray, but new letters came almost every day" (50). These letters begin arriving when Maxine is nine years old—Kingston would have been nine in 1949, when the Communists take power:

> The other letters said that my uncles were made to kneel on broken glass during their trials and had confessed to being landowners. They were all executed, and the aunt whose thumbs were twisted off drowned herself. Other aunts, mothers-in-law, and cousins disappeared. . . . They kept asking for money. . . . If we overseas Chinese would just send money to the Communist bank, our relatives said, they might get a percentage of it for themselves. (50)

The timing corresponds to the rise of particularly virulent anti-Communism in the US, with Joseph McCarthy beginning his "Red Scare" campaign in 1950, when Kingston was ten years old and one year after the Chinese Communist government took control of the country. That same year, the US passed a series of Refugee Relief Acts that demanded refugees swear they were not Communists, as noted in *China Men* (157-58). Maxine relates that her parents grew frustrated at times with the letters from China demanding money. That situation would have become even more fraught in 1954 when the US Supreme Court, in Mao v. Brownell, upholds laws forbidding Chinese Americans to send money to relatives in China. These laws come into being only after Communists come to power in China.

Mao Tse-Tung later spearheads the Cultural Revolution in China. In 1958, he had declared the "Great Leap Forward," a plan to transform China's largely agrarian society. By the mid-1960s, famine plagued much of China and Mao was under attack for the failure of his plan. He reasserted authority in 1966 with the beginning of his Cultural Revolution, which demanded the erasure of the "Four Olds": old ideas, old customs, old culture, old habits (Ramzy). An anti-intellectual movement, the Cultural Revolution led to the persecution and deaths of many millions of people, as well as the destruction of many historical sites and cultural relics. So-called Red Guards terrorized—shaming, torturing, even killing—"class enemies," intellectuals and people with ties to the West; universities were especially a target, with well-educated people being "sent-down" to work on farms in the countryside (Ramzy). Maxine's father, who had been a scholar in China, and her mother, a well-educated woman, must have felt particularly the trauma of these attacks on people with similar backgrounds in their former home. For Maxine's parents and the other "emigrant villagers" of their community, to view from afar attempts to do away with "old ideas, old customs, old culture, old habits" of the homeland must have felt like the destruction of one's home, history, and, in a sense, future. It erased the ability to return "home." Mao's revolution to change customs, culture, and habits erased the way of being Maxine's parents considered fundamental to life in China. During an adult Maxine's visit home in the mid-1970s, in "Shaman," Maxine's mother tells her,

> Now it's final. We got a letter from the villagers yesterday. They asked if it was all right with us that they took over the land. The last uncles have been killed so your father is the only person left to say it is all right, you see. He has written saying they can have it. So. We have no more China to go home to. (106)

While her mother speaks explicitly of the land, implicitly the China she dreamed of returning to no longer exists as the culture she knew. Of course, China presents not the only instance of the injustice of land seizure: in the US, Maxine's parents' laundry is lost to urban renewal.

Historical and cultural events in the US also continue making their mark on Maxine's life. With the brief phrase "Berkeley in the sixties" (45), Kingston evokes the countercultural revolution, the anti-war movement, and the Civil Rights Movement: "I went away to college—Berkeley in the sixties—and I studied, and I marched to change the world" (47). This time in Kingston's life, although presented without details about classes or marches, clearly had a profound effect on her life, philosophy, and sensibilities. The civil rights movement shapes her experiences at this time; she references both CORE (Congress for Racial Equality) and the NAACP (National Association for the Advancement of Colored People). She acts on the principles of these organizations during her stints as an employee at an art supply store and as a secretary for a land developers' association, where she is faced with the racist language and practices of her employers. She finds it physically difficult to speak up, but speak up she does "in my bad, small-person's voice that makes no impact" (48) and, in one instance, loses her job. The impact of "Berkeley in the sixties" can further be witnessed in Kingston's later life. She demonstrates her commitment to pacifist causes through her formation with her husband, Earll Kingston, of a sanctuary in Hawai'i for conscientious objectors and soldiers who were AWOL and through the establishment of writing workshops for veterans (the latter documented in part in *The Fifth Book of Peace* and the anthology, *Veterans of War, Veterans of Peace*). In one of the most humorous moments in *The Woman Warrior*, Kingston alludes to the drug culture of the sixties and seventies, when Brave Orchid informs her visiting, now grown-up daughter that, "I swallowed that LSD pill you left on the kitchen counter." Maxine replies, "That wasn't LSD, Mama. It was just a cold pill" (100).

Historical Collisions = Postmodern and Multicultural Sensibility

Literary criticism on contemporary American fiction and writing—especially criticism from the 1970s through the early 2000s—has tended to take up either postmodern texts or multicultural texts, treating them as two different kinds of literature, with differing purposes, audiences, modes of presentation, and effects. Seldom, if ever, did anthologies of contemporary fiction include writing identified as multicultural along with postmodernist writing. Many scholars are now recognizing that in fact they overlap in many respects, formal and philosophical, and that postmodernist approaches are employed by key figures in the prominence of ethnic American literature from the 1970s to the present: Toni Morrison, Ishmael Reed, Colson Whitehead, Louise Erdrich, Gerald Vizenor, Sherman Alexie, Leslie Marmon Silko, Junot Díaz, and, most certainly, Maxine Hong Kingston.

Postmodernism in common usage is sometimes employed to designate the cultural productions appearing after (and somewhat overlapping with) the era of modernism. However, most scholars use "postmodern" to signify a certain set of sensibilities, assumptions, conventions, and techniques employed by writers, artists, and intellectuals. Fredric Jameson famously declared postmodern work the "cultural productions of late capitalism." He sees it as embodying disconnected images and styles, resulting in a sense of fragmentation and a flattening effect, with few or no distinctions made between high art and popular culture. While Kingston weaves connections across her text in an almost dizzying array, she very much employs a structure of collage that characterizes much postmodern writing. The postmodern suspicion of "metanarratives," overarching, all-encompassing explanations, also structures *The Woman Warrior* and can arguably be traced to the author/narrator's experience of the colliding, contrasting, and sometimes oddly similar histories of China and the US in the twentieth-century. Postmodernism insists on cultural relativity and that there can be no one, universal, absolute truth, something Kingston illustrates in her comparisons of both gender roles and social justice issues in the US and China in the twentieth century. The self-awareness and at times even metafictional stance of her text signal a common postmodern technique and attitude—there is more than one version of any story, and meanings seldom remain stable. Kingston's genre-bending certainly comes from a postmodern sensibility, one that insists that telling her story, the story of how her psyche, her way of being in the world developed, requires reaching into the conventions of memoir, autobiography, novel, myth, and legend without being bound by the conventions of any one of those. And, of course, Kingston represents multiculturalism, rendering the lives and experiences of a vibrant but underrepresented population in the US. As much multicultural writing does, she grapples with conflicts between immigrant generations and their offspring and depicts the process of adapting to a new culture, new foods, and different cultural codes.

In the twenty-first century, scholars have begun redrawing the lines that define late twentieth-century writing, with many arguing for seeing postmodern writing as a fairly solipsistic phenomenon of the 1960s and 1970s, quickly giving way in the late 1980s to what Rachel Adams terms "American literary globalism" (250). In American literary globalism, voices from ethnic writers and a rejuvenated emphasis on emotional storytelling become prominent. While early postmodernism reacts with paranoia to a sense of hidden connections behind the surface of life (think, for instance, of Thomas Pynchon's *The Crying of Lot 49* or Don DeLillo's *Underworld*), American literary globalism understands the interconnectedness of life across the planet. Adams notes,

> many works of contemporary US fiction recognize a planet that is tied together through the increasing interpenetration of economies, cultures, and kinship. If postmodernism [through the 1980s] is governed by a sense of paranoia, which suggests that these connections may be figments of an individual imagination, the literature of globalization represents them as a shared perception of community whereby, for better or worse, populations in one part of the world are inevitably affected by events in another. (268)

Perhaps Kingston even anticipated conceptualizing contemporary literature as transnational and moving toward American literary globalism. As she says to Brave Orchid near the end of "Shaman": "We belong to the planet now, Mama. Does it make sense to you that if we're no longer attached to one piece of land, we belong to the planet? Wherever we happen to be standing, why that spot belongs to us as much as any other spot" (107).

Works Cited

Adams, Rachel. "The Ends of Postmodernism, the Ends of America." *Twentieth-Century Literature*. 53.3 (Fall 2007): 248-72.

Bergère, Marie-Claire, *Sun Yat-Sen*. Transl. Janet Lloyd. Stanford: Stanford UP, 2000.

Kingston, Maxine Hong. *The Woman Warrior: Memoirs of A Girlhood Among Ghosts*. 1976. New York: Vintage/Random, 1989.

_____. *China Men*. 1980. New York: Vintage/Random, 1989.

_____. *The Fifth Book of Peace*. New York: Vintage/Random, 2003.

_____. *Veterans of War, Veterans of Peace*. Kihei, Hawai'i: Koa, 2006.

Jameson, Fredric. *Postmodernism, or, the Cultural Logic of Late Capitalism*. Durham, NC: Duke UP, 1991.

Lim, Shirley Geok-lin. *Approaches to Teaching Kingston's* The Woman Warrior. New York: Modern Language Association, 1991.

Ramzy, Austin. "China's Cultural Revolution, Explained." *New York Times*. The New York Times Company, 14 May 2016. Web. 12 Sept. 2016. <http://www.nytimes.com/2016/05/15/world/asia/china-cultural-revolution-explainer.html>.

She Wore a Yellow Ribbon. Dir. John Ford. Perf. John Wayne, Joanne Dru, & John Agar. *IMDb*, IMDb.com, Inc., 2016. Web. 20 June 2016. <http://www.imdb.com/title/tt0041866/>.

Sharman, Lyon. *Sun Yat-Sen: His Life and Its Meaning, a Critical Biography*. Stanford, CA: Stanford UP, 1968.

Taylor, Jay. *The Generalissimo: Chiang Kai-Shek and the Struggle for Modern China*. Cambridge, MA: Harvard UP, 2009.

Waldron, Arthur. *From War to Nationalism: China's Turning Point, 1924–1925*. New York: Cambridge UP, 1995.

Wong, Sau-ling Cynthia. "Kingston's Handling of Traditional Chinese Sources." Lim, 26-36.

The Woman Warrior: An Examination of Genre, Representation, and Reception_____

Rickie-Ann Legleitner

Maxine Hong Kingston's *The Woman Warrior: Memoirs of a Girlhood Among Ghosts* (1976) has been simultaneously praised and admonished for its blending of genres, its incorporation of Chinese folktales and aspects of "authentic" Chinese and Chinese American culture, and its feminist retelling of coming-of-age. This varied reception reflects the book's own defiance of categorization, highlighting the limitations of literary, ethnic, and gender categories, while calling for a more heterogeneous mode of interpretation.

In terms of genre, the novel tests the limitations of autobiography by incorporating elements of fantasy, folktale, myth, history, and fictional representation alongside more traditional conventions of the coming-of-age memoir. Although this boundary-pushing novel has been praised for its experimentation, some critics feel that the decontextualized depiction of traditional Chinese folktales and cultural practices exploits Chinese culture, problematically appealing to a Western audience in its invocation of Orientalism without a concern for historical or cultural accuracy. Orientalism is broadly defined by Edward Said as the tendency of Western cultures to diminish the accomplishments of the East through methods of feminization and infantilization while making sweeping generalizations about a widely varied and diverse segment of the world population. Correspondingly, critics also take issue with the novel's failure to represent a wider or more authentic Chinese and Chinese American viewpoint or experience, while others find the novel's critique of patriarchy both in Chinese and American culture too brash or, conversely, altogether ineffective.

Despite this criticism, *The Woman Warrior* was a recipient of the National Book Critics Circle Award for General Nonfiction, and it continues to be one of the most widely taught works of literature in higher education by a living author. By examining the novel's critical reception over the past forty years, we can gain insight into the reasons this work continues to be debated and taught, while additionally gaining an appreciation for the complexity of hybridity in relation to identity, writing, and language.

Initial Reception

Overall, American critics supported this unknown author upon the novel's release, and this support only grew after the book received the National Book Critics Circle Award. Before this commendation, John Leonard composed a review for *The New York Times* applauding the novel's shifts between genres and ghosts of past and present, in addition to Kingston's razor sharp ability to capture the reality of a moment and of characters in a direct approach that abandons romantic nostalgia: "[T]his shuttling on an electric line of prose, between fantasy and specificity, is wonderfully original. I can't remember when a young writer walked up to and into every important scene in a book and dealt with it outright, as Mrs. Kingston does, without any evasions whatsoever" (69). Shortly after, a lengthier article appears in *The New York Times* reviewing the book and providing biographical detail about the author. In this article, Jane Kramer writes: "It is a brilliant memoir. It shocks us out of our facile rhetoric, past the clichés of our obtuseness, back to the mystery of a stubbornly, utterly foreign sensibility . . . *The Woman Warrior* is about being Chinese, in the way that *The Portrait of an Artist* is about being Irish." After the book received the award, the article "'Ghosts' of Girlhood Lift Obscure Book to Peak of Acclaim" by Nan Robertson appears detailing the life of the author, echoing the praise of the initial reviews, as well as affirming the strength of its author and characters:

> Mrs. Kingston has told her mother that she, too, "talks story" in her book. Brave Orchid—who, at the age of 80, was queuing up with men to demand a day's work in the tomato fields—already has an idea for her daughter's next book. What is it? "She says I ought to write about discrimination in hiring." (29)

In each of these reviews, we see the work consistently celebrated for its experimentation and authenticity as well as for its strong female characters.

However, the reviews of Kingston's first published book were not exclusively positive, especially within the Chinese American community. Yuan Shu explains that initial criticism centered on "autobiographical accuracy, cultural authenticity, and ethnic representativeness . . . [Critics] accused Kingston of distorting Asian American reality on the one hand, and catering to the demand of the dominant culture for exoticism and stereotypes on the other," specifically noting Frank Chin's critique that "autobiography with its basis in Western metaphysical tradition and the Christian confession would never capture the sensibility or the imagination of Chinese America" (Shu 200). Chin stands as one of Kingston's harshest opponents, going so far as to reproach her writing for attacking Chinese culture "with a stroke of white racist genius" (Chin 27). Deborah L. Madsen contends that Chin privileges the "'low,' or working-class, tradition of Chinese American writing as the 'authentic' tradition—and the tradition of Chinese American writing with which Kingston does not align herself. Chin accuses Kingston of practicing an inauthentic Orientalism inherited from the apologetic autobiographies written in the Chinese American 'high' tradition" (258). Chin narrowly defines authentic experience, demanding a more unified or homogenous idea of Chinese American culture than Kingston's work follows. Deborah Woo further explains that "[Kingston's] artistry per se is not questioned so much as the way she has manipulated cultural myths for her literary purposes. Her creativity in this regard is seen to threaten the foundations of Chinese American culture, destroying elements of a tradition which have served as an historical basis of identity" (175). *The Woman Warrior* calls into question constructions of authenticity, representation, and essentialism as well as the limits of autobiography and the boundaries of creative license. This questioning leads to more careful examinations of her novel and its techniques in later critiques that explore issues related to genre, authenticity, ethnicity, and feminist studies.

Defining Genre

The Woman Warrior is a text that defies the traditional limits of genre, more specifically autobiography, through the incorporation of elements of fiction, folktale, myth, and fantasy. Sau-Ling Cynthia Wong explains that "[t]he most fundamental objection to *The Woman Warrior* concerns its generic status: its being billed as autobiography rather than fiction, when so much of the book departs from the popular definition of autobiography" (30). Wong further explains that critics accused the publisher of using the nonfiction label to increase sales, as literary fiction by an ethnic author would be critically overlooked (30).

Despite the possible motivations of the publisher, *The Woman Warrior* stands as a work that defies simple identification, much like the work's protagonist who appears caught between two cultural worlds. Paul Outka additionally notes that, "Debates and discussions continue over whether the book is fiction, history, autobiography, or some strange mix, and over Kingston's fidelity to her sources and culture(s). While such issues are vitally important, the debates seem . . . to have established the book's clear resistance to definitions" (447). Outka goes on to affirm Kingston's complex denial of cohesion and the book's use of postmodern play, a critical stance that is reaffirmed by many other critics—yet this affirming interpretation is far from exclusive.

Some critics, such as Chin, assert that the designation of the book as autobiography aligns the novel too intimately with Western culture and literary practices. Feng Lan summarizes the critical view that Kingston's revision of Chinese history and use of the Mulan myth is "a reckless hodgepodge of autobiography, history, and myth . . . . Kingston's reconfiguration reinterprets an indigenous legend from an Orientalist perspective, it perpetuates . . . Western prejudices about social relations in Chinese history" (229). Kingston's work defies any clear categorization within the genre of memoir, though critics seem most concerned by its supposed alignment with Western ideals. As LeiLani Nishime explains,

To her critics, Kingston violates the commitment to "factuality" that the name autobiography implies and, in doing so, confronts two differing traditions of autobiography. She challenges, on the one hand, the non-fiction appellation of autobiography, and, on the other hand, the anthropological information retrieval concept of ethnic autobiography. (71)

Ultimately, Nishime concludes that "Despite her attempts to subvert or write alternatives to the many master narratives of Anglo-American history, Chinese-American nationalism, feminist autobiography, and Chinese-American biography, among others, she can never completely escape those narratives" (81). Kingston challenges the gendered ideologies that dictate rules of form and genre, yet she cannot write beyond these pervasive institutional structures. Despite these sometimes harsh critiques regarding the novel's failure to fit neatly within or break free from genre conventions, many critics recognize the potential for expansion and defiance in Kingston's manipulation of the traditional memoir.

The notion of autobiography and its limits are questioned by many of Kingston's critics, who applaud what they see as a transcendence of genre in *The Woman Warrior*. Bonnie Melchior explains that "Western culture is preoccupied with the idea of 'self-making,' and in autobiography, individuality accounts for itself as made and gives the how of the making," invoking ideas of the self-made man and the need for a truthful account of events (112). While this initially seems to mirror early critiques of the novel, Melchior moves to claim that Kingston's work "challenges the assumptions of the genre and the shared assumptions of American culture," by exploring "the distinctions between oral and written discourse," or the distinctions between Western and Eastern traditions, in essence deconstructing autobiography by calling into question "the nature of fact" (282). Similarly, Bobby Fond asserts that "Kingston's narrative strategy expands our perception of what materials and techniques can be used to construct a usable past" in its use of myth and folktale; it further breaks convention by placing the narrator in the background, telling a circular story, and leaving the establishment of self unfinished, challenging the idea that "the normative pattern of personal growth should be a linear journey to individual autonomy" (116, 117). By breaking down traditional forms, Kingston makes way for new forms that better reflect hybridity and an identity that is constantly evolving—problematizing the idea of linear development and the ability to achieve a fully realized idea of Self.

Through this experimentation in form, critics see the possibility for new modes of expressing complex notions of multicultural community and identity. Victoria Myers asserts that autobiography enables Kingston to come "to terms with the community which, through language, structures her experience," moving away from elucidation of experience to interpretation of her multiple cultural contexts (113, 123). Rather than emphasizing events as crucial to development, Kingston reveals the importance of place, community, and history in identity formation. Sue Ann Johnston additionally avows that "[i]n its shifting line between history and memory, fiction and nonfiction, dream and fact, Kingston challenges western rational ways of seeing, classifying, and ordering" (136), insisting that Kingston does not play into Western definitions of autobiography but breaks from them. Johnston goes on to argue that "[b]y laying claim to her own language, her own voice, Kingston refuses the role of racial or sexual Other and invents herself as speaking subject," while drawing from and challenging "all the traditions she has inherited" (137). Kingston asserts the power of her own voice that was both shaped by and defies Western and Eastern influence. In Johnston's analysis, Orientalism is interlinked with the idea of the Other—minority groups who are depicted or stereotyped by the dominant culture as "lesser than." As Homi K. Bhabha explains,

> An important feature of colonial discourse is its dependence on the concept of "fixity" in the ideological construction of otherness. Fixity, as the sign of cultural/historical/racial difference in the discourse of colonialism, is a paradoxical mode of representation: it connotes rigidity and an unchanging order as well as disorder, degeneracy and daemonic repetition. (37)

By challenging the fixity of limiting gender roles and ethnic stereotypes, Kingston gives a voice to her diverse heritages and experiences and affirms her own unique coming-of-age. In these analyses, critics recognize the potential in Kingston's simultaneous use and defiance of traditional genre to explore a hybrid identity formation continually in flux.

Authenticity and Ethnicity

Another point of contention surrounding *The Woman Warrior* is the level of authenticity that Kingston brings to the text when depicting Chinese and Chinese American cultures. As Jeehyun Lim notes, "The debates regarding Kingston's text that flared up immediately after the book's publication primarily concerned authenticity and representation. These conflicts centered on whether Kingston's representation of Chinese culture and Chinese Americans was faithful" (49). Moreover, Woo explains that Kingston "has been more appreciated by her Anglo audience than by Chinese Americans," especially feminist critics who applaud Kingston's critique of the universal oppression and silencing of women. Yet Kingston's use of creative license and altering of cultural myths has attracted criticism, which Woo claims calls attention to "the dilemma which faces ethnic minority writers" in being expected to take on the role of spokesperson in their work rather than that of autonomous artist (173). These critiques question the role of the ethnic writer and the level of responsibility they carry in relation to their ethnic community and to themselves as artists.

One of the largest critiques of the novel is its use, whether purposeful or unintended, of the problematic codes of Orientalism. In her article, "The Mother as Other: Orientalism in Maxine Hong Kingston's *The Woman Warrior*," Sheryl Mylan contends that Kingston distances herself from her mother and her Chinese traditions through a veil of Orientalism. Su-lin Yu takes this critique further to claim that:

> [o]n the one hand, [Kingston] unwittingly constructs Chinese women in terms of her Orientalist desire and fantasy, inserting them into the context of American culture for self-empowerment. On the other, she is trapped within an Orientalist discourse she cannot escape . . . the

Orientalizing of oneself is often the price a Chinese-American writer has to pay to be accepted in America. (83)

Yu portrays Kingston as a victim of larger Western influences that cause her to misunderstand or betray her Eastern roots. In "A Chinese Woman's Response to Maxine Hong Kingston's *The Woman Warrior*," Ya-Jie Zhang writes that "*The Woman Warrior*, a favorite book of many of my American friends . . . did not appeal to me . . . because the stories in it seemed somewhat twisted. Chinese perhaps in origin but not really any more, full of American imagination" (17). She goes on to say that, "I felt that Kingston held too much bitterness against her mother and her Chinese origin" (Zhang 17). Moreover, Lim also acknowledges the concern that Kingston may "misrepresent the Chinese American community as barbaric while accommodating the mainstream readership's expectations for Orientalist tales," yet moves forward to assert that Kingston uses the seemingly barbaric image of tongue cutting to exhibit how "[t]he demand for conformity leaves its mark on the narrator's body, a mark that will impact all her social interactions involving language . . . The cut tongue begins as a sign of the bodily regulation that meets the social pressure of standardization, yet it ultimately becomes the figure through which Kingston resists" (49, 51, 62). Lim argues that Kingston's work doesn't fall victim to Western notions of Orientalism but uses these concepts to rebel against both limiting Western and Eastern ideals. This shift in recognizing Kingston's pluralistic approach to ethnic and multicultural experience is prevalent in much of the novel's criticism.

Many of Kingston's critics attest that her work pushes against not only the limits of genre but also against the limits of ethnic "authenticity." Qun Wang acknowledges that "[i]n the study of Asian American literature, the issue of 'authenticity' is as problematic as the definition of the term Asian American itself." As he examines the critique of Asian American writers who, "not only represent their own cultural heritage but also betray the values of that culture," Wang contends that we need to allow for a more varied interpretation of Asian American experience (278). In "'Don't Tell': Imposed Silences in *The Color Purple* and *The Woman Warrior*," King-

Kok Cheung stresses that "[b]linkering the authors by historical or ethnographic criteria denies their freedom as artists to mingle history and myth, fact and fiction" (163) and that writing the Self provides a form of defense and articulation, reflecting the multicultural legacy that speaks through these texts; these authors' voices remain distinct rather than assimilated, stereotyped, or homogenized. Katherine Hyunmi Lee asserts that Kingston portrays identity as a "perpetual negotiation between rebellion and concession" (20). Ultimately, for Lee, Kingston argues that identity is never complete or fully realized, destabilizing the categories of autobiography and Asian American woman. Similarly, Pirjo Ahokas notes that the conflict surrounding the reception of *The Woman Warrior* has "centered around questions of 'authentic' ethnic representation. Moreover, it has given expression especially to the anxieties of some male members from the Asian-American community over the 'correct' representation of Chinese-American gender relations" (103). In Kingston's work, we see how "the experience of gender is inextricably linked with race relations" (Ahokas 105) and how heterogeneous subjectivity and writing of the Self can transcend and connect generations and cultures. As we will see in other examinations of *The Woman Warrior*, Kingston's groundbreaking exploration of ethnicity enables new considerations of identity formation and understandings of the Self through language, culture, and history.

In investigating issues of ethnicity, authenticity, and identity, several critics focus specifically on the importance of voice and language. Victoria Chen recognizes the connections among subjectivity, voice, and identity in the works of Amy Tan and Kingston, asserting that the double voice needed to move through different languages and cultures results in a bicultural identity. Rufus Cook concentrates on what he sees as Kingston's preoccupation with "cultural and linguistic differences," asserting that wordplay bridges the gap between cultures and the male-female social dichotomy (133, 134, 146). Cheung looks at how "ethnicity is reinvented by Kingston," by making use of "an old myth and a traditional metaphor to discover new possibilities," especially for the protagonist Maxine, a character whose personality departs from "the original Chinese models and from the stereotypes of Asian women in America" (143). Cheung claims that Maxine seeks "refuge respectively in legend and in metaphor, and subsequently, to endow both with new significance" (144) to become self-made and powerful (152). Additionally, Steven V. Hunsaker observes that there is a "tense conflict between linguistic, ethnic, and familial identities" (437) and that the final scene of the novel captures the intricacy of pluralistic identity:

> Ts'ai Yen thus sings a barbarian song in Chinese, creating in the process surprising beauty through the fusion of cultures. By blending—and holding in sustained tension—Chinese culture, American culture, and the English language to create an identity based on a Chinese-American nationality, . . . Kingston accomplishes something very similar. (458)

By acknowledging the significance and limitations of multiple cultural, linguistic, and ethnic influences, we can begin to appreciate and analyze the complexity of hybridity and self-actualization.

Feminist Writing

Similar to the debates regarding genre and authenticity, gender and feminism are contended subjects in analyses of *The Woman Warrior*. While much criticism focuses on the successes within Kingston's work in terms of pushing against patriarchal limitations in both American and Chinese culture, some critics take issue with Kingston's limited view of female experience and her invocation of Orientalism and female stereotypes.

In critiques of the novel's failures in consideration of gender, we find a range of analyses that claim Kingston is shortsighted regarding the gender issues at stake in explorations of multiculturalism and hybridity. For example, Shu asserts that "Kingston does make a great effort to rewrite Chinese-American female subjectivity . . . but such an effort has been limited by her own vision, which is embedded in contradictory discourses of Western autobiography, US Orientalism on China and Chinese-America, and Chinese patriarchal tradition" (219). In essence, Kingston's work cannot escape the paradigms it merely responds to rather than breaks away from in her failure to "consider the specific historical and cultural contexts of minority and third-world women's experiences" (Shu 219). Likewise, Daphne P. Lei argues that "[t]hrough the images of tokenized and stereotypical Chinese culture (female oppression, tattooing cruelty, Confucian family value) . . . on the American stage, one realizes that . . . the Chinese woman remains oppressed and sexualized for the American gaze" (122). Lei positions Kingston as an American author appealing to a Western audience, translating Chinese cultural practices without historical context. Lei perceives this work as a poor translation that has negative results: "Oppressed Chinese womanhood seems to become a universal truth that needs no interpretation. Sexual inequality translates better than culture across space and time. This easy translatability of Chinese sexuality becomes the most telling (mis)interpretation of cultures" (122). For Lei, Kingston fails to see beyond Orientalist perspectives of Chinese female oppression, which is all the more problematic given the popularity of her work in the American multicultural literary tradition.

Although these critics fault Kingston for lack of context and criticism in her work, other scholars find validity in Kingston's engagement with feminist issues. Jennifer Griffiths argues that in *The Woman Warrior*, we find a break in the narrative reproduction of traumatic repetition and that the opening crisis symbolizes "a change from perpetuating narratives that reinscribe the female body with the indelible mark of trauma to experimental testimony that attempts to release the female body from the collective anxiety projected onto it" (354), giving transgenerational trauma of female oppression "a form and a voice" (369). Moira Gatens also examines the use of narrative, claiming that the active role of storytelling and transforming "the cultural and social imagery through the presentation of new cultural understandings" (50) can challenge traditional patriarchal power structures and lead to social change, as:

> Kingston's considerable talent allows her not only to join a conversation that long proceeded her but to open a *new, feminist, transformative,* topic of conversation. Kingston's memoir has made a significant impact on the social imaginary and is now a feminist

resource for challenging the power of subordinating gender norms and narratives. (50)

Antje Lindenmeyer examines the specific power of the feminist autobiography, claiming that Kingston "seeks to forge connections by rewriting and refashioning myths and stories, turning them from an instrument of oppression into a source of strength" (428), thereby grappling with two cultures that denigrate women. She concludes that Kingston's narrator must create a Chinese American Self: "[S]he remains fragmented and shaped by contradictory cultures. Retaining the position in the middle, wandering and mediating between the imaginary China and the concrete United States, she can at the same time reject and reshape the myths that formed her childhood" (429), finding matrilineal connections that provide relief from the isolation of diaspora. In comparing the autobiographies of Kingston and Kim Chernin, Jeanne Barker-Nunn claims that both authors are:

> entrusted with their immigrant mothers' stories, a legacy that they shape as both empowering and burdensome. The works they shape from these stories not only present us with a different perspective on our national history, but also offer a conception of history and of its relation to the self substantially different from that of the conventional, male-centered history. (55)

Instead, they locate a female history in which "past, present, self and other, are inextricably intertwined" (Barker-Nunn 56). Each of these critics finds power in Kingston's retelling and reshaping of her ethnic and familial history in order to locate a pluralized and autonomous Self.

Other feminist critics move to an examination of the power of silence, language, and the supernatural within Kingston's work. Jill M. Parrott argues that *The Woman Warrior* "expresses silence in three distinct ways: suppression by self-restraint, suppression by force, and suppression in translation" and asserts that we must reduce the privilege given to spoken/written language and more critically examine the meaning-making capability of silence (376). This assertion positions Kingston's work as powerful in its engagement with the rhetoric of silence in relation to ethnic and gendered identity: "She turns the expected obedience of her culture and family into a rhetorically powerful strategy, simultaneously embracing, rejecting, and manipulating it by translating it into her *own* version of the story" (Parrott 386). In Ken-fang Lee's analysis of translation and feminist studies, he posits both literary acts as being critically perceived as "secondary," driving their concern with the production of meaning. He further argues that ghosts capture the "in-betweeness" of struggling between two cultures and languages, and that "[g]hosts are exorcised by writing and translating the past to construct the future" (Lee 106). He asserts that Kingston "negotiate[s] and translate[s] cultural differences into identity formation and foreground[s] the process of hybridization . . . [thus] 'in-betweenness' opens up possibilities to bring ambiguity to the production of meaning and to challenge wholesale hegemony" (123), echoing critics who affirm Kingston's explorations of ethnicity. Likewise, Ruth Y. Jenkins asserts that the "use of the supernatural by women may also serve as a specific rhetorical strategy both to expose and counter the androcentric social and literary scripts that circumscribe 'acceptable' behavior" (61). She claims that Kingston and Isabel Allende, "through their appropriation of ghosts and spirits to authorize female voice, produce narratives doubly at odds with the traditional Anglo-American literary canon" (Jenkins 63). She concludes that "[t]he supernatural, then, provides women writers a means to challenge monolithic histories, narrative styles, evaluative standards, and scripts that dictate what experience is worthy of record and how that experience is to be articulated" (70). By examining Kingston's reshaping of myth, history, and cultural experience, as well as her attention to silence and language and inclusion of the supernatural, critics position *The Woman Warrior* as an important feminist work that affirms the power of the ethnic female voice and the possibilities of the female transnational memoir.

Throughout the collective criticism of *The Woman Warrior*, we can recognize the complications and interconnectedness of issues relating to genre, authenticity, ethnicity, and gender and how identity formation and its telling are fraught with political, social, and cultural implications. At the very least, Kingston's novel has elicited a significant conversation on identity, categorization, language, and writerly discourse, providing critics with a powerful piece that continues to speak to hybridity and multicultural experience decades after its initial publication.

Works Cited

Ahokas, Pirjo. "'Crossing the Sun and Lifting into the Mountains?' The Eccentric Subject in Maxine Hong Kingston's *The Woman Warrior.*" *American Studies in Scandinavia* 27 (1995): 103-125. Print.

Barker-Nunn, Jeanne. "Telling the Mother's Story: History and Connection in the Autobiographies of Maxine Hong Kingston and Kim Chernin." *Women's Studies* 14 (1987): 55-63. Print.

Bhabha, Homi K. "The Other Question." *Contemporary Postcolonial Theory: A Reader.* Ed. Padmini Mongia. London: Arnold, 1996. Print. 37-47.

Chen, Victoria. "Chinese American Women, Language, and Moving Subjectivity." *Women and Language* 13.1 (1995): n.p. *ProQuest.* Web. 11 Feb. 2016.

Chin, Frank. "Come All Ye Asian American Writers of the Real and the Fake." *The Big Aiiieeeee! An Anthology of Chinese American and Japanese American Writers.* Ed. Jeffrey Paul Chan, Frank Chin, Lawson Fusao Inada, and Shawn Wong. New York: Meridian, 1991. 1-93.

Cheung, King-Kok. "'Don't Tell': Imposed Silences in *The Color Purple* and *The Woman Warrior.*" *PMLA* 103.2 (1988): 162-174. *JSTOR.* Web. 2 Mar. 2016.

_____. "Self-fulfilling Visions in *The Woman Warrior* and *Thousand Pieces of Gold.*" *Biography* 13.2 (1990): 143-53. *Project MUSE.* Web. 12 Feb. 2016.

Cook, Rufus. "Cross-Cultural Wordplay in Maxine Hong Kingston's *China Men* and *The Woman Warrior.*" *MELUS* 22.4 (1997): 133-146. Print.

Fong, Bobby. "Maxine Kingston's Autobiographical Strategy in *The Woman Warrior.*" *Biography* 12.2 (1989): 116-26. *Project MUSE.* Web. 12 Feb. 2016.

Gatens, Moira. "Let's Talk Story: Gender and the Narrative Self." *Critical Horizons* 15.1 (2014): 40-51. Print.

Griffiths, Jennifer. "Uncanny Spaces: Trauma, Cultural Memory, and the Female Body in Gayl Jones's *Corregidora* and Maxine Hong Kingston's *The Woman Warrior*." *Studies in the Novel* 38.3 (2006): 353-70. *MLA International Bibliography*. Web. 2 Mar. 2016.

Hunsaker, Steven V. "Nation, Family, and Language in Victor Perera's *Rites* and Maxine Hong Kingston's *The Woman Warrior*." *Biography* 20.4 (1997): 437-61. *MLA International Bibliography*. Web. 2 Mar. 2016.

Kramer, Jane. "On Being Chinese in China and America: *The Woman Warrior*." *New York Times* (7 Nov 1976): n.p. *ProQuest*. Web. 1 May 2016.

Jenkins, Ruth Y. "Authorizing Female Voice and Experience: Ghosts and Spirits in Kingston's *The Woman Warrior* and Allende's *The House of Spirits*." *MELUS* 19.3 (1994): 61-73. Print.

Johnston, Sue Ann. "Empowerment Through Mythological Imaginings in Woman Warrior." *Biography* 16.2 (Spring 1993): 136-46. *Project MUSE*. Web. 12 Feb. 2016.

Lan, Feng. "The Female Individual and the Empire: A Historicist Approach to Mulan and Kingston's Woman Warrior." *Comparative Literature* 55.3 (2003): 229-45. *MLA International Bibliography*. Web. 2 Mar. 2016.

Lee, Katherine Hyunmi. "The Poetics of Liminality and Misidentification: Winnifred Eaton's *Me* and Maxine Hong Kingston's *The Woman Warrior*." *Studies in the Literary Imagination* 37.1 (2004): 17-33. *MLA International Bibliography*. Web. 2 Mar. 2016.

Lee, Ken-fang. "Cultural Translation and the Exorcist: A Reading of Kingston's and Tan's Ghost Stories." *MELUS* 29.2 (2004): 105-27. *MLA International Bibliography*. Web. 2 Mar. 2016.

Lei, Daphne P. "The Blood-Stained Text in Translation: Tattooing, Bodily Writing, and Performance of Chinese Virtue." *Anthropological Quarterly* 82.1 (2009): 99-128. Print.

Leonard, John. "In Defiance of 2 Worlds." *New York Times* (17 Sept. 1976): 69. *ProQuest*. Web. 1 May 2016.

Lim, Jeehyun. "Cutting the Tongue: Language and the Body in Kingston's *The Woman Warrior*." *MELUS* 31.3 (2006): 49-65. Print.

Lindenmeyer, Antje. "The Rewriting of Home: Autobiographies by Daughters of Immigrants." *Women's Studies International Forum* 24.3/4 (2001): 423-32. Print.

Madsen, Deborah L. "Chinese American Writers of the Real and the Fake: Authenticity and the Twin Traditions of Life Writing." *Canadian Review of American Studies* 36.3 (2006): 257-271. *EBSCOhost*. Web. 2 May 2016.

Melchior, Bonnie. "A Marginal 'I': The Autobiographical Self Deconstructed in Maxine Hong Kingston's *The Woman Warrior*." *Biography* 17.3 (1994): 281-95. *Project MUSE*. Web. 12 Feb. 2016.

Myers, Victoria. "The Significant Fictivity of Maxine Hong Kingston's *The Woman Warrior*." *Biography* 9.2 (1986): 112-25. *Project MUSE*. Web. 12 Feb. 2016.

Mylan, Sheryl A. "The Mother as Other: Orientalism in Maxine Hong Kingston's *The Woman Warrior*." *Women of Color: Mother-Daughter Relationships in 20th-Century Literature*. Ed. Elizabeth Brown Guillory. Austin: U of Texas P, 1996. 132-52. Print.

Nishime, LeiLani. "Engendering Genre: Gender and Nationalism in *China Men* and *The Woman Warrior*." *MELUS* 20.1 (1995): 67-82. *ProQuest*. Web. 11 Feb. 2016.

Outka, Paul. "Publish or Perish: Food, Hunger, and Self-Construction in Maxine Hong Kingston's *The Woman Warrior*." *Contemporary Literature* 38.3 (1997): 447-82. *MLA International Bibliography*. Web. 2 Mar. 2016.

Parrott, Jill M. "Power and Discourse: Silence as Rhetorical Choice in Maxine Hong Kingston's *The Woman Warrior*." *Rhetorica* 30.4 (2012): 375-91. Print.

Robertson, Nan. "'Ghosts' of Girlhood Lift Obscure Book To Peak of Acclaim." *New York Times* (12 Feb. 1977): 29. *ProQuest*. Web. 1 May 2016.

Said, Edward W. *Orientalism*. New York: Vintage Books, 1994. Print.

Shu, Yuan. "Cultural Politics and Chinese-American Female Subjectivity: Rethinking Kingston's *Woman Warrior*." *MELUS* 26.2 (2001): 199-223. Print.

Wang, Qun. "Border Crossing, Cultural Negotiations, and the Authenticity of Asian American Voices." *Passages: Journal of Transnational and Transcultural Studies* 1.2 (1999): 278-89. Print.

Wong, Sau-Ling Cynthia. "Autobiography as Guided Chinatown Tour? Maxine Hong Kingston's *The Woman Warrior* and the Chinese American Autobiographical Controversy." *Maxine Hong Kinsgston's* The Woman Warrior: *A Casebook*. Ed. Sau-ling Cythnia Wong. New York: Oxford UP, 1999. 29-53. Print.

Woo, Deborah. "Maxine Hong Kingston: The Ethnic Writer and the Burden of Dual Authenticity." *Amerasia* 16.1 (1990): 173-200. Print.

Yu, Su-lin. "Orientalist Fantasy and Desire in Maxine Hong Kingston's *The Woman Warrior*." *Transnational, National, and Personal Voice: New Perspectives on Asian American and Asian Diasporic Women Writers*. Ed. Begona Simal and Elizabeth Marino. New Brunswick: Transaction, 2004. 67-86. Print.

Zhang, Ya-jie. "A Chinese Woman's Response to Maxine Hong Kingston's *The Woman Warrior*. *Maxine Hong Kingston's* The Woman Warrior: *A Casebook*. Ed. Sau-ling Cynthia Wong. New York: Oxford UP, 1999. 17-21. Print.

"'What is Chinese tradition and what is the movies?': A Transnational Approach to Maxine Hong Kingston's *The Woman Warrior: Memoirs of a Girlhood Among Ghosts*

Linda Trinh Moser

Early in Maxine Hong Kingston's *The Woman Warrior*, the narrator asks: "Chinese-Americans, when you try to understand what things in you are Chinese, how do you separate what is peculiar to childhood, to poverty, insanities, one family, your mother who marked your growing with stories, from what is Chinese? What is Chinese tradition and what is the movies?" (5-6). In the forty years since its publication, critics have taken up the narrator's preoccupation, leading to a well-known debate over the "authenticity" of Kingston's representation of Chinese and Chinese American culture. Much of the debate centers on Kingston's use of the Fa Mu Lan (Hua Mulan in the Pinyin transcription system) legend in the "White Tigers" chapter. Her earliest and most vocal critics include Jeffrey Chan, Frank Chin, Lawson Inada, and Shawn Wong, editors of the groundbreaking 1974 anthology *Aiiieeeee! An Anthology of Asian American Writers* and its expanded edition, *The Big Aiiieeeee! An Anthology of Chinese American and Japanese Literature*, published in 1991. In the latter, Chin attacked Kingston for inventing a "fake" Chinese American culture to appeal to white readers. His approach can be described loosely as "cultural nationalism," reflecting the belief that all those with Chinese ancestry share a single culture. Cultural nationalists and other like-minded critics argue that Kingston perpetuates stereotypes and prejudice by reinterpreting Chinese legends from an "Orientalist" perspective; in other words, in a way that patronizes and looks down upon Asian cultures. Those on the other side of the debate have responded directly to what has been described as a "wholesale endorsement of traditional classics," which "risks reinstalling patriarchal mores and even smacks of patriarchal ancestral worship" (Cheung 238). Highlighting Kingston's concern with gender inequality, for example, King-kok Cheung defends Kingston against what she perceives to be exclusionary definitions of Chinese American identity based on masculine or "heroic" traits. Critics have also supported *The Woman Warrior* by highlighting its fictional aspects; Sau-ling Wong takes this approach, arguing that Kingston's use of Chinese myths and folklore should "be read as a fantasy, not historical reconstruction" (29). Deborah L. Madsen, likewise, challenges notions of cultural "authenticity" by examining "the strategies by which elements of an ethnic cultural tradition are reworked so that they become expressive of a feminist voice instead of expressing traditional patriarchal values" (220). By calling attention to literary techniques and challenging patriarchal values, these approaches provide a necessary corrective.

Additional support for Kingston's revisions come from critics who invoke the idea of transnationalism. As an adjective, transnational describes practices that occur between or beyond national boundaries and that involve several nations or nationalities. As a noun, it describes an entity operating in multiple countries. By conveying the back-and-forth dynamics and interplay of various cultures, the concept of "transnational" builds upon the term "multicultural," which designates the existence of multiple cultures but not necessarily the relationship between them. As such, transnational approaches highlight the state of being outside of, in between, across, or beyond nations. Thus, a transnational approach to literature, in addition to recognizing the multicultural resonances of a work, will also question lines of inquiry that attempt to promote notions of culture as static and, therefore, challenge distinctions between "real" and "fake" versions of culture. It overthrows the notion of discrete national literatures or the idea that ethnic works belong only to minor categories of national literatures. In the case of Asian American literature, these arise from what Shirley Lim and the other editors of *Transnational Asian American Literatures: Sites and Transits* (2006), describe as:

The diasporic, mobile, transmigratory nature of Asian American experience, a history characterized by disparate migratory threads, unsettled and unsettling histories churned by multiple and different Asian ethnic immigrant groups each with a different language and cultural stock, different value and belief systems, and different notions of literary aesthetics, albeit most largely mediated through the English language. (1)

This chapter uses examples from "At the Western Palace," the fourth chapter of *The Woman Warrior*, to show how Kingston draws from her trans-Pacific roots to express a "transnational sensibility" (Friedman 5). The narrator of *The Woman Warrior* does not physically experience transnationalism in the way outlined by Lim; in other words, she does not physically migrate to another country. Instead, as Schultermandl notes, her "negotiation of the cultural differences and similarities she perceives between herself and her Chinese ancestry" (40) enacts the same journey as her paternal aunt, the "no name woman" who seeks to "[cross] boundaries not delineated in space" (Kingston 8). Her cultural negotiation requires reimagining the shape and scope of nations, the cultures associated with them, and the boundaries between them. Like the other sections of *The Woman Warrior*, "At the Western Palace" imagines, negotiates, and undermines the boundaries between Chinese, American, and Chinese American by overlapping narrative forms associated with both the narrator's Chinese mother and American culture. The narrator can only begin to understand her life in the US when she can see the lives of her female ancestors "branch[ing]" into hers.

"At the Western Palace" begins in stark contrast to the previous sections. Told in the third- rather than first-person, the section seems more realistic with characters who are "no longer distanced by time, space, or a frame tale" and "correspond to Kingston's living kin" (Yalom 111). But, like previous sections, "At the Western Palace" is also filtered through the author's imagination. The narrator emphasizes her imaginative intervention into the story about Moon Orchid at the beginning of the next section, "A Song for a Barbarian Reed Pipe," when she says: "What my brother actually said was. . . . 'I drove Mom and Second Aunt to Los Angeles to see Aunt's husband who's got the other wife'" (163). This is a highly condensed version of the events described in "At the Western Palace." The story's veracity is further undermined when the narrator reveals her brother's imperfect memory. He insists, not once but twice, that he doesn't remember anything about the conversation between Moon Orchid and her husband: "I don't remember . . . [Moon Orchid] saying one thing" (163). And to further demonstrate the narrator's removal from the events, she provides another surprising detail: She was also not present when her brother recounted the story. Instead, she heard it—second hand—from her sister who did hear it from her brother. In short, the narrator is three times removed from Moon Orchid's story; it is told by her brother, who told it to a sister, who told it to the narrator.

In this way, the narrator makes obvious that she has elaborated and "twisted into designs" (163) her version of Moon Orchid's story. Before this chapter, the narrator provides multiple clues that her characters are never exact duplicates of living people. About this particular chapter, Kingston has said:

> Students want you to come to class and tell them, . . . "Yes I have this aunt, Moon Orchid." They want that. But what I want is to see the stories change. . . . I try to keep that extra doubt in the stories. I throw it in. I can't help it, it seems to be part of every story." (Islas 31; qtd. in Yalom 111-112)

Even without this admission, readers perceive textual evidence that the purpose of "At the Western Palace" is not merely to reproduce objective historical events. Kingston, for example, indicates Brave Orchid's magical thinking and her belief in her own supernatural ability in the description of her mother "add[ing] her willpower to the forces that keep Moon Orchid's airplane up" in the air as she flies to San Francisco from Hong Kong (113). Kingston does not merely recount autobiographical details but crafts her story to convey a transnational sensibility. Her use of cultural content from both the US and China, however, does not merely promote an unreflective multiculturalism that ignores social inequity. As the narrator strives to reconcile an "American life" with her Chinese

Critical Insights

heritage, she explores the way both cultures in which she grows up are "interpenetrating," (Fishkin 21). In other words, she creates new combinations of Chinese myth and Western narrative forms, not merely to make her story seem more "exotic" or palatable to Western audiences, but to expose and challenge racism and gender inequality no matter where it exists.

Kingston draws from several Chinese sources in "At the Western Palace." Kathryn VanSpanckeren identifies "a myth 'Goddess Chang [sic] Ascends to the Moon,' told during the Mid-Autumn Harvest Festival" (48), which occurs on the night of the full Moon in the eighth lunar month when Chang'e, who lives on the moon, is reunited temporarily with her husband, who lives on the sun. Multiple versions of this myth exist, but in all, Chang'e is eventually rewarded (by the gods) for her faithfulness and duty to her husband after long suffering his absence. Kingston signals the similarities between Moon Orchid and Chang'e in several ways. Most obviously, like Chang'e, Moon Orchid is separated and forced to live apart from her husband. When her husband immigrates to the US, Moon Orchid, with their daughter, stayed in Hong Kong where "[f]or thirty years she had been receiving money from him" (124). The two characters are also linked by their association with the moon, where Chang'e has been forced to reside. Details that Kingston introduces, however, create stark differences between the myth and adaptation. In contrast to the joyful anticipation of being reunited with her husband that Chang'e experiences, Moon Orchid is anxious and fearful. From the beginning of her US sojourn, she regrets following her sister's advice to attempt a reunion. Kingston's revision also deflates the celebratory aspects of the myth when she reduces the elaborate Mid-Autumn feast to "lunch. . . . [a]t a good restaurant" (114), extorted by Brave Orchid when she finally realizes that her brother-in-law has no intention of welcoming his wife and daughter into his American life.

Kingston clearly makes changes to the Chinese original, but viewing the adaptation as a "fake" version that diminishes Chinese experience by perpetuating a Western Orientalist position (as she has been accused of doing) is too simplistic. By foregrounding the pressures immigrants face to adapt and assimilate to new surroundings, "At the Western Palace" does present a "real" issue. Unable to adapt to new surroundings and a "foreign" culture, Moon Orchid loses everything: her husband, her home in Hong Kong, and eventually her mind. She spends her last days in an asylum for the mentally ill after being prescribed thorazine to alleviate symptoms of schizophrenia (an irony, given that her estranged husband is a neurologist). Brave Orchid understands her sister's illness as a lack of discursive power:

> Brave Orchid saw that all variety had gone from her sister. She was indeed mad. "The difference between mad people and sane people," Brave Orchid explained to the children, "is that sane people have variety when they talk-story. Mad people have only one story that they talk over and over." (159)

The doctor-husband, too, presents his life in terms related to stories, describing his assimilation into American culture and transformation in terms of myth: "It's as if I had turned into a different person. The new life around me was so complete; it pulled me away. You became people in a book I had read a long time ago" (154). In contrast to his first wife, the doctor-husband is fully assimilated. Wealthy and married (albeit bigamously) to an ethnic Chinese wife who has an "American look" and "[speaks] less like a Chinese than Brave Orchid's children" (148), he "look[s] and [smell[s] like an American" and "talk[s] like a child born here" (152; 153). His ability to adapt to new surroundings has even surpassed that of Brave Orchid who "could not practice openly in the United States because the training here was so different and because she could never learn English," despite having "been a surgeon too" in China (149). Reflecting the rags-to-riches trajectory of the American Dream, his life has been transformed by his cultural assimilation and the financial and professional success he has found.

Although the doctor and Moon Orchid seem to represent opposite responses to American culture by immigrants, like Moon Orchid, he also has "only one story" that excludes the kind of "variety" Kingston introduces in *The Woman Warrior* through her narrator. Like the cultural nationalists whose either/or categories designate Asian American literature as either "real" or "fake," the doctor's single-sided narrative leaves room for either American or Chinese culture, not both. For him, the stories of his American present and Chinese past are mutually exclusive. Despite his pledge to continue his financial support of Moon Orchid, he relegates her (and their daughter) to the past and refuses to make a place for her in his life. Although the doctor's story represents success in professional and financial terms, he is not the hero of this tale. Thus, rather than praising the American Dream, Kingston's story challenges it. Transplanting Chinese myth into an immigrant context provides a cautionary tale that highlights the difficulties of cultural adaptation while also dramatizing the potential dangers faced by individuals who grow up in more than one culture. In particular, it draws attention to the negative consequences of assimilating to the point of cultural erasure. In "At the Western Palace," attaining the American Dream comes at great cost.

Kingston juxtaposes the tragedy of Moon Orchid's inability to rekindle a relationship with her husband and to live independently with humorous comments and elements. One example is a description of Brave Orchid's encouragement: "[she] gave her sister last-minute advice for five hundred miles" (143). Comedic elements also emerge in the observations Moon Orchid makes as she stalks her nieces and nephews around their home. As if narrating a documentary about a "primitive" culture, she "described them aloud. 'Now they're studying again. They read so much. Is it because they have enormous quantities to learn, and they're trying not to be savages?'" (140). From her perspective, living in the US is "roughing it in the wilderness" and her American-born relatives are "savages." Mimicking an anthropologist, Moon Orchid attempts to "translate" American culture, but she gets much of it wrong. She renders, for example, a pair of beaters for an electric mixer as "spiders" that "spin the eggs" (140) and butter as "cow oil" (141). Kingston uses humor to highlight the potential for bias in cultural representations. Here, she turns the tables on the Western tradition of exoticizing and "Orientalizing" the East.

Kingston's addition of transnational elements to Moon Orchid's story also includes a feminist critique. While Moon Orchid's tragedy elicits great sympathy, it also serves as a warning to women not to become like Moon Orchid, who like Chang'e, "merely lives a life of reflected light, dependent on her absent husband" (VanSpanckeren 49). Kingston undermines the myth's implicit glorification of female passivity; in the contemporary version, the gods do not offer any "reward" to a woman who waits for an absent spouse. The criticism, however, is not directed at China only. A criticism of US patriarchy emerges in her use of elements from *I Love Lucy*, a television sitcom that originally aired from 1951 to 1957. Highly popular, "in one form or another, the program has reportedly never been out of syndication in the United States" (Desjardins 56). In explaining the switch from first- to third- person in "At the Western Palace," Kingston described the show as an influence:

And actually what gave me a lot of help was thinking of "I Love Lucy." I thought, what an easy form; I could work in that form. The first half of the show is Lucy and Ethel. . . . and they are stirring up everything. They are plotting to do something that will get their husbands into a lot of trouble. And then, by the second half, there's the confrontation, where all of them, Ricky and Fred, and everybody, they all clash, and they're chasing all over the place, and there's all this excitement, and then the resolution. (Chin 87)

In Kingston's adaptation, Brave Orchid and Moon Orchid take the roles of Lucy and Ethel, respectively. Like Lucy, Brave Orchid is a schemer whose plans never turn out as intended. She is presented as the leader, bold and self-assured, while Moon Orchid, her follower, is unsure and susceptible to being bossed around. Brave Orchid's plan is elaborate. She encourages her sister to give up her home in Hong Kong and immigrate to the US. She tells Moon Orchid: "Your husband is going to have to see you. We'll make him recognize you. Ha" (124). Five years before her sister's arrival, Brave Orchid had also arranged a marriage between Moon Orchid's daughter and a Chinese American, making the US a more attractive location with her child and grandchildren already living there. Although Moon

Orchid reveals that she is "scared" and "want[s] to go back to Hong Kong" (125), Brave Orchid masterfully counters her sister's every objection just as Lucy deflects any protest put up by Ethel. When Moon Orchid worries that her husband will be angry, Brave Orchid tells her: He deserves your getting angry with him. For abandoning you and for abandoning your daughter" (125). At each step, Brave Orchid tells her sister what to say, crafting and helping to her to rehearse responses to possible objections from her husband.

Despite Brave Orchid's efforts, her carefully constructed plan begins to unravel, following a pattern featured in almost every episode of *I Love Lucy*. But in Kingston's version, the ensuing events are not funny. Moon Orchid becomes increasingly fearful and reluctant; her daughter backs out on the plan to lend support. Brave Orchid, like Lucy, however, remains undaunted. When Moon Orchid attempts to delay her reunion with a detour to visit her grandchildren, Brave Orchid turns them into a "reward." "You take care of this other business," she tells her sister, "and [then] you can play with your grandchildren without worry" (146). Whereas Moon Orchid is intimidated by evidence of her husband's success and wealth, her sister is emboldened. "It would serve a rich man right to be humbled" (147), she thinks. Like Lucy, Brave Orchid's plans also involve trickery. To gain access to her brother-in-law's office, she feigns illness. When she is turned away by his nurse-wife, Brave Orchid, undeterred, improvises another "new plan" (149) on the spot. She enlists her reluctant son, a stand-in for Ricky and Fred, "to go up to his office and tell [his] uncle that there has been an accident out in the street" (150). Brave Orchid's own husband had backed out much earlier, as soon as she announced: "Now! We have to get down to business" (123).

Just as Moon Orchid's story subverts the fantasy of Chang'e, it also subverts the humor of television sitcoms. In *I Love Lucy*, the schemes of women, despite turning out badly, end in comedy. In "At the Western Palace," they lead to tragedy. Lucy's relentless defiance of Ricky provides the foundation for humor; however, no laugh track accompanies Brave Orchid's continual defiance of the reality of her sister's life. When the trick to get her brother-in-law to meet with the sisters succeeds, Brave Orchid believes she has the upper hand. But his failure to recognize them breaks the illusion of Brave Orchid's fantasy of power. "What's wrong," he asks, "What is it, Grandmothers?" (152). The reminder of the thirty years that have passed since he left China and his wife abruptly snaps the story from the realm of Hollywood sitcom and fairy-tale possibility. Unlike characters on television or in a fable, Moon Orchid and her sister have aged. Although Brave Orchid manages to coerce the husband into taking them to lunch, she has lost the upper hand; in fact, she may never have had it.

Kingston's revision of a well-known television show highlights the unequal power relations between men and women in both Asian and American cultural productions. Much of the show's humor comes from Lucy's failed attempts to enter "show biz" and to succeed in the public realm of business. Although Lucy relentlessly defies Ricky, male dominance is always reinstated and reaffirmed at the end of each episode. The show "ultimately does the cultural work of promoting the patriarchal nuclear family with husband/father working outside the home and wife-mother taking care of house and children" (Desjardin 58). Similarly, at the end of "At the Western Palace," Moon Orchid remains dependent on her husband. Borrowing the sitcom formula reminds us that patriarchy is not a Chinese institution and that sexism is also an inherent part of American culture.

The incongruity between the "moral" or lesson offered at the end of "At the Western Palace" and the story's tone further challenges the dual problems of Western ethnocentrism and patriarchy. After learning of their aunt's fate, "Brave Orchid told her children they must help her keep their father from marrying another woman," and her "daughters decided fiercely that they would never let men be unfaithful to them. All her children made up their minds to major in science or mathematics" (Kingston 169). In knee-jerk fashion, the women attribute Moon Orchid's downfall to polygamous marriage. By implicating a cultural practice associated with China, they obscure and deflect attention from their own bias. Their proposed strategies reinstate the notion that a woman's worth is dependent on her relationship with a man. The tidy moral-at-the-end associated with Western fables also undermines itself. By invoking the stereotypes of Asian Americans as "model minorities" predicated on the (incorrect) belief that are naturally or genetically predisposed to be good at math and science, the second-generation sisters reveal that they have grasped only one meaning of Moon Orchid's life in their determination to become self-supporting women. They have failed to gauge the story's equal condemnation of American forms of patriarchy and ethnocentrism.

"At the Western Palace," like the other stories in *The Woman Warrior*, illustrates the importance of adaptation and improvisation, qualities that are important to a transnational sensibility. Like Lucy, Brave Orchid is a woman who struggles to break free of the domestic realm. And she does. As a "Gold Mountain" widow—one of thousands of women left behind in China when their husbands immigrated to the US—she challenges social norms to get an education that enables her to support herself and family as a medical practitioner. After a long period of separation, she accomplishes what Moon Orchid cannot. She immigrates to the US, reclaims her husband, and rebuilds her family. Brave Orchid momentarily fails to understand that her strategies cannot be imposed upon or reproduced successfully by another whose situation and circumstances differ greatly from her own. Her success, in both China and the US, comes from her ability to transform and adapt, an important lesson that her American-born daughter has learned. Using a transnational lens to read "At the Western Palace" highlights the intentional use of both Chinese and American stories. By allowing different narrative forms to interpenetrate, Kingston highlights the cultures that influence her own identity while also criticizing both Chinese and North American cultures. By blending Chinese and American stories, Kingston insists that transnational elements are very much a part of US cultures. Rather than singling out and separating traditional Chinese motifs from popular American culture, readers should look for ways they converse with one another to create new forms better equipped to combat gender and racial bias.

Works Cited

Cheung, King-Kok. "Slated Allusions: Transnational Poetics and Politics of Marilyn Chin and Russell Leong. *[P]ositions* 22.1 (Winter 2014): 237-262. Print.

Chin, Marilyn. "Writing the Other: A Conversation with Maxine Hong Kingston." Skenazy & Martin. 86-103. Print.

Desjardins, Mary. "Lucy and Desi: Sexuality, Ethnicity, and TV's First Family." *Television, History, and American Culture: Feminist Critical Essays.* Ed. Mary Beth Haralovich & Lauren Rabinovitz. Durham, NC: Duke UP, 1999. 56-74. Print.

Fishkin, Shelley Fisher. "Crossroads of Cultures: The Transnational Turn in American Studies: Presidential Address to the American Studies Association, November 12, 2004." *American Quarterly* 57.1 (2005): 17-57. Web.

Friedman, May & Silvia Schultermandl. Introduction. *Growing Up Transnational: Identity and Kinship in a Global Era.* Toronto: U of Toronto P, 2011. Print.

Islas, Arturo with Marilyn Yalom. "Interview with Maxine Hong Kingston." Skenazy & Martin. 21-32. Print.

Kingston, Maxine Hong. *The Woman Warrior: Memoirs of a Girlhood Among Ghosts.* 1976. New York: Vintage-Random, 1989. Print.

Lim, Shirley Geok-lin. *Approaches to Teaching Kingston's* The Woman Warrior. New York: Modern Language Association, 1991. 26-36. Print.

Madsen, Deborah. *Feminist Theory and Literary Practice.* London: Pluto, 2000. Print.

Schultermandl, Silvia. "The Politics of Transnational Identity in and of Maxine Hong Kingston's *The Woman Warrior. On the Legacy of Maxine Hong Kingston: The Mullhouse Book.* Ed. Sämi Ludwig & Nicoleta Alexoae-Zagni. Zurich and Berlin: Lit Verlag, 2014. 33-44. Contributions to Asian Literary Ser. Print.

Skenazy, Paul & Tera Martin, eds. *Conversations with Maxine Hong Kingston.* Jackson: UP of Mississippi, 1998. Print.

VanSpanckeren, Kathryn. "The Asian Literary Background of *The Woman Warrior.*" Lim. 44-51. Print.

Wong, Sau-ling Cynthia. "Kingston's Handling of Traditional Chinese Sources." Lim. 26-36. Print.

Yalom, Marilyn. "*The Woman Warrior* as Postmodern Autobiography."
Lim. 108-115. Print.

Deliberately Forgetting: The Invention of Unnamed Ancestors in Maxine Hong Kingston and Maya Angelou

David Borman

> You hear a version of the music, and then you go out and make your own music.
>
> (Maxine Hong Kingston, 2006)

If Maxine Hong Kingston's *The Woman Warrior* is widely regarded as the most frequently taught text in American universities by a living author, the book's opening segment, "No Name Woman," is easily the most anthologized portion of that text. In a 2006 interview, Kingston told Nicoleta Alexoae-Zagni that one of the central narrative devices—the melding of fiction and memoir—was a strategy meant to reflect the rhetorical position of narrator and subject:

> I was working with a form that was a melting of fiction and non-fiction. This is because I was writing about actual people who had wild imaginations and the narrator herself had a wild imagination. She had to have an imagination, because nobody would tell her the truth, so she had to imagine the truth. (25)

Such a situation, in which truth must be imagined, is central to the book's opening story, in which the adult narrator (whom I'll refer to as Maxine) retells her mother's story from before immigration and then proceeds to interpret that story through a number of possible lenses. In telling the history of her aunt who committed suicide after having a baby out of wedlock, "No Name Woman" gives definition to a family history that was not meant to be remembered.

This essay explores Kingston's act of imagining the truth about her aunt as a rhetorical choice that allows for a transnational sense of affiliation to emerge in Kingston's narrator. I compare the approaches of "No Name Woman" and Maya Angelou's 1986 memoir *All God's Children Need Traveling Shoes* as texts that imagine and invent specific ancestry in the face of active forgetting. Angelou—an African American "returnee" to Ghana in the 1960s—imagines ancestors from Ghana just before their moments of capture into Atlantic slavery. Her invented Ghanaian grandmothers and grandfathers are historically rooted, but in the end, they lack the power to explain her deep sense of transnational affiliation with Ghana and the African continent. Such connection, for Angelou, can only come through contact and dialogue with contemporary Ghanaian citizens. By contrast, Kingston's approach in "No Name Woman" focuses solely on the invention, on the unable-to-be-named aunt who serves as an inspiration to and counterpart for Kingston herself.

Kingston's "No Name Woman"

The opening story of Kingston's memoir is many things: a retelling of her mother's cautionary tale, an exploration of her family's past in China, and an examination of her own identity as Chinese American. "No Name Woman" begins with the story itself, as Kingston relays the words her mother told her twenty years earlier about her father's sister. The mother opens the story by telling Maxine, "In China your father had a sister who killed herself. She jumped into the family well. We say that your father has all brothers because it is as if she had never been born" (3). Her mother continues to tell of the aunt, who became pregnant while her husband was away working in the United States. The home the two women shared was attacked by villagers who "threw mud and rocks at the house," "began slaughtering our stock," and tore apart sacks of rice and clothing throughout the home (4). The night of the attack, the unnamed aunt gave birth to her baby in the pigsty and then drowned herself and the child in the family well. Maxine's mother warns her, "Now that you have started to menstruate, what happened to her could happen to you. Don't humiliate us. You wouldn't like to be forgotten as if you had never been born" (5).

In the story, Kingston then proceeds to unpack her mother's cautionary tale, suggesting rationales for why the aunt may have become pregnant, or what motivated her to drown herself and the child in the well. Key to Kingston's interpretation is her belief that her mother's story "tested our strength to establish realities" (*Woman Warrior* 5). This, according to Kingston, was a defining feature of growing up in a Chinese American household: "Those of us in the first American generations have had to figure out how the invisible world the emigrants built around our childhoods fits in the solid America" (5). In her attempts to fit the two together, Kingston reanimates her unnamed aunt's life, giving her actions meaning well beyond a cautionary tale of transgression and humiliation. Kingston imagines the no-name woman just as she has given birth and the simultaneous shock and love that accompany the moment:

> She reached down to touch the hot, wet, moving mass, surely smaller than anything human, and could feel that it was human after all—fingers, toes, nails, nose. She pulled it up on to her belly, and it lay curled there, butt in the air, feet precisely tucked one under the other. She opened her loose shirt and buttoned the child inside. (14-15)

Similarly, Kingston gives the no-name woman thoughts at the moment of her death that indicate purposeful and defiant action: "Carrying the baby to the well shows loving. Otherwise abandon it. Turn its face into the mud. Mothers who love their children take them along" (15).

Such details and interpretations give a more rounded portrait of the unnamed aunt. Although she is denied an identity through the family's deliberate amnesia, Kingston's narrative offers actions and thoughts as a substitute. The loving act of pulling the newborn close after birth is paired with a different act of love, taking the child to the well with her. Kingston's interpretations here do more than simply give life to the story. They imagine and feel a connection to her family's past in China—a connection not available in her mother's version of the story.

The initial narrative that Kingston relays from her mother is deliberately devoid of details. Perhaps because it is impossible to detail the life of one who "had never been born," the opening story cannot explain the aunt's death beyond a simple observation, as Maxine's mother tells her, "The next morning when I went for the water, I found her and the baby plugging up the family well" (5). In light of such a non-specific vision of her aunt, Kingston's project of reconstructing a life for her ancestor becomes something heroic in itself. To tell the story of the "No Name Woman," for Kingston, is to defy the non-detailed version of family history she has received for years. In the pages that follow her mother's initial story, Kingston reimagines her aunt and invents a sense of self that aligns her aunt's (assumed) act of resistance with Kingston's own resistant text.

This flattening of history and circumstance is perhaps the most controversial aspect of "No Name Woman." As Yuan Shu convincingly argues, Kingston's story is aimed at a non-Chinese American audience, and many of these potential readers are less attuned to cultural circumstance. Shu claims that these readers "often construe the story in terms of the American cultural imagination of China and the Chinese people and thus confirm the US Orientalist construction of China as misogynist and irrational" (207). The lack of broader cultural context in the story thus reinforces a vision of China that does not match with the contemporary nation, according to Shu. Other readings of the story, which focus on Kingston's powerful adoption of her aunt's story as a method for ending the family's punishment by silence, similarly view Kingston's rhetorical act as a rebellion in itself. Jill Parrott sees the actual narration as "Kingston's rhetorical choice to extend existence back to that long-dead relative by telling the story, gaining power for herself and her aunt" (379).

These readings address important aspects of the story. Kingston does gloss over a number of cultural complexities and present an image of China aligned with Anglo America's imagined China. And the overt power struggle centered on the ability to tell a story is a significant push in the story's conclusion. However, I want to suggest an alternative reading of Kingston's motivation to reimagine her aunt's life: giving the no-name woman a story in this fashion is Kingston's effort to animate her family's history for herself.

Kingston herself has recognized the individual nature of her writing, as she stressed individuality in her essay "Cultural Mis-readings by American Reviewers." But she also stresses, in a 1991 interview with Shelley Fisher Fishkin, that her stories are meant to affect readers as individuals:

> And what I want is to give people questions (which I think are very creative things)—and then when people wrestle with them and struggle with them in their own minds and in their own lives, all kinds of exciting things happen to them. I don't want people to throw the responsibility back on me. (785)

I see the personal nature of "No Name Woman" in the act of animating an unnamed ancestor with thoughts, feelings, and a deep sense of morality, which I claim suggests that Kingston's tale is one attempt to come to terms with a place and a history she never truly understood at the outset. The attempts to remember an ancestor who had been willfully forgotten are key to the narrator's attempts at defining herself in any cultural sense. Although, as Carole Center points out, the story does focus on "the instability of the self and of reality," the narrative continually pushes towards stability through the act of inventing an aunt (232). Rather than look to the fragmentation evident in the narrator's sense of Self—rather than see Maxine as divided between acting "American pretty" or "dignified and honorable"—I suggest that Kingston's "No Name Woman" foregrounds the act of telling the story as one of simultaneous discovery and invention of a cultural Self (12).

In a 2006 interview, Kingston explained the role of telling stories anew throughout human history:

> Before any people had discovered writing, we all told one another stories and told one another our ancestry, our adventures, our history and our imaginings. We listened to those stories and then we passed them on. From the very beginning, every time a story is being told, it changes in order to fit the circumstances and needs of the people who hear it. (Alexoae-Zagni 20)

She continues, comparing storytelling to jazz music: "You hear a version of the music, and then you go out and make your own music" (Alexoae-Zagni 20). Inspiration, in this case, is important, but not as important as the uses one makes of the music. In Kingston's case, her mother's story (or, at the very least, her memory of her mother's story) is a vital connection to the past but not one that can explain Kingston's specific connection to the past. For her mother, this is a tale about a place and time she experienced; for a young Maxine, China is a secondhand memory. Making her own music—narrating her own China—is both an act of love and defiance for Kingston, as she can use her no-name aunt to "fit the circumstances and needs" of the child and adult who cannot feel stably situated in the US.

Near the end of the story, just after Kingston has lovingly described the unnamed child's birth and her aunt's act of suicide, she situates the story once again in relation to the narrative her mother tells. She says that the decades of silence about this unnamed ancestor were partially caused by the family's migration to the US: "I have thought that my family, having settled among immigrants who had also been their neighbors in the ancestral land, needed to clean their name, and a wrong word would incite the kinspeople even here" (16). In a way, the silence is an inheritance from China, the only inheritance that "No Name Woman" points to for its readers. By investigating and unpacking that silence—by actually working to give her aunt a voice and a perspective—Kingston connects with the only cultural transfer from China in her mother's story. She goes further, comparing her opening story to paper replicas of houses, clothes, and automobiles: "My aunt haunts me—her ghost drawn to me because now, after fifty years of neglect, I alone devote pages of paper to her, though not origamied into houses and clothes" (16). Remembering, animating, and writing about the no-name woman is Kingston's connection to the Chinese past that is only mentioned in passing throughout the story.

Yet at the same time, Kingston acknowledges that her work—as much as it may connect her to a Chinese past she does not understand—is an act of rebellion against what she understands to be her cultural heritage. Initially, she takes blame for participating in the swift and continued forgetting of her aunt: "But there is more to this silence: they want me to participate in her punishment. And I have. In the twenty years since I heard this story, I have not asked for details nor said my aunt's name; I do not know it" (16). But to the degree that she has perpetuated this punishment, her story also pushes against the cultural logic of forgetting the one who caused family humiliation. She identifies this punishment for what it is to her from the US: "The real punishment was not the raid swiftly inflicted by the villagers, but the family's deliberately forgetting her. Her betrayal so maddened them, they saw to it that she would suffer forever, even after death" (16). Such an act of identification, when combined with the lovingly described scenes from her unnamed aunt's life, suggests a willed connection to her family's Chinese past, even when her mother insists on treating the no-name woman "as if she had never been born" (3). Kingston explained the impulse further to Fishkin: "I realized that by writing about her I gave her back life and a place in history and maybe immortality. And then I thought, it's a duty of mine to save her in this way" (786). The duty, at least in part, is to remember her family's unspoken cultural past and to further find history's place within Kingston's own life as well.

Angelou's *All God's Children Need Traveling Shoes*
In her seven volumes of autobiography, along with countless poems and essays, Maya Angelou established herself as a key voice in African American and global literature. The autobiographies in particular chronicle her ever-changing roles: poor southern black girl, working-class single mother, nightclub calypso singer, globetrotting actress, freelance journalist, African "returnee," civil rights coordinator, and professor for life. Because of the sheer variety of roles Angelou inhabits in her autobiographies, her works convey a sense of Self larger than an individual life, and she is often cited as an influential black voice who "write[s] the story of the developing black female subject" (Manora 359). In her fifth autobiographical installment, *All God's Children Need Traveling Shoes*, Angelou specifically questions how to form an African-based identity in diaspora when she narrates her time in Ghana as

an expatriate and "Revolutionist Returnee." As Gregory Smithers notes, Angelou's story of return narrates how a diasporic's imagined Africa, contemporary Ghana, and the history of slavery clash in unexpected ways that disrupt Angelou's sense of self. In contrast to Kingston's "No Name Woman," Angelou's work asserts that, rather than projecting cultural unity on an often-invented past and an unrealized future, connection found in the present—between living African and diasporic subjects—is actually the only reliable means of diasporic unification with contemporary Africa.

Angelou's narrative begins with the basic assumptions of dispersal at the heart of a diaspora worldview. A diasporic perspective, as theorized by Paul Gilroy, begins with the assumption that African-descended people are connected by a common ancestry that was literally displaced by the Atlantic slave trade. When thinking of Ghana—or Africa in general—Angelou considers her relationship to her "homeland" as something that has been lost through generations of disconnect, beginning with slavery. Her vision of homecoming, then, necessarily engages Ghana as a space that can explain her present sense of self by capturing a lost piece of her distant past. Upon settling in Ghana's expat community, Angelou notes her feelings of finding her place and the welcome she assumes will follow:

So I had finally come home. The prodigal child, having strayed, been stolen or sold from the land of her fathers, having squandered her mother's gifts and having laid down in cruel gutters, had at last arisen and directed herself back to the welcoming arms of the family where she would be bathed, clothed with fine raiment and seated at the welcoming table. (21)

Of course, Angelou recognizes that her initial vision of Ghana is more akin to fantasy than the actual, lived conditions of return, but feelings of belonging and comfort underlie her expectations at each moment in this narrative of return. Even when Ghanaians are anything but welcoming, Angelou asserts that the returnees need not "earn the right to return"—rather, through hard work and productivity, they would show their belonging and "then snuggle down into Africa as a baby nuzzles in a mother's arms" (19). In focusing on her place as a descendant of slaves and then on the necessary belonging that "homecoming" is supposed to enable, Angelou effectively invents a long family history of disruption in the past and potential wholeness again through meaningful belonging in Ghana. In Angelou's account, the most important moment in her family's African past is that of capture—indeed, she does not entertain any sustained moment of family or cultural unity before her ancestors were sold into slavery. Without sustained engagement of Ghana as a space with a distinct history unrelated to the slave trade, Angelou can only imagine "return" in terms of reunion. Yet, the most telling moments of cultural unity come through recognizing Ghanaian contemporariness, when she is able to explore modes of belonging in Ghana that do not quite measure up to her expectations of a seat at the welcoming table.

But this recognition of contemporary Ghana only comes after she has imagined ancestors in much the way Kingston does in "No Name Woman." I want to stress two critical moments in which Angelou invests Ghana with long-lost ancestors. The first happens on a weekend excursion outside the capital. Angelou drives through Cape Coast, deliberately avoiding the slave fort from which many were sent across the Atlantic. Although she does not enter the castle, memories of the slave trade come to Angelou anyway, as she begins to imagine long-lost relatives and "the eternal melodrama":

> What did they think and feel, my grandfathers, caught on those green Savannahs, under the baobab trees? How long did their families search for them? Did the dungeon wall feel chilly and its slickness strange to my grandmothers who were used to the rush of air against bamboo huts and the sound of birds rattling their grass roofs? (78)

On a personal level, the history of slave trading in Ghana is a barrier to Angelou's complete sense of belonging. To a certain extent, she holds modern Ghanaians accountable for their ancestors' sales of their people to slave traders. The anguish of knowing that her ancestors suffered and that many like them died in the slave trade seriously affects how Angelou approaches her daily life as a returnee.

In some cases, as in her passing through Cape Coast, the memory of these ancestors is at the moment of capture and transportation. It is a distinctly diasporic narrative of slavery in which capture, sale, and slave ship are the only salient moments. Yet, Angelou also fills her return imagining these ancestors as Ghanaians, even if only briefly: "I loved to imagine a long-dead relative trading in those marketplaces, fishing from that active sea and living in those exotic towns, but the old anguish [of having ancestors sold into slavery] would not let me remain beguiled" (47). Although Angelou's imagined ancestor is ultimately sold into slavery, it is notable that, in this moment, the ancestor exists as an individual before he or she becomes a slave. In these moments, Angelou wills a long family history into being via narrative, presenting an African identity for herself based on these imagined fisherman and day traders. In a sense, "knowing" these long-lost ancestors ultimately allows for knowing oneself, but Angelou's ties to Ghana are explicitly invented, as in the manner of Kingston's unnamed aunt.

The memoir ends with a final familial gesture, this time from Ghanaian market women toward Angelou. Although Angelou had spent three years seeking belonging in Ghana, she finally actively creates that belonging just before departure. On a final trip through the country, to see the eastern part of Ghana for the first time, Angelou stops in Keta, a small, vibrant market town inhabited chiefly by the Ewe people. While walking through the market with her guide, Angelou is suddenly stopped by a woman who insists she has seen Angelou before. Unsurprisingly, Angelou's descriptions of the woman bind the two together as almost-family members: "[S]he had the wide face and slanted eyes of my grandmother. Her lips were large and beautifully shaped like my grandmother's, and her cheek bones were high like those of my grandmother" (204). Suddenly, the woman begins to rock from side to side with "a pitiful little moan," in an act of Ewe mourning (204). Although the experience jars Angelou, her friend and guide explains the particulars of the situation, noting that Angelou reminds the market women "of someone, but not anyone they knew personally" (205).

This explanation is followed by a story of slavery and its place in local memory.

According to her guide, the women mourn for Angelou because they consider her to be the descendant of those abducted and sold into slavery from Keta long ago. The town has a particularly devastating story of slavery—the tale that is passed down through history is that Keta was emptied of all adults and destroyed, with the children of the town escaping to hide in the bush. These children saw and recounted captures and deaths at the hands of slavery: "What they saw they remembered and all that they remembered they told over and over" (Angelou 206). The women in the marketplace are the descendants of those children, and they came of age listening to stories of Keta and the slave trade. When Angelou walks through the market, these women claim her as a physical reminder of their past, as her guide explains:

> They have heard the stories often, and the deeds are still as fresh as if they happened during their lifetimes. And you, Sister, you look so much like them, even the tone of your voice is like theirs. They are sure you are descended from those stolen mothers and fathers. That is why they mourn. Not for you but for their lost people. (206)

In these final moments, the market women interpellate Angelou into a distinct family structure, where she is a distant, lost relative who has come home. Angelou responds by forging these bonds even further, creating a stronger sense of shared identity: "The women wept and I wept. I too cried for the lost people, their ancestors and mine. But I was also weeping with a curious joy. Despite the murders, rapes and suicides, we had survived. The middle passage and the auction block had not erased us" (207). In a sense, this final scene is the culmination of Angelou's efforts to create a sense of family in Ghana, and the abrupt nature of this encounter only serves to highlight the very invented quality of her new "family." From the beginning, she acknowledges that the arrival of two hundred black Americans had little impact on most of Ghana, as "the citizens were engaged in their own concerns" (Angelou 21). The mourning of the market women suggests a melding of Angelou's imagined ancestors and the living, contemporary Ghanaians she meets. Similarly, Angelou finds an outlet for her desire to belong, which she describes from the outset as paramount to the returnee state of mind: "our need for belonging allowed us to ignore the obvious [lack of effect the returnees had on Ghanaians] and to create real places or even illusory places, befitting our imagination" (19). In weeping together with the Keta women, Angelou creates that structure of belonging by constructing an African family as a knowable entity in an uncertain return to Africa. In the end, Angelou writes her family's past into existence and actively creates a global family in the present.

Connecting to the Ancestor

In Angelou's memoir, the acts of imagination and inventing unnamed ancestors come when she is physically in Ghana. Her "return" to Africa is importantly about connecting with a long-lost past, and this begins through her thinking about those who were forced to leave their homeland during the time of Atlantic slavery. However, the real connections that take place between Angelou and Ghana happen in the present day. She imagined ancestors and commits to an understanding of Ghana that is perpetually marked by the slave trade. Yet the memoir's final moments, when she is recognized as a descendant of one of these imagined ancestors, stresses the transcultural connections available in contemporary Africa.

By contrast, Kingston does not visit her ancestral home in "No Name Woman." Exploring her cultural heritage, and similarly reinventing her unnamed aunt's life, is the only act of cultural connection to China available for her. She writes the no-name woman into her book; indeed, she "resolved questions that would not resolve in life" (Fishkin 786). While it may be that the story's version of China is far from the lived realities in the modern nation, Kingston's imagined China—and the imagined ancestry who lived there—is the only avenue available for connecting between cultures.

Works Cited

Alexoae-Zagni, Nicoleta. "An Interview with Maxine Hong Kingston." *Revue française d'études américaines* 110.4 (2006). Web.

Angelou, Maya. *All God's Children Need Traveling Shoes*. 1986. New York: Vintage, 1991. Print.

Center, Carole. "'Desperately Looking for Meaning': Reading Multiethnic Texts." *MELUS* 30.2 (2005): 225-241. Print.

Fishkin, Shelley Fisher & Maxine Hong Kingston. "Interview with Maxine Hong Kingston." *American Literary History* 3.4 (1991): 782-791. Print.

Gilroy, Paul. *The Black Atlantic: Modernity and Double-Consciousness*. Cambridge, MA: Harvard UP, 1993. Print.

Kingston, Maxine Hong. "Cultural Mis-readings by American Reviewers." *Asian and Western Writers in Dialogue: New Cultural Identities*. Ed. Guy Amirthanayagam. London: MacMillan, 1982. 55-65. Print.

_____. *The Woman Warrior: Memoirs of a Girlhood Among Ghosts*. New York: Vintage, 1989. Print.

Manora, Yolanda M. "'What you looking at me for? I didn't come to stay': Displacement, Disruption, and Black Female Subjectivity in Maya Angelou's *I Know Why the Caged Bird Sings*." *Women's Studies* 34.5 (2005): 359-375. Print.

Parrott, Jill M. "Power and Discourse: Silence as Rhetorical Choice in Maxine Hong Kingston's *The Woman Warrior*." *Rhetorica* 30.4 (2012): 375-391. Print.

Shu, Yuan. "Cultural Politics and Chinese-American Female Subjectivity: Rethinking Kingston's 'Woman Warrior.'" *MELUS* 26.2 (2001): 199-223. Print.

Smithers, Gregory. "Challenging a Pan-African Identity: The Autobiographical Writings of Maya Angelou, Barack Obama, and Caryl Phillips." *Journal of American Studies* 45.3 (2011): 483-502. Print.

CRITICAL
READINGS

Kingston's *Woman Warrior* in the Context of Life Writing Studies: An Exploration of Relational Selfhood

Anne Rüggemeier

The Woman Warrior as Autobiography?

Discussing Kingston's *The Woman Warrior* in the context of autobiography's generic classification, it soon becomes clear that the book does not fulfill "the law of genre," which the French critic Jacques Derrida defined as follows: "as soon as a genre announces itself, one must respect a norm, one must not cross a line of demarcation, one must not risk impurity" (Derrida 57). Even though Kingston's book is classified as *Memoirs* in the subtitle, this exceptional work of art clearly transgresses conventional ideas of both memoir and autobiography and conspicuously deviates from the "law" of the genre 'autobiography.' As a consequence, the generic classification of *The Woman Warrior* has been widely disputed among critics.

The "law of genre" that still determines what is regarded as autobiography and what is not was mainly designed by critics at the beginning of the twentieth century. A quite general first definition was offered by Georg Misch, a German historian, who described autobiography as "the description (*graphia*) of an individual human life (*bios*) by the individual himself (*autos*)" (5). Misch also had strong opinions about the kind of lives that should be represented in autobiography, namely the life of the representative 'great man' who could be regarded as an example of "the spirit of his time" (13).

Misch's definition triggers certain questions concerning the notion of representativeness, which have been summarized by Smith and Watson: "What is at stake when a life is described as 'representative'? Whose lives can be considered representative of a culture or a historical moment? Who determines which lives are representative?" (196). By defining what is representative, genre critics are actually not only able to favor specific types of lives while discriminating against others but they are also in a position to decide which narrators or authors are allowed to participate in the discourse of life writing and which are not. This is why later critics, especially postmodern and postcolonial theorists, characterize the generic politics of autobiography as exclusionary. By implying that other kinds of life writing, that is, texts produced by women or non-Western subjects, were not appropriate for the canon, early theorists of autobiography generated an idea of the autobiographical Self as an autonomous and enlightened individual. Paul Eakin notes that the "individualistic assumptions" (58) that underwrite this system of generic classification have been influential ever since. Thus, the legacy of individualism continues to present an important template, especially for Western lifestyles.

The concept of individual identity is closely bound up with the idea of a coherent and universalizing life story, which generates the unity of the autobiographical Self. Scholars once assumed that autobiographies should be written late in life from a retrospective perspective that allows for teleological patterns, linear plots, and conclusions. The idea of narrative coherence is especially stressed by the Belgian critic Georges Gusdorf in his essay "Conditions and Limits of Autobiography," in which he describes autobiography as an act of "reconstructing the unity of a life across time" (37). Gusdorf conceptualizes autobiography as a 'Western' genre and, therefore, defines the concept of the isolated individual (as opposed to collective formations common in non-Western countries) as indispensable for autobiography. It is thus clear that as a literary institution, the genre of autobiography is inscribed with the prevalent assumptions, norms, and values of the European Enlightenment and its formative ideas about individuality, autonomy, and logical coherence. Measured against early definitions of autobiography that define the genre as a factual account of one's own life, giving order and shape to episodic events, Kingston's literary debut really must be disqualified as an autobiography. Scholarly discussions focus especially on the question of its status as fact or fiction and criticize Kingston for not sticking to the chronological order suggested by Wayne Shumaker in his laconic remark: "Autobiography characteristically opens with the cry of an infant and closes with the chair tilted against a sunny wall" (130). Actually, "the cry of the infant," or put differently the birth of the autobiographical protagonist, is only mentioned in the middle of *The Woman Warrior*: "I was born in the middle of World War II" (96).

The question arises: Can a book that starts with a chapter focusing on a paternal aunt ("No Name Woman"), that continues with the mythical figure of Fa Mu Lan ("White Tigers"), that further includes a chapter that tells the story of Maxine Hong Kingston's mother ("Shaman"), and that interchanges first- and third-person narrative perspectives (especially in the chapter "At the Western Palace") be described as autobiography? As all these derivations and breeches from traditional conventions of autobiography make clear, *The Woman Warrior* is a hybrid piece of life-writing that transcends clear generic boundaries. The generic tension pervasively present in Kingston's autobiographical art has been summarized by LeiLani Nishime: "Kingston never fully escapes genre because she must write within and against the constraints of generic forms in order to comment upon them and manipulate them" (67). If she resents the constraints of the generic form, one might ask, why does she not abandon the form completely and make use of a different literary form? One of many possible answers lies in the fact that Kingston chooses to enter into a dialogue with the traditions of Western life-writing and the cultural hegemonies upon which it is based. If she had abandoned the form completely, the cultural resonances so crucial to her disruptions of hegemonic conceptions of gender, culture, and identity would have been lost. To make fully visible the ideologies that inform the genre of autobiography, she has to keep them present, without giving in to the "law of genre." As will be shown in the following paragraphs, *The Woman Warrior*, Kingston's unusual work of autobiography, is a milestone in the genre of life-writing as it provokes us to re-evaluate to what extent the Self and the story of the Self is formed in relation to Others. Neither purely factional nor entirely fictional, neither autobiography, nor biography, nor traditional memoir, readers are confronted with the insight that this narrative fosters a view of the individual that highlights entangledness and stresses the relationality of the Self.

Relational Self Concepts in *The Woman Warrior*

The Woman Warrior offers an inspiring example to think of autobiography as auto/biography, a term that underlines the close interrelation between one's own life and the lives of the proximate Others that exist in a reciprocal relationship with the Self. One of the first scholars to discuss *The Woman Warrior* as a piece of relational autobiography was Paul John Eakin in his groundbreaking work *How Our Lives Become Stories* (1999). The concept of relationality with regard to life writing was originally developed by feminist scholars who based their studies on autobiographies by women. In contrast to Gusdorf and other early scholars of autobiography who studied only autobiographies by male writers and who fostered a model of autonomous identity that was based on hegemonic European discourses, the advent of female writing on autobiographies caused a remarkable change of view on autobiographies and their subjects. From the 1980s on, the model of relational identity was repeatedly described and claimed for female autobiographers. However, even though the feminists' critique of the Gusdorf model of Selfhood paved the way for a fruitful and sustained study of women's life writing, it also fostered an unfortunate polarization by gender that Eakin describes as follows: "If female, then relational, collectivist and, for some reason non-narrative; if male, then autonomous, individualistic, and narrative" (50). However, relational identity is, by no means, restricted to female characters and writers. Rather, the stress on relationality seeks to resist the use of a monologic, authoritative narrative voice, in preference for multiperspectivity and dialogue.

Eakin contextualizes *The Woman Warrior* in a corpus of memoirs that stress the idea of "a relational model of identity, developed collaboratively with others, often family members" (57). He introduces his concept of relational autobiography as follows:

We tend to think of autobiography as a literature of the first person, but the subject of autobiography to which the pronoun 'I' refers is neither singular nor first, and we do well to demystify its claims. . . . [A]*ll* autobiography is relational, and . . . the definition of autobiography, and its history as well, must be stretched to reflect the kinds of self-writing in which relational identity is characteristically displayed. (Eakin 43 f.; emphasis in original)

The quotation emphasizes several issues. Firstly, Eakin draws attention to the fact that the expression "I," whose meaning is very much dependent on the context and therefore can be called deictic, has been used dominantly in a very simplifying way within the topic of autobiographies, while it actually is a very complex, plural, and changing referent in autobiographical texts. Secondly, he indicates the power of genre theory to define not only genres but also conventionalize their specific outlook on the world and thereby establish a concept of reality that is informed by specific 'myths' and 'illusions.' And, thirdly, Eakin shows the necessity not only of redefining the term but also of re-conceptualizing its history and the ideologies this history has been based on. Finally, and some might even say surprisingly, Eakin's introduction of the term 'relational autobiography' insists on the continuity of the genre. Instead of arguing that autobiography is nowadays displaced by family memoir, Eakin draws attention to the fact that relational autobiographies have always been there. At the same time, he argues that in contrast to memoir, the story of the Self is not "ancillary to the story of the other" (Eakin 58); rather, the Other is conceptualized as a constitutive element of the autobiographer's construction of the Self. Apart from drawing attention to the fact that "relational lives represent the most prominent form of life writing in the United States today" (69), Eakin has proposed a first typology of relational life writing found in contemporary literatures:

I want to preserve the usefulness of the label by applying it to those autobiographies that feature the decisive impact on the autobiographer of either [1] an entire social environment (a particular kind of family, or a community and its social institutions – schools, churches, and so forth) or [2] key other individuals, usually family members, especially parents. (69)

In the following paragraphs, it will be argued that Kingston's *The Woman Warrior* qualifies as a relational piece of life-writing in both ways. On the one hand, the relational Self of the autobiographical protagonist (conventionally called Maxine, although Kingston does not name her in the text), is constructed in an ongoing dialogue with her mother, Brave Orchid. On the other hand, the process of identity formation is also shown to take place in relation to the particular social environment of a Chinese immigrant family that provokes the American-born daughter to negotiate the specific values and traditions her parents transfer to her (via talk-story) in the context of the American culture in which she grows up. By interweaving her own life story with those of her ancestors, she expands the spatial and temporal boundaries implicated in earlier definitions of autobiography as an individual person's life story. Thus, she also permeates the borders between personal experience, family history, and the broader cultural context of Chinese immigration to the United States. In this frame of reference, she especially draws attention to the impact that stories (listened to and internalized from childhood on) have on the supposedly 'autonomous' Self.

Instead of conveying the events of her life in a straightforward narrative, Kingston tells her story in an episodic manner, often jumping from one event to another without overtly clarifying the connection. Critics have repeatedly pointed to the fact that the book is made up of five autonomous chapters. The autobiographer does not describe her life as a linear progression from birth to adulthood. Instead, she begins with the story of an aunt from her father's side of the family, continues with a fantasy of herself as the fabled Chinese woman warrior Fa Mu Lan, then describes the life of her mother Brave Orchid, and further includes the story of another aunt, Brave Orchid's sister, upon her arrival in America. The book closes with a chapter that is, finally, specifically about herself. Only this last chapter, it seems, is overtly about the life of Maxine. However, the preceding chapters also relate to her in meaningful ways, as they narrate events and stories that have deeply affected her life as a Chinese American female. The narrative structure of the book reveals something fundamental about the relational structure of the autobiographer's identity, about her roots and involvement in these women's lives: "The space of autobiography, the space of the self, is literally occupied by the [auto]biographies and the sel[ves] of the other[s]" (Eakin 61). In *The Woman Warrior*, Kingston identifies herself "as part of a web of relations without which [her] own story would be incomplete" (Egan & Helms 223) and therefore includes a variety of intertexts—that is, embedded narratives—most prominently the biography of her mother.

Especially in "Shaman," Kingston focuses entirely on the life story of her mother. The title of the chapter hints at the fact that Brave Orchid received an accomplished education as a midwife in China and was a well-reputed medical practitioner before she left China to join her husband in the US. Although most of the events in "Shaman" take place before Maxine's birth, it is appropriate that Brave Orchid has a prominent presence in *The Woman Warrior* because of her enormous influence on Maxine's thoughts and perception of the world: Maxine's head is "stuffed" with Brave Orchid's talk-stories. During the daytime, she banishes Brave Orchid's tales from her mind. Yet at night, these stories haunt Maxine's dreams. Through stories, her mother and the specific Chinese values she wants her daughter to internalize are always present in Maxine's thinking.

At the same time, Maxine's Self will not be determined solely by her ancestral roots. Rather she performs a dialogic renegotiation that is based on her position as an emphatic listener and a creative re-teller of tales. While her parents want her to be silent about the fate of her aunt, the autobiographer not only tells, but even publishes her aunt's story and thereby breaks the taboo that frames the story as a guiding principle: "You must not tell anyone," she is warned (11). While Kingston provides a space for Brave Orchid's life story and allows her words and experiences to be read by Americans and thereby is able to enter into dialogue with American cultural discourses, she, at the same time, subjects her mother to her narrative, making her a biographical object in the story written by the daughter. This mirrors the activity of the storytelling mother who continuously tries to subject her daughter to the traditional Chinese values exerted and expressed in her talk-stories. It thus becomes clear that the field of relationality is a contested one; it consists of opposing forces that include identifications and dis-identifications, or, put differently, strategies of affiliation and strategies of separation.

This can best be demonstrated by the complex relationship between the narrator and her mother as it becomes obvious in their struggles over the meanings of stories. "No Name Woman" again serves as an example: After breaking the silence and thereby breaking the injunction against talking about the disgraced aunt, Brave Orchid uses the story as a warning and as a reminder of what binds her daughter to her family tradition and her responsibility as a Chinese female: "Her meaning was just don't fool around or you're going to get pregnant and get in big trouble. . . . Then the trouble on my part was to say no to that meaning" (Kingston qtd. in Skenazy 123). The mother is "preserving the traditions that authorize the old way of life . . . , she dominates the life, the landscape and the language of the text as she dominates the subjectivity of the daughter who writes that text" (Smith 58). The narrator's strategy of embedding her mother's story within her own autobiographical text can be interpreted as an attempt to balance the distribution of power in terms of storytelling. She subjects her mother's story to her own narrative voice, just as her mother had tried to dominate the life of the daughter with the help of her storytelling: "Before we can leave our parents," the narrator observes, "they stuff our heads like the suitcases which they jam-pack with homemade underwear" (87). Nevertheless, while the mother stifled the daughter's own voice by commanding her obedience to traditions, she, at the same time, opened up possibilities to claim power through the practice of storytelling. "When we Chinese girls listened to the adults talk-story, we learned that we failed if we grew up to be but wives or slaves. We could be heroines" (19). Making her daughter familiar with the story of Fa Mu Lan, the Woman Warrior, Maxine's mother opens up new possibilities for her daughter to break the mold of the typical woman: "She said I would grow up a wife and a slave, but she taught me the song of the warrior woman, Fa Mu Lan" (20).

Relational Storytelling and Chinese Talk-Story

One of the relational entanglements Kingston inevitably finds herself in is the narrative practice of the Chinese talk-story. As her mother tries to educate, warn, and make her understand Chinese values via the often rather frustrating talk-stories ("They scramble me up," [202]), the daughter's consciousness is deeply informed by these stories. In *The Woman Warrior* the power of storytelling dissolves the conventional (Western) borders between fact and fiction, I and you, Self and Other, and the individual and collective evaporate. The narrator's "recourse to talk-story—which blurs the distinction between straight fact and pure fiction—accomplishes two key objectives: to reclaim a past, and more decisively, to envision a different future" (Cheung 121). Framed in this context, the daughter's imaginative enrichment and negotiation of the disgraced aunt's behavior depicted in the first chapter is an act of appropriation. Rather than listening to her mother's interpretation of the story, Maxine engages with the silences of the story, the parts not told. Thus her dialogic engagement with her mother's version of the story paves the way for alternative meanings. She arises from a past that was dominated by the stories told to her to a future in which she herself is the storyteller and thereby a shaper of meanings. Maxine affiliates herself with her mother and the Chinese tradition of talk-story, yet while she forms her own narrative voice out of the experience of listening to her mother, she denies the rules established by her forerunner ("Don't tell") and the meaning and values transmitted via her mother's talk-story. Thus, she is simultaneously aligning herself with the cultural tradition of talk-story while breaking complicity and identification with the value system inherent in her mother's stories. The Chinese tradition of talk-story embodies a collectivity of voices; by listening to her mother, Maxine becomes part of this collectivity. Simultaneously her own re-imagination and re-framing of the stories enable her to generate new meanings and interpretations. Like a voice-over, she uses the collectively imagined source narration to enrich her own singular interpretation.

The talk-story form allows the autobiographical narrator to subsume under her narrative voice the divergent stories of different generations and perspectives. She thus positions herself in the social and historical environment of other people—be they actual or mythical—and includes their experiences and perspectives in her own story. The autobiographical narrator thereby demonstrates that the lives and voices of her proximate Others, her mother, her aunts, and the traditions they are positioned in, are also part of her own autobiographical voice and part of her Self. The critical observation that Kingston allows those other female figures to take central stage in her own story "to the extent that at times the figure of Kingston herself disappears from view" (Grice 39) is by no means atypical but rather a key characteristic of relational life writing. In an interview with Shirley Geok-Lin Lim, Kingston explains: "That was the function of *The Woman Warrior*: self-understanding, understanding myself in relation to my family, to my mother, my place in my community, in my society, and in the world." Just as the mother's night-time stories smoothly transform into night-time dreams, so the mythical figures and stories from Chinese tradition link inseparably with stories about her real life experiences. From these stories and her reaction to them the autobiographical protagonist derives her own voice. This is why, at the end of the work, Maxine's voice interconnects with her mother's: "Here is a story my mother told me. . . . The beginning is hers, the ending, mine" (206). Maxine's voice is not an imitation, but a dialogic counter-part to her mother's. Her voice is formed in dialogue as her self is shown to be deeply relational.

Actually, it can be argued that the whole text of *The Woman Warrior* resembles a talk-story that is partially Brave Orchid's and partially Maxine's. This especially becomes clear in the closing chapter, "A Song for a Barbarian Reed Pipe," when Maxine finally overcomes her silence and tells her mother what she really thinks: "I don't want to listen to any more of your stories; they have no logic. . . . You can't stop me from talking. You tried to cut off my tongue, but it didn't work" (202). The moment the adolescent daughter finally talks back to her mother has often been described as the discovery of Maxine's voice. If we reconsider Maxine's outburst within the context of the whole book, however, the teenage daughter's embrace of American concepts of logic and success did not make it into her practice as a writer, and she does not follow through on her declarations to her mother: "I'm not going to Chinese school anymore. I'm going to run for office at American school, and I'm going to join clubs. I'm going to get enough offices and clubs on my record to get into college" (202). While as a girl she devalued the Chinese traditions of storytelling ("I push the deformed into my dreams, which are in Chinese, the language of impossible stories," [87]), the older narrator includes and celebrates these traditions. The cultural artifact of *The Woman Warrior* shows that she no longer wishes to make her life "American-normal" (87). This implies that as a Chinese American writer, she has undergone a process of reevaluating Chinese and American myths and value systems. While the young Maxine suffered from the incompatibility of Chinese and American criteria for success and a good life, noting the saying within her family that "You can't eat straight A's" (46), the mature narrator (and writer) uses her Chinese background to consciously question and critique Western standards regarding both the representative life and the appropriate story to express it.

The Woman Warrior continuously negotiates between and balances two very different cultural frames of reference. While Western readers might first experience the mixture of myth, cultural history, and personal experience as, in the words of Sau-Ling Cynthia Wong, a "sabotage of factuality" (279), a second and more careful reading might unmask the ideologies that shaped the expectation for truth to be inherent in conventional generic formula. Using autobiography to create identity, Kingston unmasks the ideologies of conventional autobiography and breaks out of the Western schema of self-representation to create a relational self that questions the concept of autonomous individualism and the "myth of autonomy" (Eakin 43) that influences Western culture like virtually no other:

"Why do we so easily forget that the first person of autobiography is truly plural in its origin and subsequent formation? Because autobiography promotes an illusion of self-determination: *I* write my story, *I* say who *I* am, *I* create myself" (Eakin 43). The dominance of the first person singular is by no means representative for all cultures as Maxine's confusion in her English lesson demonstrates: "I could not understand 'I.' The Chinese 'I' has seven strokes, intricacies. How could the American 'I' . . . have only three strokes, the middle so straight?" (166). Recognizing the inextricable relationship between an individual's sense of Self and the community's stories of Selfhood, Kingston's position between two cultures enables her to see the value-creating system inherent in generic expectations. The initial frustration readers might feel because they cannot easily find Maxine's autobiography among all the other stories and myths might finally lead to the insight that the Self's story is, to a great extent, constructed through the story of and in relation to Others.

Relationality in Kingston's Other Books

That the idea of relational selfhood is central to Kingston's work can also be demonstrated with regard to her second book, *China Men* (1981), and her latest, *I Love a Broad Margin to My Life* (2011). Like *The Woman Warrior*, *China Men* can be described as a multilayered narrative that defies any attempt at generic definition. The hybrid text consists of a "blend of research, essays, talk-story, fiction, and reinvented myths" (Davis 96). The basic difference, in comparison to its literary forerunner, however, lies in the fact that Kingston writes about her male ancestors. Though the autobiographer originally set out to reconstruct her father's story of immigration, her endeavor seems to be doomed because her father refuses to talk. Thus, the narrator performs her own research, which draws her deeply into the past of other *men* and their stories of immigration from China. Rather than presenting substantial data in a chronological manner, Kingston imaginatively re-envisions her father's possible story as a version of the ones transmitted by other immigrants and constructs a (possible) individual life from collective experience: "I'll tell you what I suppose from your silences and few words, and you tell me that I'm mistaken. You'll just have to speak up with the real stories if I've got you wrong" (*China Men* 15). Meant as a provocation to make him talk, her father only responds and enters into a dialogue with his daughter when he writes comments in the margins of her published version of the book. He writes "responses, corrections and additions" (Skenazy 155). As a consequence, the meaning of margins, the spaces that are awaiting comment and response, the spaces kept free to invite readers to enter into dialogue with the writer, become a telling metaphor in Kingston's work, giving rise to the title of her later book.

In *I Love a Broad Margin to My Life*, Kingston's negotiation of the American myth of autonomous individualism continues; she asks, "How be American unless 'I'?" (219). She counters it with a story of her sixty-five-year old self that includes and even focuses on Others, this time not family members, but fellow human beings like Fred, an unemployed engineer, born in Iran (*Broad Margin* 13), millions of homeless in China, displaced by dams, industrial zones and the Olympics (87), work migration from the Philippines to Hong Kong, from Mexico to the United States (55), and concludes: "Each life impacts every life" (77)—"all related" (112). Kingston's consciousness for relationality started to take shape in dialogue with the females in her family, but it did not stop there. Especially as Chinese American, the daughter of immigrants, living in between cultures, she had already developed a sense for the planetary in *The Woman Warrior*, where she says, "We belong to the planet now, Mama. Does it make sense to you that if we're no longer attached to one piece of land, we belong to the planet?" (107). In *Broad Margin* this sense for planetary relationality has grown into its full potential.

Works Cited

Cheung, King-Kok. *Articulate Silences: Hisaye Yamamoto, Maxine Hong Kingston, Joy Kogawa*. Ithaca, NY: Cornell UP, 1993. Print.

Davis, Rocío G. *Relative Histories: Mediating History in Asian American Family Memoirs*. U of Hawai'i P, 2001. Print.

Derrida, Jacques. "The Law of Genre." *Glyph* 7 (1980): 55-81. Print.

Eakin, Paul John. *How Our Lives Become Stories: Making Selves*. Ithaca, NY: Cornell UP, 1999. Print.

Egan, Jennifer & Gabriele Helms. "Life Writing." *The Cambridge Companion to Canadian Literature*. Ed. Eva-Marie Kröller. Cambridge, UK: Cambridge UP, 2004. 216-240. Print.

Gusdorf, Georges. "Conditions and Limits of Autobiography." *On Autobiography: Essays Theoretical and Critical*. Ed. James Olney. Princeton, NJ: Princeton UP, 1980. 28-48. Print.

Hong Kingston, Maxine. *The Woman Warrior: Memoirs of a Girlhood Among Ghosts*. 1976. New York: Vintage/Random, 1989. Print.

_____. *China Men*. 1980. Vintage/Random, 1989. Print.

_____. *I Love a Broad Margin to My Life*. New York: Vintage/Random, 2011. Print.

Lim, Shirley Geok-lin. "Reading Back, Looking Forward: A Retrospective Interview with Maxine Hong Kingston." *MELUS* 33.1 (2008): 157-170. Print.

Misch, Georg. *A History of Autobiography in Antiquity*. 1907. London: Routledge and Paul, 1950. Print.

Nishime, LeiLani. "Engendering Genre: Gender and Nationalism in *China Men* and *The Woman Warrior*." *MELUS* 20.1 (1995): 67-82. Print.

Shumaker, Wayne. *English Autobiography: Its Emergence, Materials, and Form*. Berkeley/Los Angeles: U of California P, 1954. Print.

Skenazy, Paul. "Kingston at the University." *Conversations with Maxine Hong Kingston*. Ed. Paul Skenazy & Tera Martin. Jackson: UP of Mississippi, 1998. 118-158. Print.

Smith, Sidonie. "Filiality and Women's Autobiographical Story Telling." *Maxine Hong Kingston's* The Woman Warrior. *A Casebook*. Ed. Sau-Ling Cynthia Wong. Oxford: Oxford UP, 1999. Print.

_____. and Julia Watson. *Reading Autobiography. A Guide for Interpreting Life Narratives*. Minneapolis: U of Minneapolis P, 2010. Print.

Wong, Sau-Ling Cynthia. "Autobiography as Guided Chinatown Tour? Maxine Hong Kingston's *The Woman Warrior* and the Chinese American Autobiographical Controversy." *Multicultural Autobiography: American Lives*. Ed. James Robert Payne. Knoxville: U of Tennessee P, 1992. 248–279. Print.

"The Words at My Back": Maxine Hong Kingston's *The Woman Warrior* and the Power of Discourse

Lorna Martens

Maxine Hong Kingston's *The Woman Warrior*, subtitled *Memoirs of a Girlhood Among Ghosts*, does not resemble a traditional memoir or autobiography in shape. It does not offer a chronological, first-person account of the author's life and times, but consists of five discontinuous, disparate narratives. The first three recount stories the autobiographical protagonist heard when growing up. The fourth tells of an event that she did not witness herself. The autobiographical protagonist, the narrator's younger self, plays above all the role of a listener, a recipient of the stories. The narrator only starts to tell her own story in the fifth and final part, "A Song for a Barbarian Reed Pipe," although her voice comes in to comment in all sections except part IV. Nevertheless, we learn of the child's reactions to the earlier stories, each of which transmits a radically different message about what it means to be female, and to be a Chinese American in the United States. This memoir, therefore, is about how a child is shaped and socialized, and how verbal discourse is instrumental in this process. All of us hear a variety of messages about what is expected of us, but this child, whom I shall refer to as Maxine although Kingston does not name her, is the target of irreconcilably contradictory messages from her parents, older Chinese immigrants to the United States, and her immediate American environment, the California context where she grows up. In breaking with the traditional shape of autobiography and initially assigning the protagonist the role of listener, Kingston demonstrates the effects of discourse on identity. She makes a compelling case for the formative influence of talk on children and particularly on children who grow up in multicultural contexts. All children pick up on values transmitted by adults' talk, but if their parents come from a different culture and convey a set of cultural values that are radically different from the dominant ones in their surroundings or that are taught in school, they can struggle to figure out which one is right.

Maxine's mother is the source of the first three stories. They are calculated to have a strong impact on the girl's consciousness. To the child's ear, the messages she gets from her Chinese relatives, and above all from her mother, are strident, unforgettable, and opaque. They do not add up, much less allow themselves to be reconciled with the realities that she sees and hears around her. Kingston has the gift for making the strange seem strange. Instead of laboriously telling us how confused the child has become, she mainly lets the Chinese discourse, the mother's stories, work directly on the Western reader's own sensibilities. Sau-ling Cynthia Wong points out that far from giving the reader a "guided Chinatown tour," far from transmitting information about Chinese culture to the Western reader, Kingston presents a protagonist who "from fragmentary and haphazard evidence . . . has to piece together a coherent picture of the culture she is enjoined to preserve against American influence" (44). Kingston constructs her story so as to make the reader live her protagonist's experience, to hear with her and to think along with her. While the splintered form of the narrative corresponds to the divergent messages the child receives in her implicit attempt to construct her identity, the five pieces are astutely sequenced so as to unfold the complexity of the book's themes gradually.

The first section, entitled "No Name Woman," starts with the mother's story about Maxine's paternal aunt in China, told verbatim in quotation marks. The aunt became pregnant after her husband had emigrated to America. The villagers terrorized the family, organizing a raid on their home on the eve of the birth. That night, the disgraced aunt gave birth in the pigsty and drowned herself and her baby in the family well. She suffered a terrible punishment: her family decided to erase her from memory, to treat her as if she had never been born, never to speak her name. Maxine's mother's concise, horrific tale, which she tells because her daughter has "started to menstruate," is followed by the narrator's own lengthy and inconclusive exegesis. The narrator notes that the story exemplifies her mother's style of teaching. Yet she remains mystified: "Those of us in the first

American generations have had to figure out how the invisible world the emigrants built around our childhoods fits in solid America" (5). She reflects that it is useless to ask her mother for more details about this story; her mother has told her "once and for all the useful parts" (6). So she speculates extensively about her aunt, about what went on in her mind, about the unknown man who made her pregnant, about the circumstances. She spins out a variety of further narratives, strewn with "I wonder" and "perhaps," that attempt to make sense of the story and turn her aunt into a comprehensible person. One imagined scenario follows the next. The mother's narrative thus fails in its purpose of directly communicating its intended message to her American-born daughter: "Now that you have started to menstruate, what happened to her could happen to you" (5). Instead, like a stone thrown in the water, it causes unintended ripples in the girl's mind. It reinforces two other cultural messages that are not its main point, but that the girl already knows: a woman, in China, is an underling; and in China, family is all-important. In her elaboration of her aunt's story, the narrator tries to undercut these cultural messages about female inferiority and passivity and about the priority of communal over individual needs. Having to grapple with the messages, she implies, is part of what shaped her identity and socialization.

Kingston's parents were born in pre-Nationalist China, in the era of foot binding, invoked in the book as an obvious symbol for the Chinese oppression of women. They brought with them to the United States the mindset of an older China, not the Communist China of the time of writing. In accordance with her parents' stories and United States perspectives of China, the child conceives of China as a scary place where parents sell girl children and men marry multiple wives—a place where she does not want to go (99). Story after story tells of the Chinese preference for boys. Saying after saying, quoted throughout the book, convinces Maxine of the Chinese contempt for girls.

Just when the reader thinks that the Chinese image of women has been established, Kingston provides an utterly contradictory image in the second section, "White Tigers," by invoking the story of Fa Mu Lan, the woman warrior. She learns this story from her mother, and she hears it much earlier in her childhood than the story of "No Name Woman": "I remembered that as a child I had followed my mother about the house, the two of us singing about how Fa Mu Lan fought gloriously and returned alive from war to settle in the village" (20). The Fa Mu Lan story opens the child's imagination to the idea that women can become warriors: "When we Chinese girls listened to the adults talk-story, we learned that we failed if we grew up to be but wives or slaves. We could be heroines, swordswomen" (19). The story of the woman warrior, which dates to a sixth-century ballad, is well known and often retold. Whereas the image of woman as slave has its basis in history, the image of woman as warrior comes to the child through literature. The effect on the child is to instill in her a sense not just of the potential power of a woman but of the power of literature.

"White Tigers" is the child's fantasy. Fantasizing that she will grow up a warrior woman, she imagines being led, at age seven, by a bird into the mountains for her training. As a young woman of twenty-two, her imagined self fights in her father's stead for her people with "Kuan Kung, the god of war and literature riding before [her]" (38). In all of her many battles, she is victorious, a superwoman. Commentators have shown that Kingston considerably changes the content of the original ballad (Zhang 17), amplifying the story with a strong subjective element (Simmons 61-70). Her fantasy details not only her marvelous fighting skills, deployed in phantasmagoric combats, but expands, casually, to encompass all the young girl's wishes: "My parents killed a chicken and steamed it whole, as if they were welcoming home a son" (34); she marries and has a baby, all the while continuing to fight; she beheads an oppressor who echoes sayings she hates ("'Girls are maggots in the rice.' 'It is more profitable to raise geese than daughters'" [43]); and she liberates locked-up women with bound feet. After deposing and killing the emperor and setting a peasant on the throne, she achieves great recognition from her family and in her village.

Coming back to real life after her woman warrior story, the narrator concludes that her "American life has been such a disappointment" (45). Despite her straight A's, her parents and the

Chinese community, apparently unimpressed, continue to repeat misogynistic sayings: "Feeding girls is feeding cowbirds" and "Better to raise geese than girls" (46). If "No Name Woman" presented Chinese customs as cruel, barbaric, misogynistic, and superstitious from the point of view of a supposedly enlightened America, the second story flips the moral scales: Chinese values (specifically filiality) appear highly meaningful, eclipsing the American ideal of personal success. Chinese aspirations open glorious, heroic vistas, whereas the goals of American life are petty and prosaic. Thus, far from divorcing herself from her parents' values, Maxine yearns to merit their approval the way a son traditionally might be able to earn it. She avoids doing things that are coded feminine, like cooking and housework. She feels she must become something similar to a warrior.

Within the child's woman warrior fantasy her parents carve the grievances they want her to avenge "on her back." Kingston borrows this striking and violent image from the story of the general Ngak Fei (transcribed in *China Men* as Yüeh Fei [56]). The image fits the main theme of *The Woman Warrior*: the child is formed by the parents' words and stories. It shows the hold of the past, of the parents, over a child. The back is a part of the body that one cannot properly see. The words carved into the young woman's flesh are like a "postmemory," poorly understood, yet indelible and controlling. Past wrongs, which the woman warrior herself has not endured, propel her forward.

The narrator seizes upon the image of writing on the female warrior's back and rewords it so that it forms her response to her present circumstances. Today's America is far from perfect; it is a place where many people are oppressed. Particularly relevant is the fact that Chinese immigrants are targets of racism and unfair or exploitative labor practices. As she grows up, Maxine recognizes her real-life oppressors and by extension those of her family and of all Chinese immigrants: American businessmen, racists. In the real world, anger takes away her voice. She can't speak, but only squeak. The strong desire to have a voice merges with her warrior fantasy. Reflecting that the Chinese idioms for "revenge" are "report a crime" and "report to five families," she envisions seeking her revenge through words. "The swordswoman and I are not so dissimilar. ... What we have in common are the words at our backs" (53). The change of preposition is significant. Kingston specifies "at" rather than "on" their backs. To have someone "at one's back" implies a backup and the presence of allies. "At one's back" also occurs in the common idiom "to have wind at one's back," which signifies having an advantage. Whereas words "on" the back are a compulsion imposed by others, words "at" the back are an asset. Although the narrator must contend with her enemies' backbiting words, like the swordswoman she has weapons at her disposal, in the form of words. In her case, these words might not just be those she has heard, past wrongs that push her forward, of which, she says, she has too many to fit on her skin, but her own original words, the words of a talented writer. Her pen has become her sword.

Running through these two contradictory narratives about Chinese female identity are allusions to another role model, namely the "American-feminine" model (11, 47), which presses in on her—"or no dates" (47). What "American feminine" means is left up to the American readership to supply, aside from the narrator's observation that it means "speaking in an inaudible voice" (11), in contrast to a loud Chinese voice. Maxine's story is the story of how Kingston found her voice, how she learned to speak out, how she became a writer. Kingston makes plain that this did not mean simply renouncing a Chinese voice in favor of adopting an American voice—for if a Chinese woman's voice, loud and bossy, sounded jarring in an American context, an American woman's voice in that era was not effective either.

The third section, "Shaman," tells the life of Brave Orchid, the narrator's mother, in China. In her third-person retelling, the narrator preserves much of her mother's point of view and imaginatively recreates her mother's thoughts and feelings. This story adds another role model to the narrator's childhood: her mother. Strikingly, this model absolutely does not confirm the negative construction of femininity suggested by "No Name Woman" and buttressed by the platitudes spouted by the immigrant generation. If it does not quite live up to the narrator's fantasy of the warrior woman, it nevertheless is the story of a brave, energetic woman and her real-life successes. As such, it translates the "woman warrior" story into the Chinese reality of the 1930s. We find out that under the Nationalist Government of the Republic of China, an intelligent and determined Chinese woman, with enough money, could get away from the family, study, establish a career, and become a respected person in society. In that era, according to Brave Orchid's story, impoverished families and "professionals" would sell a girl child as a slave (although slavery had been illegal in China since 1910). But Brave Orchid, in her thirties, waiting for her husband to come home or send for her, becomes one of the "new women, scientists who changed the rituals" (75). She uses the money he sends from the United States to go to medical school in Canton and becomes a successful village doctor.

The historical truth of the mother's story is debatable. One of its high points is a ghost story: her mother allegedly braves, struggles all night with, and vanquishes a ghost who haunted a room in her dormitory. She then tells an even more fanciful version of the story to her fellow medical students in which she dies, wanders the world for ten years, returns from the dead, and finally defeats the ghost with her will. Lurid creatures, bizarre practices, and brutal acts then pepper her stories of her years as a doctor in China. The narrator ends the re-narration of her mother's story by commenting that her mother's stories haunt her dreams. At once inspirational and incredible, they are to American reality as dream is to waking.

"Shaman" also introduces the further themes of stuffing and eating. Both themes have a metaphorical as well as a literal dimension. Initially, the text connects "stuffing" to the chain of maternal stories we have heard thus far: "Before we can leave our parents, they stuff our heads like the suitcases which they jam-pack with homemade underwear" (87). But "stuffing" also suggests eating and thus links the theme of storytelling to that of food. The narrator declares her mother omnivorous: "my mother won in ghost battle because she can eat anything" (88). Correspondingly, her mother cooks for the family in the United States with a wide range of ingredients: "raccoons, skunks, hawks, city pigeons, wild ducks, wild geese, black-skinned bantams, snakes, garden snails, turtles that crawled about the pantry floor and sometimes escaped under refrigerator or stove, catfish that swam in the bathtub"(90). By including game not included in the diets of most Americans, especially those living in urban settings, Kingston's descriptions of eating can be understood as metaphor for the integration of the foreign. The narrator's underlying point with the food theme is that eating is a winning strategy, and the more one eats, and the more disparate things one eats, the likelier one is to win. The narrator states, "All heroes are bold toward food" (88). She tells four seemingly digressive tall tales about phenomenal legendary Chinese eaters. She concludes: "Big eaters win" (90).

Since stuffing and eating are linked to storytelling, they thus bear a twofold message, negative and positive. The negative message has to do with inappropriate, confusing, and troubling indoctrination. Her mother has the power to "overfeed" her with ideas: "She pries open my head and my fists and crams into them responsibility for time, responsibility for intervening oceans" (108). The positive message is that the child who grows up amid multicultural influences has the potential to be particularly strong, a winner—if only she is able to stomach, absorb, and integrate the different elements she encounters. By extension, this goes for any immigrant who is strong enough to survive, adapt, and succeed in a different culture. The narrator intimates that there are some "foods" so revolting that one has to draw the line; she recalls thinking at her mother's table, "I would live on plastic" (92). But basically, the message here is similar to that in Dr. Seuss's *Green Eggs and Ham:* "Eat them, eat them!" This message ushers in the next narrative, which concerns an aunt who failed to become a big cultural eater.

"At the Western Palace" tells the story of Moon Orchid's visit to California. Moon Orchid comes from Hong Kong to see her sister Brave Orchid, rejoin her married daughter, and meet her three grandchildren. Brave Orchid, however, is intent on a different agenda: she wants Moon Orchid to confront and reclaim her husband, who lives in Los Angeles, has a successful medical practice, but has never called for her to join him. Timid Moon Orchid shrinks from doing anything of the kind. Both sisters are in their sixties.

Moon Orchid, helpless and delicate, a woman who never worked, presents a fourth and very different version of Chinese womanhood. Brave Orchid's attempt to get her sister's husband back fails miserably. Subsequently, Moon Orchid cannot adapt to life in the United States, gradually loses her mind, and eventually has to be institutionalized. In "Shaman" big eaters, those who can adapt their palates, are the winners; here, an inability to adapt marks the loser. Insanity also robs Moon Orchid of her voice, for as Brave Orchid tells her children, "mad people have only one story that they talk over and over" (159). In a context where not just hard work and resourcefulness, but also flexibility and a ready tongue are deemed important for success, Moon Orchid fails on all counts and becomes a negative role model.

This story opens a new perspective on Brave Orchid. Although she is the same strong woman she was in China, here we see her as she is in the United States. She is a very poor judge of Americans and American realities. She grotesquely misjudges the extent to which Moon Orchid can exercise her rights as the first wife of her Americanized brain surgeon husband, who is now married to a younger Chinese American woman. Brave Orchid fights for Chinese-style women's rights. In the United States, women do not have these particular rights. Brave Orchid argues for women's rights based on traditional practices related to polygamous Chinese marriages, which are alien and not effective in a American context.

In confronting Chinese with American women's rights, the narrative takes on a feminist dimension. Brave Orchid and her daughters all blame Moon Orchid's insanity on her husband's infidelity. We recall that in "Shaman" big eating had its limits. *Some* foods were pronounced inedible. Here, all the women in the family react with revulsion to the behavior of Moon Orchid's husband. Her sister's sad end causes Brave Orchid to reevaluate and reject Chinese polygamy, while her daughters resolve never to put up with an unfaithful husband. All of the children in the family decide to protect themselves from the kind of fate that befell Moon

Orchid by pursuing studies in subjects that are firmly grounded in empirical reality and moreover transcend cultural differences: science or mathematics. The narrator's account of the children's reaction demands to be read with a grain of salt: solutions are rarely that simple, and, although in her actual life Kingston entered the University of California, Berkeley, to study engineering, she soon changed her major to English.

The final section, "A Song for a Barbarian Reed Pipe," picks up on the story of Moon Orchid told in the previous section, but introduces a striking shift from third to first person. The narrator writes: "What my brother actually said was . . ." "A Song for a Barbarian Reed Pipe" presents something that the narrator withheld from the reader up to this point: her story of growing up as told from her own perspective. Speaking and storytelling reemerge as themes when the account of Moon Orchid's story is revealed to be her brother's story, which the narrator is further distanced from because she hears it second-hand from a sister. The narrator re-problematizes these themes when she adds that her brother's "version of the story may be better than [hers] because of its bareness, not twisted into designs" (163). Kingston thus identifies herself as a designing storyteller, comparable, in her metaphor, to the ancient Chinese knot-makers who tied strings into complicated knots. The risk of such designs, it seems, is above all to the knot-maker, not to the listener. One knot was said to be so complicated that it blinded the person who tied it and had to be outlawed. Kingston admits her passion for tying such potentially self-destructive knots: "If I had lived in China, I would have been an outlaw knot-maker" (163). Thus she admits that she tells complicated stories, or complicates stories, in a way possibly fatal to herself.

Wherein lies the fatality of this art? It once again splits the culturally divided self, conjecturally unified with the metaphor of eating and hypothetically protected through the study of science or mathematics, into two. On the one hand, the girl abjures her mother's and, by extension, Chinese storytelling as deliberately confusing. This message, which builds up throughout the book, peaks toward the end of "A Song for a Barbarian Reed Pipe," when she tells how she confronted her parents in a screaming tirade of accusations. On the other hand, she implicates her own practice of storytelling in Chinese tradition. With her knot metaphor, she acknowledges what the reader may have surmised all along: her own mode of storytelling resembles Brave Orchid's. If Maxine's mother tells highly fanciful and metaphoric stories, so does she. Emulating her mother's story of a "Sitting Ghost" who sits on her all night, the narrator tells a story, which she admits she might have made up, of a "mentally retarded boy who followed [her] around" (194) at Chinese school (and whom she and her classmates "suspected was [. . .] an adult" [195]) and sits in her parents' laundry on boxes filled with what she learns later is pornography, watching her. If her mother tells allegedly true stories heavy with deeper meaning, like "No Name Woman," so does the narrator; for example, she tells the story of torturing a silent little Chinese girl, who, as critics have surmised and Kingston has agreed, is her alter ego, the part of herself that she hates (Islas 30).

The narrator's most complex narrative knot comes in this final section, when she takes up the threads of the theme of voice. Particularly ambiguous is her story of her mother cutting her tongue. She herself attributes her speaking problems to the fact that her mother (as her mother told her) cut her frenum when she was an infant. Whether this tongue-cutting is a metaphor for familial censorship or a genuine operation is left up in the air. Did her mother "cut her tongue" to keep her voiceless, as she believes, or did she undertake a necessary operation to loosen her tongue, so that she would not be tongue-tied in the new country, as her mother asserts? (164).

In this final section, the multifaceted theme of voice takes center stage. Maxine gradually realizes that it is imperative to speak, to speak up and to speak out. For a Chinese American girl to remain silent is, as shown in the story of the mute classmate she tortures, a misguided form of self-defense, one ultimately destined to fail. It is a source of endless embarrassment and frustration to Maxine that, to her mind and also in the opinion of others, she cannot articulate properly. She has a speech impediment; her voice comes out broken, as a squeak. A Chinese acquaintance says, "She quacks like a pressed duck" (192). What is her problem? Her inability to speak may be understood metaphorically or literally (Kingston acknowledges that she has "had problems speaking" [Bonetti 34]), but either way, the import is the same: her status as a member of a racial minority group in the United States, as someone who precariously straddles two cultures, undermines her ability to speak. She grows up bilingual and at first has trouble untangling the two languages. Then she realizes how utterly different the two cultures are. As a Chinese American child, she has the privilege and the liability of two different visions that refuse to come together into one. The first is the complex, internally inconsistent, yet emphatic vision of her "champion talker" of a mother, the most impressive and competent figure in her life, yet one who is blind to American realities, and indeed calls all Americans "ghosts"—i.e., possibly dangerous creatures of another order who are not to be trusted. The second is the American vision, which looks with the uncomprehending eyes of power on all minority groups, including the Chinese. Finding one's footing in this uneven terrain, where everything appears through a double focus, is difficult. From what place can she speak? Speaking implies communicating, and communicating implies an audience. Specific audiences have a predefined receptivity for certain types of content, articulated in certain ways by certain categories of people. A prerequisite for speech is the instinctive confidence that one's words will not fall on deaf or uncomprehending ears because of what one says or because of what one is. A young Chinese girl does not occupy a good spot for speaking "freely" in either the Chinese or the American communities. Both sides push her to say certain things, in certain ways. "My mouth went permanently crooked with effort" (171). Her parents constantly tell her not to talk freely to the Americans; Chinese have to be secretive in the United States or risk trouble. Not only does she lack confidence to speak; she is boxed in by a censorship that becomes self-censorship. She bottles her feelings up and thus feels that she is full of unspeakable things, mainly her petty misdoings and sinful wishes, but also some questions she never dared ask. She maintains an ever-growing interior list of things she'd like to say, specifically to her mother. Telling would be cathartic. But after she blurts out a few of the items over the course of several nights, her mother reacts uncomprehendingly and tells her to stop and leave her alone.

The narrator has spent much of her childhood believing that her family and the Chinese immigrant community want to push her into traditional Chinese womanhood. The motif of sitting as oppression, specifically the oppression of Chinese women by Chinese men, made a first brief appearance in "White Tigers," in the woman warrior's vision of "fat men [who] sat on naked little girls" (30). Sitting then becomes a central motif in "Shaman" in Brave Orchid's account of the Sitting Ghost who sat on her chest all night and nearly suffocated her. The implication of a struggle between the sexes becomes apparent when this "new woman" reproaches the ghost: "'You will not win, Boulder, [. . .]. You do not belong here'" and "'You have no power over a strong woman'" (70). In "A Song for a Barbarian Reed Pipe," the narrator tells the story of an intellectually disabled rich boy who stalks her and morphs into someone who "started sitting at [her parents'] laundry" where he "panted, the stubble rising and falling on his fat neck and chin" (195). Maxine is terrified that her parents want to marry her to this person, whom she describes as a "monster" and "were-person" (196). His continued presence in the laundry finally loosens her tongue. Far from confessing her sins as she had in mind, she screams accusations at her parents in front of the entire family. In a geyser of expressive language, she says exactly what she thinks—if indeed she clearly knew what she thought before her throat burst open and the words came rushing forth. In a torrent of confrontational language, Maxine demands that her parents get rid of the "sitter"; proclaims she's "smart"; insists that she's not going to get married because she "can win scholarships" and "get into colleges" (201); and finally, refuses "to listen to any more of [their] stories; they have no logic" (202). This is the climax of the book, the moment of push-back up to which all of the previous narratives have been building. The American-born child embraces her American life, rejects the ways of her parents, and talks straight.

Following this outpouring, the narrative builds toward a resolution. Even during the girl's tirade, her mother steps up in defense of Chinese ways and talks back. The narrator writes: "My mother, who is champion talker, was, of course, shouting at the same time" (202). Her mother calls her a "dummy" and "stupid" for thinking she wanted to marry her off and for not being able to "tell a joke from real life" (202). Moreover, the narrator herself begins to speak in tones that recall a Chinese art form: her items "kept pouring out anyway in the voice like Chinese opera" (203). This duet, where the girl sounds operatic and the mother speaks clearly, undermines the truth implied by the expressive outburst and dissolves black and white into gray. To what extent has she misunderstood her parents and their motives all along? If she cannot discern a clear message behind "the language of impossible stories" (87), might not this be her—and not her parents'—fault? When Maxine accuses her mother, "You lie with stories" (202), her mother counters with, "Can't you take a joke? . . . We like to say the opposite" (202-203).

The narrator, speaking from a present-day perspective, tells us that she had to leave home so as to see the world logically. Yet her relationship with her mother, the "champion talker," remains double to the end. Consistent with the two possible interpretations of the tongue-cutting, with the two-pronged messages of "No Name Woman" and Fa Mu Lan, with her mother's wisdom and simultaneous blindness, her mother ultimately both hobbles and empowers her, obstructing her integration yet giving her a positive model. At the conclusion of the book, in present time, the narrator tells her mother that she also talks story. This final moment is one of rapprochement: the daughter of the champion storyteller has become a writer. The narrator and her mother reach of moment of resolution when they combine stories in the final section "A Song for a Barbarian Reed Pipe." After Brave Orchid recounts a story about the narrator's grandmother and her belief that "our family was immune to harm as long as they went to plays" (Kingston, *Woman Warrior* 207), the narrator imagines a performance featuring the songs of the Chinese poetess Ts'ai Yen who had been taken captive by "barbarians." But hearing the sound of the barbarians' flutes, the poet herself is moved to sing her story. Although the barbarians don't understand the words, they understand her song because she sings of universal emotions, sadness and anger, and common experiences like forever wandering. As critics have pointed out, the story could be about her mother and the stories her mother directs at her, her "barbarian" child; but it could also be her own story (Smith 80-81; Rabine 97-98; Simmons 104-107). The duet, a testimony to the ability of art to transmit universal experience and foster understanding, suggests what this autobiography—itself a song for a barbarian reed pipe—accomplishes, namely to give voice to two utterly different cultures in such a way that the American barbarians will comprehend what it is like to grow up Chinese American. By extension, this means understanding what it is like to grow up split between two cultures, two languages, two sets of values, and two or more conflicting discourses. It means understanding how a person nonetheless can, little by little, learn to put these disparate things together, taking the best of each, and be the stronger for it.

Works Cited

Bonetti, Kay. "An Interview with Maxine Hong Kingston." *Conversations with Maxine Hong Kingston.* Ed. Paul Skenazy & Tera Martin. Jackson: UP of Mississippi, 1998. 33-46. Print.

Islas, Arturo & Marilyn Yalom. "Interview with Maxine Hong Kingston. *Conversations with Maxine Hong Kingston.* Ed. Paul Skenazy & Tera Martin. Jackson: UP of Mississippi, 1998. 21-32. Print.

Kingston, Maxine Hong. *China Men.* 1980. New York: Vintage/Random, 1989. Print.

_____. *The Woman Warrior: Memoirs of a Girlhood among Ghosts.* 1976. New York: Vintage/Random, 1989. Print.

Rabine, Leslie W. "No Lost Paradise: Social Gender and Symbolic Gender in the Writings of Maxine Hong Kingston." *Maxine Hong Kingston's* The Woman Warrior*: A Casebook.* Ed. Sau-ling Cynthia Wong. New York: Oxford UP, 1999. 85-109. Print.

Simmons, Diane. *Maxine Hong Kingston.* New York: Twayne, 1999. Print.

Smith, Sidonie. "Filiality and Woman's Autobiographical Storytelling." *Maxine Hong Kingston's* The Woman Warrior: *A Casebook.* Ed. Sau-ling Cynthia Wong. New York: Oxford UP, 1999. 57-83. Print.

Wong, Sau-Ling Cynthia. "Autobiography as Guided Chinatown Tour? Maxine Hong Kingston's *The Woman Warrior* and the Chinese American Autobiographical Controversy." *Maxine Hong Kingston's* The Woman Warrior: *A Casebook*. Ed. Sau-ling Cynthia Wong. New York: Oxford UP, 1999. 29-53. Print.

Zhang, Ya-Jie. "A Chinese Woman's Response to Maxine Hong Kingston's *The Woman Warrior*." *Maxine Hong Kingston's* The Woman Warrior: *A Casebook*. Ed. Sau-ling Cynthia Wong. New York: Oxford UP, 1999. 17-21. Print.

The Mother's Mark on the Daughter's Speech in *The Woman Warrior*

Jeffrey Westover

In *The Woman Warrior*, Maxine Hong Kingston draws on many resources to develop a story about her protagonist's individual development. As the daughter of Chinese immigrants, she finds herself investigating selfhood in more than individual terms. Her story is suffused with uncertainty, fantasy, and ambiguity, all of which she navigates through dramatic metaphors of voice and writing. The book as a whole challenges its readers to consider the ways that language frames and generates meaning, showing that selfhood is shaped by culture. In this essay, I will draw upon three categories the narrator negotiates in her quest for maturation and insight—prohibition, inscription, and incision—to examine Kingston's responses to her mother and her own legacy as the child of Chinese immigrants. In particular, I will focus on the fact that, in a book rich with ambiguities, Kingston makes it clear that selfhood is not achieved in isolation. Although individuation is important for self-development, selves mature in relation to family, history, language, and the contemporary world.

Kingston figures these relationships in several ways, but the mother's role in embodying or mediating most of them is a consistent theme throughout the book (for more on this issue, see Ho [118] and Sabine [2]). By focusing on Kingston's references to prohibited speech, writing, and scarification (in the form of tattooing or surgical cutting), I will demonstrate some of the ways *The Woman Warrior* portrays selfhood in dynamic and contingent terms, as a process. Kingston prominently features the role of writing in the articulation of this process, implying that selfhood is an ongoing negotiation instead of a finished condition.

Prohibition

The first chapter of *The Woman Warrior*, "No Name Woman," begins with a dramatic prohibition: "'You must not tell anyone,' my mother said, 'what I am about to tell you'" (3). The injunction is part of a plot to erase the life of the protagonist's aunt from the record of her family. However, the very existence of the chapter, as Kingston's narrator makes clear, is an ironic violation of that prohibition. The mother's telling her daughter not to speak becomes the occasion of the daughter's speech. The prohibition inaugurates the book, striking a keynote of repression, but also enacting the narration that constitutes the very book in readers' hands. By writing down her mother's words, as Shirley Geok-lin Lim explains, Kingston "is both subordinate to and repudiating the mother's request for silence" ("Chinese American" 260). Moreover, by beginning her book in this way, Kingston shows that her protagonist must engage with the burdens of the past in order to grow up.

In interviews with Donna Perry (1991) and Eric J. Schroeder (1996), Kingston points out that, like her, both Alice Walker and Toni Morrison begin important books with references to silence (Skenazy & Martin 177, 215). By aligning the opening of *The Woman Warrior* with "the feminist topos of imposed silence" (Cheung, *Articulate* 74) in *The Color Purple* and *The Bluest Eye*, Kingston invites her readers to view the narrator's mother as a representative figure as well as the protagonist's mother. According to David Leiwei Li, moreover, Lawrence Yep begins his 1975 novel *Dragonwings* with "a mother who is unwilling to break the taboo subject" (46). In the case of "No Name Woman," the narrator is an agent of repressive patriarchal culture, for the admonition not to speak is obviously a way of policing her daughter's behavior. "You see, everybody has that same line," Kingston tells Perry. "[I]t's the same struggle to break through taboos, to find your voice. It's that same 'exile, secrecy, and cunning' that [James] Joyce was talking about" (Skenazy & Martin 177).

For an individual to find her voice, she must respond to other people's speech. Jill M. Parrott analyzes the narrator's response in *The Woman Warrior* by making an important distinction between

Critical Insights

action and representation: "Although the legend of the woman's downfall continues as a form of social control," Parrott writes, "the name does not" (378). By speculating about her aunt's life, Kingston offers interpretations that defy the sinister impact of her legend while testifying to her existence. Instead of passively accepting that legend, she improvises her own mode of storytelling in an attempt to understand and honor her dead relative. Indeed, the very etymology of *legend* (that which must be read) indicates that the story is told in order to be weighed and worked through: "Whenever she had to warn us about life, my mother told us stories that ran like this one, a story to grow up on. She tested our strength to establish realities" (Kingston, *Woman Warrior* 5). In this formulation, Kingston indicates that listening to stories is an intellectual and psychological challenge. Stories provide an opportunity for the attentive listener to develop her imagination, judgment, and self-knowledge. If, as King-Kok Cheung observes, "No Name Woman" is a variation on the Philomela myth, "in which the tongue of the raped woman is cut off" ("'Don't Tell'" 163), then the anonymous aunt's violation is not the last word of the story, for Kingston uses her artistry to commemorate her aunt. In this respect, Kingston's chapter honoring No Name Woman is analogous to the tapestry Philomela makes in order to communicate her violation to her sister Procne and thereby overcome her voicelessness (Ovid recounts the myth in *Metamorphoses*, VI: 517-619).

Moreover, by working through several potential versions of her aunt's story, the narrator tries to compose for her "a local habitation and a name" even as she acknowledges the necessarily provisional nature of her efforts (*A Midsummer Night's Dream* 5.1.17). In the very process of making the speculations, Kingston commemorates her aunt, striving for a tentative, scaled-down form of immortality: "after fifty years of neglect, I alone devote pages of paper to her, though not origamied into houses and clothes" (*Woman Warrior* 16). Despite the negation here, the narrator's pages turn out to be as artistically crafted as origami. While lacking the visual appeal and three-dimensionality of folded paper objects, the narratives offer a robust roundedness on their own terms, in the domain of the textual.

"No Name Woman" paradoxically attributes a name to the aunt, but a name which is more a generic category than a personal noun, more a representative term than an individual moniker.

Kingston makes her reverence for the social and psychological power of words quite clear in the course of an interview with Shirley Geok-lin Lim:

> "As a writer, it seems to me that growth takes place when I can put it into words. If I can say who I am, if I can say what powers I want, then I can have them. That was the function of *The Woman Warrior*, self-understanding, understanding myself in relation to my family, to my mother, my place in my community, in my society, and in the world" (Lim, "Reading Back" 158).

In *The Woman Warrior*, the narrator must violate the prohibition against telling the story of No Name Woman in order to articulate her sense of herself and the world that has produced her, and readers must conspire with her in the violation in order to proceed with the text. To accompany Kingston's protagonist on her adventure of self-knowledge—the adventure of becoming a woman with a well-defined identity—readers must collude with her in breaking a taboo.

Inscription

Beyond reclaiming an unknown female ancestor, what does this violation lead to or make possible? One answer seems to be that the narrator is now freer to invent and test new models of identity, a process that depends on the imaginative use of language. As Helena Grice observes, "The woman warrior is, often, a *word* warrior" (50). This idea is borne out by the fact that Kingston rewrites certain aspects of "No Name Woman" in the course of her next chapter, "White Tigers." By referring to the onset of the protagonist's menses, for example, both chapters focus on the process of the protagonist's maturation (Kingston, *Woman Warrior* 5, 30). In "No Name Woman," the villagers curse the family by shouting "Pig" and "Ghost," and No Name Woman gives birth in a pig sty (4-5, 14-15). In "White Tigers," by contrast, the woman warrior is fêted upon her return home with the sacrifice of a pig (45). While she hides her pregnancy from her soldiers, the baby's birth is celebrated by her husband and her family (40-41, 45). In "No Name Woman," the villagers ritually plunder and defile the family's property and home (4-5, 13), whereas in "White Tigers," they send the woman warrior off to battle by providing her with gifts (35-36). The gifts are too bountiful for her to carry away, and she even likens them to "wedding presents" (35). This festive send-off is diametrically opposed to the ritualistic punishment meted out to No Name Woman and her family. The narrator of "White Tigers" revises the legend of "No Name Woman," adjusting its storyline in an attempt to benefit her own identity and self-esteem in the context of her culture: "From the words on my back, and how they were fulfilled, the villagers would make a legend out of my perfect filiality" (45). This envisioned harmony reverses the dramatically broken social bonds of No Name Woman (4). The narrator's revision of No Name Woman's story in "White Tigers" is incremental and incomplete, but it is also based on materials inherited from her family and from Chinese culture. The Fa Mu Lan story provides elements of empowerment to Kingston's protagonist, but the story is not without its limitations, as the end of the chapter makes clear. I will return to this issue, but first let me turn to a consideration of Kingston's emphasis on the act of representation in her second chapter.

In "White Tigers," Kingston foregrounds the role of writing in the development of her protagonist, partly through metaphors of Chinese script, as when she likens a bird to "the ideograph for 'human'" (*Woman Warrior* 20) and partly through depicting writing in the form of scarification, as when the litany of revenges is carved into the skin of her protagonist's back:

> My father first brushed the words in ink, and they fluttered down my back row after row. Then he began cutting; to make fine lines and points he used thin blades, for the stems, large blades.
>   My mother caught the blood and wiped the cuts with a cold towel soaked with wine. It hurt terribly—the cuts sharp; the air burning; the alcohol cold, then hot—pain so various. . . . If an enemy should flay me, the light would shine through my skin like lace.

At the end of the last word, I fell forward. Together my parents sang what they had written, then let me rest. (Kingston, *Woman Warrior* 34-35)

By slicing words into their daughter's skin, the parents provide a purpose for her and encourage her to internalize the duties and norms codified in their culture. Daphne Lei goes so far as to argue that "The woman warrior does not own her own body. Her body is claimed by her parents and her village." For this reason, Lei concludes that "[s]he becomes the ultimate Orientalized object under the American gaze" (121). But "ultimate" is a strong word to use about a book that is constantly shifting perspectives. Indeed, one might even say that *The Woman Warrior* thematizes such shifts in perspective as part of its effort to depict the development of the narrator as multifaceted, open-ended, and incomplete. As Bonnie TuSmith argues, "Structurally, each story of the woman warrior—whether of the legendary Fa Mu Lan, the narrator's mother Brave Orchid, or the narrator herself—tests the potential for reconciliation between the individual and her community" (289). This reconciliation is necessary to the process of individuation, whereby the narrator develops and strengthens her personal identity by orienting it in relation to others. Thoughtfully responding to cultural scripts, such as that of Fa Mu Lan, is a significant feature of this process, but it is only one part of the process. In the episode above, the parents write upon their daughter's body, but it is the daughter herself who narrates this event as part of her story.

Moreover, this scene is not the culmination of "White Tigers," for Kingston chooses to burst the bubble of her Fa Mu Lan episode, revealing it to be a fiction—an impressive and compelling one, but nonetheless a fantasy. In doing so, she shows her readers that even though the storyline is a revision of a traditional story, that revision is inadequate to her protagonist's era, personal taste, and circumstances. As Martha J. Cutter claims, "Kingston struggles in the book not to be a text, an icon of divided, marked, scarred ethnic American body/self, but rather to speak a text that transcodes this body/self into a new entity" (49). While the Fa Mu Lan myth provides one important model of assertive femininity, Kingston's narrator goes on to reject its violent and romanticizing elements. The image of the woman warrior's flayed skin shining like lace in the sun, for instance, is a stunning one, but the narrator's subsequent decision to deflate the heroic storyline is an acknowledgment of the dangers of aestheticizing or ritualizing such bodily violence.

In addition, the warrior woman is an exception, so for that reason alone, she cannot succeed as a role model for a young woman trying to find her way in a racist and sexist environment. The woman warrior keeps her gender secret from her army because "Chinese executed women who disguised themselves as soldiers or students, no matter how bravely they fought or how high they scored on the examinations" (Kingston, *Woman Warrior* 39). Leslie W. Rabine points out the paradoxical quality of Kingston's protagonist, writing that "Fa Mu Lan has to hide the writing under the male armor in order to be able to express it" (492). In the end, Kingston's narrator demonstrates her awareness that the Fa Mu Lan story is insufficient for her needs, for it only partially aids her in rejecting those elements of her cultural heritage that impede her quest for selfhood. In the words of Feng Lan, "Kingston's Mulan . . . stands for the 'past' that her creator wants to leave behind, not a future to 'reach for'" (243).

Kingston has explicitly identified the feminist agenda behind her treatment of the Fa Mu Lan story. As she explains in an interview with Kay Bonetti,

> When the woman warrior has the words carved on her back, that's actually a man's story. It's about a man named Yüch Fei who had the vow carved on his back by his mother. Now I took that and gave that to a woman. I gave a man's myth to a woman because it's part of the feminist war that's going on in *The Woman Warrior*, to take the men's stories away from them and give the strength of that story to a woman. I see that as an aggressive storytelling act, and also it's part of my own freedom to play with the myth, and I do feel that the myths have to be changed and played with all the time, or they die. (Skenazy & Martin 40)

In comments such as this, Kingston clearly conveys her revisionist intent. Kingston rewrites "No Name Woman" in "White Tigers," but she also alters the Fa Mu Lan story itself in significant ways. As Sau-ling Cynthia Wong observes, "The heroine of 'Mulan Shi' sees herself merely as a second-best substitute for an aged father (there being no elder to take his place)," but "the little girl in 'White Tigers' is a *chosen* one, destined to be called away by 'immortals'" (45). It is important to remember Kingston's revisionist purpose when assessing "White Tigers" in particular and *The Woman Warrior* as a whole. In addition, Kingston has frequently emphasized the significance of her characters' fantasies and dreams in her writing, so an undue emphasis on the factual or pragmatic can lead readers to miss or dismiss important features of her work (Skenazy & Martin 30, 37, 75).

As I have mentioned, the subject matter of "White Tigers" is not limited to the story of Fa Mu Lan. The coda running from pages 45 to 63 (beginning with the sentence, "My American life has been such a disappointment") is not a tacked-on afterthought. It is an integral part of the chapter, for it continues the rewriting of cultural norms and storylines that structure the narrator's quest for identity. As Lan suggests, "the Mulan story is in fact the author's strategy to *negotiate* her Chinese heritage" (236), not a straightforward representation of Chinese culture or the fulfillment of her effort to clarify her identity. The key word in the subtitle of Kingston's book, *memoirs*, is plural: her protagonist's quest is marked by many memories and multiple imaginations. The book is about a singular girlhood lived among several ghosts. In the fantasy interlude in which she imagines herself as Fa Mu Lan, Kingston's narrator begins to exercise her powers of language to produce more satisfying models of selfhood, models that might withstand the negative pressures of her environment.

This experiment articulates some important lessons about personal development (such as making "room for paradoxes" [Kingston, *Woman Warrior* 29]), but it produces a model that proves only partially adequate or temporarily convincing to Kingston's protagonist. If the tattooing of the crimes upon Fa Mu Lan's back provides one example of incision as a phase in the narrator's growth, it is not the only form of bodily mutilation that she experiences. The ritual scarification results in an elegant, though grisly, script that inaugurates her hero's quest, but Kingston refers to another form of incision in the last chapter of her book.

Incision

In that chapter, "A Song for a Barbarian Reed Pipe," Kingston's narrator alleges that her mother cut her frenum, a membrane connected to the tongue: "my mother cut my tongue. She pushed my tongue up and sliced the frenum. Or maybe she snipped it with a pair of nail scissors. I don't remember her doing it, only her telling me about it" (*Woman Warrior* 163-64). (It is worth noting that Kingston relates tongue-cutting to history and truth-telling in *The Fifth Book of Peace* [45].) The narrator both posits this event as factual and undercuts it as unverifiable, since the putative action seems to have happened in infancy and the narrator has no personal recollection of it. Indeed, even the definition of the word cuts both ways, since *frenum* refers to an anatomical structure that either restricts or supports an organ to which it is attached. Kingston milks this semantic duplicity for all it's worth, investigating the ways the reputed cutting of the daughter's frenum *both* restricts and supports her capacity for speech.

Indeed, the storytelling associated with the event comes to function as a fable partly because the mother's stated purpose of cutting the frenum was to liberate the daughter's speech. (The pun on *frenum* as freedom parallels this claim). Brave Orchid's argument is that the narrator's frenum was unduly restrictive, locking her daughter's tongue in a position that marred its capacity for speech, especially for speech in more than one language. "I cut it so that you would not be tongue-tied," she tells her daughter. "Your tongue would be able to move in any language. You'll be able to speak languages that are completely different from one another. You'll be able to pronounce anything. Your frenum looked too tight to do those things, so I cut it" (Kingston, *Woman Warrior* 164). According to this logic, Brave Orchid performed her surgery to support her daughter by giving her access to multiple worlds or cultures, an access she needs in order to function as a native-born American daughter of Chinese immigrants.

Despite the mother's stated purpose, the daughter harbors doubts. Kingston portrays her mother as at once admirable and forbidding. Given that the action would have happened before she had full awareness of herself and the world, the story suggests that the mother is a force of nature or an aspect of fate, for her action could only be withstood and not altered. But since the mother is a person and not a personification of fate or nature, she exercises choice, which suggests that she is potentially culpable and may, therefore, be defending herself against accusations of injustice. That said, the daughter mimics her mother in taking up the story of her tongue-cutting. She acclimates herself to the narrative, but she also perpetuates it and tries to make it her own by putting the story in her own words, playing with its terms, and challenging her mother's authority to frame it. In the following passage, for example, she simultaneously questions, accepts, and corrects her mother's story:

> If my mother was not lying she should have cut more, scraped away the rest of the frenum skin, because I have a terrible time talking. Or she should not have cut at all, tampering with my speech. When I went to kindergarten and had to speak English for the first time, I became silent. A dumbness—a shame—still cracks my voice in two, even when I want to say 'hello' casually, or ask an easy question. (Kingston, *Woman Warrior* 164-165)

For the myth of the tongue-cutting to remain alive with meaning, Kingston must adapt it in her own way. In the words of Jeehyun Lim, "[the narrator] incorporates the story of her tongue cutting into a part of her identity" (55-56). This responsive collaboration on her part provides further evidence for the idea that selfhood is forged through the give-and-take of relationships rather than in isolation. The narrator's sense of herself is the product of her interactions with her mother and other people. As the passage indicates, such interactions include conflict as well as forms of social bonding.

The narrator also seems to mimic her mother's tongue-cutting when she bullies another girl at the Chinese school they both attend

(Kingston, *Woman Warrior* 172-181). Moreover, she overtly repeats her mother's prohibition in "No Name Woman" when she commands the girl to keep quiet about her harassment of her, saying, "'Don't you dare tell anyone I've been bad to you'" (181). This episode not only puts the protagonist in a negative light, it also seems to signal a regression in her development. She succumbs to negative social forces in her everyday world when she bullies her classmate. By portraying her younger self in this manner, Kingston suggests that she was trying to fend off something in herself that she notices in another. This mirroring accounts for the powerful emotional turmoil that the narrator experiences during this episode, turmoil that includes crying and screaming (179-181). By lashing out at the other girl, as Sidonie Smith observes, Kingston's narrator "strikes violently at her own failure to take a voice and at all her mother's prior narratives of female voicelessness" (169). Recognizing deficiencies in the other girl that she fears and loathes in herself, the narrator attempts to exorcise her own shortcomings by mistreating her classmate. After repeatedly commanding and badgering the silent girl, she starts to rationalize her behavior, albeit in increasingly hysterical terms:

"Why won't you talk?" I started to cry. What if I couldn't stop, and everyone would want to know what happened? "Now look what you've done," I scolded. "You're going to pay for this. I want to know why. And you're going to tell me why. You don't see I'm trying to help you out, do you? Do you want to be like this, dumb (do you know what dumb means?), your whole life? (Kingston, *Woman Warrior* 180)

Cruelty is cruelty, and portraying it in writing does not alter that fact. Nonetheless, the protagonist's claims that speech is necessary for the development and expression of selfhood are part of the consistent theme of the entire last chapter. There is a pragmatic truth to such claims, even though they are meant to rationalize the protagonist's misbehavior and offset her guilt about it. "If you don't talk, you can't have a personality," she argues, "You've got to let people know you have a personality and a brain" (Kingston, *Woman Warrior* 180). Speaking is a form of action in the world. It may stimulate the thinking and development of the speaker in productive ways, but it also registers the selfhood of that speaker in the social arena.

By including the episode of bullying, Kingston suggests that the problem of silenced female subjectivity is widespread or representative rather than exceptional. The bullying fails to alleviate the protagonist's problems, and it harms the other girl. However, Kingston's depiction of the event is not merely confessional. Instead it demonstrates the deforming impact of the conflicting demands to speak and keep quiet that young girls experience in both American and Chinese immigrant contexts. So intense are these contradictory demands, they eventually paralyze the narrator as much as they do the girl whom she taunts, although the narrator comically characterizes her paralysis in somewhat vacation-like terms, spending eighteen months "like the Victorian recluses I read about" (Kingston, *Woman Warrior* 181-182). As the tongue-cutting fable suggests, the narrator must speak out and speak up in order to strengthen her self-esteem and to situate herself more effectively in relation to her mother, the Chinese-American immigrant community, and the rest of the world. As a result, in the final chapter of *The Woman Warrior*, Kingston figures the conflicts involved in becoming an adult as a sustained battle to claim one's voice. She not only begins the chapter with the tale of the tongue-cutting, but she also refers to reticence, silence, speaking, and throat pains throughout the final pages of the book.

In the following passage, for example, the protagonist speculates that her mother's tongue-cutting acknowledges (or confers) her distinctiveness: "Maybe because I was the one with the tongue cut loose, I had grown inside me a list of over two hundred things that I had to tell my mother so that she would know the true things about me and to stop the pain in my throat" (Kingston, *Woman Warrior* 197). In this sentence, the mother's character as progenitor is doubled by her power to engender the growth of her daughter's speech, although Kingston's canny syntax suggests that the narrator herself is the maker of her words ("I had grown inside me"). Like mother, like daughter: as Kingston shows in this and many other cases in *The Woman Warrior*, when it comes to the aggressive and artful use of words, it certainly does take one to know one. Kingston casts the act of writing as a form of giving birth, thereby appropriating a metaphor common among male poets in English literature. At the same time that she figures the daughter as a mother of words, Kingston portrays her in child-like terms, as dependent on her mother for nurture and encouragement. Kingston clearly shows that her protagonist needs her mother as much as she needs to be independent of her.

In an important scene of the last chapter, the protagonist makes a dramatic outburst to her parents. The scene is a kind of turning point. In it, she expresses some of the recurrent issues in many previous chapters of *The Woman Warrior*:

> "I can't tell what's real and what you make up. Ha! You can't stop me from talking. You tried to cut off my tongue, but it didn't work." So I told the hardest ten or twelve things on my list all in one outburst.
>
> My mother, who is champion talker, was, of course, shouting at the same time. "I cut it to make you talk more, not less, you dummy. You're still stupid. You can't listen right. . . . Can't you take a joke? You can't even tell a joke from real life. You're not so smart. Can't even tell real from false." (Kingston, *Woman Warrior* 202)

This exchange hearkens back to a key sentence from "No Name Woman," in which the narrator writes that her mother "tested our strength to establish realities" (Kingston, *Woman Warrior* 5). While both mother and daughter prove themselves to be engaging storytellers, spinning fantastic yarns for the entertainment and education of their listeners, in this scene, Kingston conveys the mother's subtlety in humorous and virtuosic terms. Indeed, the exchange leads the narrator to a very important conclusion: "And suddenly I got very confused and lonely because I was at that moment telling her my list, and in the telling, it grew. No higher listener. No listener but myself" (204). This moment marks a critical juncture for the protagonist, for in it she discovers the need to be independent in her judgments. Throughout the chapter called "Shaman," Brave Orchid offers her daughter a heroic model of assertive self-representation and impressive leadership. In these passages from "A Song for a Barbarian Reed Pipe," the mother fosters her daughter's self-knowledge and nourishes her courage to act on her own. The narrator's epiphany may have an element of Emersonian self-reliance to it, but her expression of it is decidedly melancholy. The passage poignantly acknowledges the need for mutuality—the love and opposition of the mother—in developing the distinctive features of the self.

In the closing pages of her memoir, Kingston tells the story of Ts'ai Yen, a woman who is captured in battle, married to one of her captors, and forced to bear children in exile for a period of years (Kingston, *Woman Warrior* 206-209). As Kingston explains, "the beginning of the story" is her mother's, but the ending is Kingston's (206). The story clearly reflects the situation of her own mother as an immigrant, but because Ts'ai Yen has children in a foreign land, it also parallels Kingston's position as the daughter of immigrants. Regardless of the narrator's conflicted feelings about the mother's role in her life, her decision to end her memoirs with the story about the barbarian flute song, which she explains is an assimilated work of art, gives the last word not to herself alone but to her mother as well, in the form of a collaboration. This choice is Kingston's final reminder that selfhood is social.

Works Cited

Cheung, King-Kok. *Articulate Silences*. Ithaca, NY: Cornell UP, 1993.

_____. "'Don't Tell': Imposed Silences in *The Woman Warrior* and *The Color Purple*." *PMLA* 103.2 (March 1988): 162-174.

Cutter, Martha J. *Lost and Found in Translation: Contemporary Ethnic American Writing and the Politics of Language Diversity*. Chapel Hill: UP of North Carolina, 2005.

Grice, Helena. *Negotiating Identities: An Introduction to Asian American Women's Writing*. Manchester, UK: Manchester UP, 2002.

Ho, Wendy. *In Her Mother's House: The Politics of Asian American Mother-Daughter Writing*. Walnut Creek, CA: Altamira-Rowman & Littlefield P, 1999.

Kingston, Maxine Hong. *The Fifth Book of Peace*. New York: Vintage-Random House, 2003.

_____. *The Woman Warrior: Memoirs of a Girlhood Among Ghosts*. 1976. New York: Vintage-Random House, 1989.

Lan, Feng. "The Female Individual and the Empire: A Historicist Approach to Mulan and Kingston's *Woman Warrior*." *Comparative Literature* 55:3 (Summer 2003): 229-245.

Lei, Daphne. "The Blood-Stained Text in Translation: Tattooing, Bodily Writing, and Performance of Chinese Virtue." *Anthropological Quarterly* 82:1 (Winter 2009): 99-127.

Li, David Leiwei. *Imagining the Nation: Asian American Literature and Cultural Consent*. Stanford, CA: Stanford UP, 1998.

Lim, Jeehyun. "Cutting the Tongue: Language and the Body in Kingston's *The Woman Warrior*." *MELUS* 31.3 (Fall 2006): 49-65.

Lim, Shirley Geok-lin. "Chinese American Women's Life Stories: Thematics of Race and Gender in Jade Snow Wong's *Fifth Chinese Daughter* and Maxine Hong Kingston's *The Woman Warrior*." *American Women's Autobiography: Fea(s)ts of Memory*. Ed. Margo Culley. Madison: U of Wisconsin P, 1992. 252-267.

_____. "Reading Back, Looking Forward: A Retrospective Interview with Maxine Hong Kingston." *MELUS* 33.1 (Spring 2008): 157-170.

A Midsummer Night's Dream. Complete Works of Shakespeare. Ed. David Bevington. Fourth Ed. New York: HarperCollins, 1992. 150-177.

Ovid. *The Metamorphoses*. Trans. Horace Gregory. Mentor-Penguin, 1958.

Parrott, Jill M. "Power and Discourse: Silence as Rhetorical Choice in Maxine Hong Kingston's *The Woman Warrior*." *Rhetorica* 30.4 (Autumn 2012): 375-391.

Rabine, Leslie W. "No Lost Paradise: Social Gender and Symbolic Gender in the Writings of Maxine Hong Kingston." *Signs* 12.3 (Spring 1987): 471-492.

Sabine, Maureen. *Maxine Hong Kingston's Broken Book of Life: An Intertextual Study of* The Woman Warrior *and* China Men. Honolulu: U of Hawaii P, 2004.

Skenazy, Paul, & Tera Martin, eds. *Conversations with Maxine Hong Kingston*. Jackson: UP of Mississippi, 1998.

Smith, Sidonie. *A Poetics of Women's Autobiography: Marginality and the Fictions of Self-Representation*. Bloomington: Indiana UP, 1987.

TuSmith, Bonnie. "Literary Tricksterism: Maxine Hong Kingston's *The Woman Warrior: Memoirs of a Girlhood Among Ghosts.*" *Anxious Power: Reading, Writing, and Ambivalence in Narrative by Women.* Ed. Carol J. Singly & Susan Elizabeth Sweeney. Albany: SUNY, 1993: 297-294.

Wong, Sau-ling Cynthia. "Autobiography as Guided Chinatown Tour? Maxine Hong Kingston's *The Woman Warrior* and the Chinese American Autobiographical Controversy." *Maxine Hong Kingston's* The Woman Warrior: *A Casebook.* Ed. Sau-ling Cynthia Wong. Oxford: Oxford UP, 1999: 29-56. Rpt. from *Multicultural Autobiography: American Lives.* Ed. James Robert Payne. Knoxville: U of Tennessee P, 1992. 248-279.

The Role of Talk-Story in Maxine Hong Kingston's and Amy Tan's Versions of the Mother-Daughter Plot

Susanna Hoeness-Krupsaw

Feminist scholars have long scrutinized the characteristics of women's relationships with their mothers and daughters. When the first detailed studies emerged in the 1970s, they applied a strong Euro-American focus, often following in the analytic footsteps of Sigmund Freud and did not yet consider multicultural texts. My essay examines how Maxine Hong Kingston's *The Woman Warrior* and Amy Tan's *The Joy Luck Club* introduce readers to innovative, ethnic talk-story versions of the mother-daughter plot. In these talk-stories, immigration and diaspora become metaphors for the mother-daughter relationship, one that is always laden with tension as American-born daughters become acculturated into a new environment while translating and decoding their Chinese mothers' messages.

"If there is no longer a Father, why tell stories?" (Roland Barthes)

Like Virginia Woolf in *A Room of One's Own*, many readers have deplored the absence of "women in literature"; that is, the paucity of literature by and about women before the twentieth century. In hindsight, the explanations for this absence are quite clear. Patriarchal society inculcated its norms into school reading and the publishing industry so that no one thought twice about reading lists dominated by works written by male authors featuring male characters in leading roles. The French philosopher and literary theorist Roland Barthes went as far as claiming that without the father, there would exist no need to tell stories and consequently there would be no literature at all: "If there is no longer a Father, why tell stories?" (47). So far went the influence of what we might call the father-son plot that female literary critics embraced the same ideas in such comprehensive studies as *Time and the Novel* in which Patricia Tobin, following an Oedipal model, posits a "genealogical imperative," ignoring the possibility that a search for one's origins does not necessarily have to lead to the father, but can just as easily lead to the mother.

No wonder audiences welcomed a shift away from this patriarchal dominance to greater awareness of matriarchal discourses. In the late 1970s and throughout the 1980s, as the field of women's studies was flourishing, so did scholarly interest in the mother-daughter plot in fiction. As evidenced in a 1983 bibliographic essay by Marianne Hirsch, both courses in and critical studies about this topic suddenly abounded. Even at that time, however, Hirsch noted the absence of much scholarship by and about minority authors ("Mothering" 38).

Interest in mother-daughter plots was dominated by white middle-class women scholars who often applied Freudian and other derivative psychological analyses to the study of literature. Together with Adrienne Rich, Nancy Chodorow and Marianne Hirsch remain the most popular contributors to the field, with Hirsch's emerging as the voice with the greatest staying power and the most pervasive influence on contemporary studies in the field of mother-daughter narratives. As the subtitle of Rich's book indicates, her *Of Woman Born: Motherhood as Experience and Institution* blends her own experiences with scholarly models and explores motherhood both as lived experience and as an institution sanctioned by the patriarchy. Based on oedipal analysis of familial structures in the West during the 1970s, Chodorow observes the prevalence of mothering tropes, a pattern she interprets as a determinant for women's self-image. In short, girls raised almost exclusively by a mother will become so acculturated to this mothering model that they, too, will become mothers and view themselves within this gendered role. Hence the title of Chodorow's study, *The Reproduction of Mothering*.

Less focused on an oedipal model of parenting and more interested in a revision of the Freudian family romance, Marianne Hirsch's *The Mother/Daughter Plot* provided an entire generation of feminist scholars with a handy tool and terminology for rereading the classics from a rich, new perspective. Centering her analysis on the silenced voice of the mother in classical mythologies, Hirsch unearths a history of mothers in Western literature. Applying these ideas to American and British novels, she reveals how mothers and mothering have been depicted in Western literature. Earlier novels tended to feature weak mother figures whose shortcomings required daughters to avoid identifying with them in order not to remain trapped within a restrictive set of behaviors. Later novels then shift to communities of women in which father figures are shown to be weaker and less influential. Yet in a turn to empower daughters, mothers remain silenced. Hirsch notes that a privileging of the daughter's voice prevents a full telling of the mother's stories.

Carol Gilligan and others focus their attention on different forms of feminine or maternal discourses and their influence on thought and behaviors. Gilligan's work reveals that male patterns of moral thought only insufficiently explain women's more relational thinking about actions and their outcomes. French theorists, such as Luce Irigaray and Julia Kristeva, in a Neo-Freudian move, attempt to create a special feminine discourse to bridge the ruptured ties with the maternal. Where Irigaray idealizes these ties, Kristeva's premise that matricide is necessary for women's individuation runs the risk of replacing the oedipal story with a similar model that still leaves the mother's story unspoken (Yu 46). Yi-Ling Yu's study of matrilineal narratives derives new insights from Jennifer Benjamin's subject-relations theory, which aims at explicating women's intimate cross-generational connections.

Yi-Lin Yu's book also offers visual schemas of the above-mentioned theories, such as family romance, feminist family romance, or new feminist romance, conveniently simplifying a comparative analysis of many of these common approaches to mother-daughter stories (116-121). For Wendy Ho and others, the theoretical work on Asian American women authors necessitates different and even more subtle reading practices that can reveal important political statements: "The politics emergent from their individual and collective locations can provide ways to rethink masculinist, nationalist, and/or capitalist configurations of the social body politic" (20). The fiction and the theoretical approaches of minority women writers, identified as "diasporic matrilineal narratives" by Yu, pay more attention to the mother's voice. Particularly, the autobiographical narratives by Kingston and Tan go a long way in reclaiming the abject maternal body from centuries of silence by letting the mothers' stories be heard alongside the daughters' narratives.

Kingston's and Tan's Diasporic Matrilineal Narratives

Maxine Hong Kingston's and Amy Tan's novels illustrate Wendy Ho's call for new approaches because their use of talk-stories foregrounds cultural and textual as well as linguistic components, rather than Western-influenced psychological elements. Ho's childhood memories of long conversations with her mother and grandmother offer a helpful definition of talk-story: "an eclectic feast of living language, culture, memory and affiliations that brings us to a more intimate knowledge of each other and our many identities in the diverse communities and daily locations we inhabit" (13). She further describes talk-story as "part of the process of rethinking the fierce heart of the matter, the politics of mother-daughter writing and its potential for radically rethinking the ways we experience our lived realities" (Ho 27). She observes the fluidity of these stories in terms of blending "Chinese myths, legends, folklore" (27, note 1). Ho also identifies talk-story as possibly influenced by Kingston's exposure to a Hawaiian term that refers to "a social or communal oral exchange in which people gather to 'chew the fat' or 'shoot the breeze' with friends and family" (28, note1).

Through this "talk-story" mechanism, the narrator of *The Woman Warrior* learns how to be a woman, both like her mother yet also quite unlike her. By retelling the maternal narrative, the narrator comes to absorb important cultural wisdom, but also develops her own story, rejecting those elements in the maternal plot that she does not find suitable or experiences as stifling. Interestingly, Tan, without using Kingston's terminology, structured her novel in very similar fashion. Talk-story thus serves as an (often painful) introduction into a community of women, but on one's own terms (that is, within one's own plot) Tan's and Kingston's respective works present not just a duplication of the mother's story by the daughter—as Chodorow viewed the daughter's narrative—but a new talk-story-telling with more options for the daughter's creativity without loss of the mother's subjectivity.

Initially, Kingston's and Tan's works raised concerns among some Chinese American scholars because of their uses of Chinese folklore and often unflattering description of Chinese cultural practices (see, for instance, Chin). Both Kingston and Tan, for that matter, adamantly insist on their artistic freedom to utilize cultural sources as needed for their craft. It is clear from the beginning of *The Woman Warrior* that the narrator is talking story and not conducting an anthropological or sociological study. Moreover, as the final book section "A Song for a Barbarian Reed Pipe" amply clarifies, the memoir is both a cultural and metaphorical translation, with the narrator assuring us that "it translated well" (209).

The translational element in the Chinese American daughter's narrative has given rise to interesting new critical reflections, for instance, in Pei-Ju Wu's recent article linking memory work to maternal body and immigration. Wu claims that authors must arrive at a "traveling awareness" in their narratives (203) because their experience of diaspora has distanced them through time and space from their mother's country of origin and context of experiences. Such awareness also requires a "transnational approach" that transcends narrow thinking along disciplinary or national boundaries (203). While the narrator, Maxine, talks story about the past, she translates cultural elements by removing them from their original context into an American context so that they may be more easily understood by their intended audience.

"Memoirs of a Girlhood Among Ghosts" (Maxine Hong Kingston)

Illustrative of the need for translation, Kingston's memoir highlights the secrets that the protagonist must reveal and the silences she must fill to understand her family's past. The formerly silenced mothers have powerful stories that convey important wisdom to their daughters, yet the daughters must learn to decipher these stories correctly because they are told by indirection and may well turn out to have been "cheat stor[ies]" (Kingston 206). The daughters must learn over time how to decode the silences in their mothers' stories and to read the symbolism in their mothers' "talk-story" correctly. At the same time, the young Chinese American women must determine whether the information imparted by their often domineering mothers still applies to their lives in contemporary American society. Kingston specifically addresses this issue of finding her own voice in the last chapter titled "A Song for a Barbarian Reed Pipe" when she describes her mother's act of cutting her frenum. As everything else, the action itself remains ambiguous. Is it, as first perceived, a violent attempt by the mother to silence her daughter, or is it the mother's means of giving her daughter the ability to speak more freely?

Originally meant to be read as a "diptych" (Grice 17) together with *China Men*, a chronicle about Chinese fathers and their immigration to the Gold Mountain, *The Woman Warrior* appears influenced by the same motivations as, for instance, Monique Wittig's *Les Guerrières* or Marguerite Duras' *Moderato Cantabile*; that is, the desire to produce a typically female, perhaps even maternal, language and a narrative that breaks free of existing patriarchal constraints. Moreover, the empowering act of telling and naming in order to remember (Kingston 15) echoes other feminist narratives of the 1970s that aimed to give voice to the formerly silenced. According to Helen Grice's study, Kingston eventually served as a role model for other female Asian American storytellers, such as Amy Tan, Shirley Geok-lin Lim, Gish Jen, Fae Myenne Ng, and Sigrid Nunez (16).

Through the mother's talk-story rendered in the daughter's voice, despite admonishments to keep the story secret, the invisible aunt of "No Name Woman" is finally made visible and given a voice. Thus Kingston's memoir is not just a retelling of the mother's talk-story by the daughter, but a fictionalized documentation of the aunt's life. Within the first chapter and throughout the entire memoir, Kingston's emphasis on the resulting communal elements goes against the grain of traditional Western autobiographies that tend to reveal the extraordinary elements of one individual life. Maxine's personal history becomes diffused within her familial and cultural history. In the light of the 1970s, this constitutes yet another anti-patriarchal and feminist element in Kingston's project, which finally creates a new talk-story that serves as Maxine's personal space for self-discovery. In return, the result is a new genre that blends autobiography with maternal narrative and operates from a new communal angle by integrating the narrative perspectives of several female ancestors, which Jeanne Rosier Smith finds a more fluid and "relational view of autobiography" (203). Ho agrees that Kingston's memoir, by transcending narrow Western genre boundaries, can "articulate complex multi-layered identities and histories that cannot be fully processed or evoked in traditional autobiographical genres" (142). It reveals more than personal history as the family's and indeed the entire community's histories are intertwined with hers. As Maxine's story creates a space for her aunt's existence, so does storytelling make room for Maxine's own emergent voice.

In this anti-patriarchal rhetorical move, the mother serves as important purveyor of secrets (Kingston 5-6), made more difficult to negotiate by the transcultural work in which Maxine must engage. It is not just a matter of "always trying to name the unspeakable" (5) but an act of bridging the rift between what is Chinese and what is American or Chinese American; what is fact and what is fiction or cliché; and what really happened and what is imagined. Even the horror movies to which Brave Orchid takes her children target her daughter's critical thinking skills, functioning as code that Maxine seeks to discern (19-20).

According to Rosier Smith, it is through such ambiguous trickster elements (205) that Maxine can become a rebel who sees women in subordinate positions all around her, but can envision herself as warrior woman Fa Mu Lan. In this vein, she writes herself into myths and imagines that she lives within the framework of folktales. As Leslie Marmon Silko manages to do with "Yellow Woman," so does Kingston here accomplish a renewal and thus endurance and adaptation of traditional lore. Simultaneously, the communal lore becomes Maxine's as she immerses herself in and becomes part of the stories, a textual move paralleled by Tan's Jing-mei taking her deceased mother's place at the mahjong table. Martha Cutter confirms that:

> These characters finally realize that it is precisely their divergent cultural/linguistic heritages that engender the ability to produce new meanings, new stories, writerly translations that break down the binary opposition between the ethnic and the American, enriching and finally re-creating both cultural terrains. (44)

Inspired by her mother's cautionary tale about her paternal aunt, Maxine's Fa Mu Lan story is striking in its multilayered physicality. She experiences menstruation, matrimony, and motherhood all the while combating her community's enemies and serving social justice. Kingston seems to embrace the belief that narrative is a kind of embodied experience, felt as deeply and lastingly as childbirth or a message of revenge carved onto Fa Mu Lan's back (40). Brave Orchid's story, including separation from husband, loss of children, and acquisition of a "medical diploma" (57), reveals a personality as strong as Fa Mu Lan's. The imaginary fight with the sitting ghost and her savvy trading and survival instincts reveal her as a character of great strength and courage (Kingston 65) and a true survivor (68), regarded by Jeanne Rosier Smith as the true "trickster mother" (Smith 202).

In America, this struggle morphs into a battle against powerful—now social—forces as Kingston counterpoints Maxine-as-Fa-Mu-Lan's famous exploits with Maxine's failures as she imagines she is perceived by her mother. Martha Cutter expands on this translational element in Kingston between China and America and interprets it as both inter-generational and between "the silenced and the spoken" (Cutter 59). Maxine must repeatedly practice her skills in deciphering her strong mother's mixed messages (Kingston 51). Heung sees the mother's language as a hybrid discourse that requires translation because of generational and cultural differences (606). Again, Rosier Smith's article helpfully addresses these textual ambiguities by pointing out how Kingston situates her readers in the same position as Maxine. Readers must also deal with textual contradictions; any lacunae left in the stories can be filled by reader experiences (Smith 206). In fact, textual ambiguities and silences play a disruptive role that underscores the fluidity not just of the text, but of gender and character (Ho 143). Maxine's reflections further reveal that her mother was a gifted storyteller who could inspire in her daughter both nightmares as well as alternative life narratives. Maxine reveals the linguistic dilemmas she navigated as a child as she identifies Chinese as "the language of her impossible dreams" (Kingston 87). The power of the mother's words is equal to the effect of her secret potions and is capable of warding off evil (91). It is a sign of a nurturing quality that manifests itself also in her watching her adult daughter fiercely while she is asleep in her old bedroom (99).

Repeatedly in this narrative, the narrow mother-daughter configuration that was so prevalent in the feminist discourses of the 1970s is accompanied by a more community-oriented narrative that may include other female family members, such as aunts or sisters, and, as we have seen, can even reach out to mythological cultural heroines (Kingston 71). The strong, rebellious role models change ancient rituals and, like Maxine and Fa Mu Lan, can themselves become the stuff of myth (77). By contrast, the mother's sister Moon Orchid (whose story is told in "At the Western Palace") remains child-like, expects others to tell her what to do, eventually becomes too fearful to live on her own, and is remanded to a mental institution. Her fear and madness limit her to just one story, which she repeats endlessly. She remains incapable of envisioning for herself a different way of life and thus remains voiceless. In Cutter's reading, such instances of insanity reveal a character's inability to acquire translational skills (63).

In "A Song for a Barbarian Reed Pipe," Maxine's individuation is completed when her voice emerges through associations with the Barbarian reed pipe and identification with the expert knot maker (an image Rosier Smith also links to the trickster tradition [205]). The mother's impact on her daughter, however, remains ambiguous through the competing versions of stories and secrets. The cutting of the frenum, for instance, intended perhaps to give her daughter the good voice of an obedient daughter, perhaps to encourage her ability to speak freely, ends up having a freeing influence (Kingston 164). Thus the mother serves as the conduit for breaking the daughter's silence in the new "ghost" country when she orders her to negotiate with the grocer and expects her to carry on family business at a young age. In the Chinese school, where memorization is required, all chant in unison; outside of it, Maxine develops a strong individual "I."

It is only when the narrator believes her parents are planning to marry her to a young man she considers slow and unappealing that Maxine's survival instincts awaken, moving her to create a list of complaints and confessions to be presented to her mother, an act that finally frees her from her filial obligations. Through the telling— through the spoken words themselves—the umbilical cord is cut and Maxine is ready to leave her mother's sphere of influence and see the world for herself (Kingston 204). As she grows older and wiser, Maxine comes to realize, however, that she needs some aspects of her mother's stories, and so the memoir ends with a blended story in which "the beginning is hers, the ending, mine" (206). For Martha Cutter, such blending requires "mutual respect" (54) and, in the end, mother and daughter admit their appreciation of and need for each other. Maxine, fully aware of her mother's strength and her role in her own development, can shed both Western stereotypes of the Chinese feminine as well as Chinese cultural expectations of women's behavior. In the process of doing so, there emerges Maxine Hong Kingston who creates a Chinese-American song.

"Feathers from a Thousand Li Away" (Amy Tan)

In symmetrically and rhythmically interwoven sections, following the 'winds' and 'directions' of a mahjong game, the four mothers and daughters in *The Joy Luck Club* tell their own stories to reveal in alternating fashion the origins of their many conflicts and deep affections. Prompted by the death of her mother, Jing-mei's search for her through her aunties' stories becomes the structuring device that integrates the other narratives. For Jing-mei (whose "American" name is June), this process constitutes a problematic beginning, since it appears that their relationship was not always a comfortable one, her mother having omitted significant details in the accounts of her past life story and Jing-mei having resisted her mother's attempt at enriching her life with Chinese folk wisdom. As Jing-mei reports, "My mother and I never really understood one another. We translated each other's meanings and I seemed to hear less than what was said, while my mother heard more"(Tan, *Joy* 27).

Tan described her own translation work most specifically in a short article titled "Mother's Tongue." Trained as a linguist and employed at one point as a language development therapist (Ling 137), Tan became keenly aware of her mother's struggle with the English language, which, during her childhood, often embarrassed Tan and "limited" her perceptions of her mother. She knew of her mother's rich experiences and linguistic and storytelling facility in the Chinese language and wished to maintain both in her narrative of these experiences. Thus Tan faced the difficulty of translating mother, experience, language, and culture without falsifying any and yet making it all understood to her American audiences. Imagining her mother as her audience, she "began to write stories using all the Englishes I grew up with" (Tan, "Mother Tongue" 34). Eventually her mother offered her approval of this linguistic tour de force: "So easy to read" (44).

As with Kingston's opening pages, Tan's foreground the mother and her memories of the "old" country, subsequent emigration, and obstacles to successful communication with her daughter. Even more pronounced than in Kingston's work, however, is Tan's attempt at recreating the mother's discourse. Although not given her own chapter, throughout the entire novel, Jing-mei's mother is invoked repeatedly as the daughter is reaching out to her mother by getting into her story and retelling it for her: "How can I be my mother at Joy Luck?" (Tan, *Joy* 15). This rhetorical move is paralleled by Jing-mei's adoption of her mother's place at the mahjong table and the acknowledgment by her "aunties," the other players, that this action is appropriate. A similar motif is repeated in the three other mother-daughter pairings. It is not until Jing-mei reconstructs her mother's "loss narrative" (a term introduced in Yuan Yuan's article)—reliving it by visiting China and reconnecting with her sisters—that she feels a sense of completion conveyed in the intricate structure of Tan's novel. Through the multiple mother-daughter stories included in the novel, Tan achieves a community of women connected by historical and familial ties resembling those in Kingston's memoir.

The ghosting of strange and forbidden elements is equally as strong in Tan's novel as in Kingston's memoir. For instance, An-mei Hsu, one of the mothers, recalls her own mother whom she was not allowed to mention by name. Over several generations, this narrative reestablishes the connections between mothers and daughters in a rebellion against patriarchal authority, an illustration of the "Grandmother-Mother-Daughter Triad" discussed by Yi-Ling Yu (117). "Othermothering" can involve members of an extended family (Yu 206), such as Kingston's aunt, the "no name woman." Through the talk-stories, those who had been unmentionable come alive again. This is necessary because the connections between mothers and daughters are so deep that they are felt in the bones (41), and they demand to be honored even when they have been lost by separations through time and space.

Wendy Ho warns us not to view these works as idealizations of mother-daughter relationships but as depictions of "the complicated struggles women confront in naming desire, self, and community" (22). Tan's "Malignant Gates" chapter illustrates how the mother's will power can influence the daughter's life and well-being—often in ambiguous ways. Like a magical spell, her admonishments become a self-fulfilling prophecy when Waverly Jong learns from her mother the art of "invisible strength" to win chess tournaments (Tan, *Joy* 89). Waverly's memories of her mother's sabotaging her chess playing and finding fault in her attachments to Rich reveal the deep-seated problems with their Chinese mothers: overpoweringly strong-willed, grudge-holding, and bossy women to whom their daughters have difficulty standing up. "In her hands," Waverly reflects about her mother, "I always became the pawn. I could only run away. And she was the queen, able to move in all directions, relentless in her pursuit, always able to find my weakest spots" (199). The puzzling depths of the mother's linguistic position are revealed particularly well in a passage in Tan's novel when Rose describes the power of maternal discourse: "[i]f I listened to her, later I would know what she knew: where true words came from, always from up high, above everything else" (206).

A section entitled "American Translations" reveals the same strained relationships and clash of values, highlighting the difficulty experienced by the older first-generation immigrant women to come to terms with their problematic beginnings as American citizens and the concomitant refusal by the second-generation American daughters to allow their mothers to indoctrinate them with traditional Chinese wisdom. Several of Tan's daughter stories illustrate the burdens of these translated lives, which can even necessitate psychotherapy. The separation from the (Chinese) maternal element required by the immigrant experience creates an imbalance that manifests itself in various forms of depression and other related disorders or social failures. They suffer from depression and bulimia, and their lives remain imbalanced until they come to terms with their mothers. Unlike the Freudian concept of separation from parental influence, Tan seems to suggest that wholeness requires a reconnection with the maternal by finding the viable Chinese elements in one's hyphenated identity. As the anecdote of the Schumann sonata illustrates, however, the two halves belong together, and the music is only perfect when they are united or unified (Tan, *Joy* 109). To find this balance in the "in-between world condition" indicates the daughter's greater level of maturity (Ling 141).

Another instance indicative of translational difficulties is narrated by Lindo Jong. Even though she thinks that "American circumstances and Chinese character" don't mix well (Tan, *Joy* 289), as she and her daughter look into their hairstylist's mirror, they recognize an intergenerational connectedness between themselves, the past and next generations, and community. Like Maxine, Lindo recalls that she had to hide her Chinese face in order to become American. Marina Heung explains how this mirror moment attributes a kind of 'double vision' to Lindo that lends subjectivity to the mother character that many other narratives lack (601). Lindo's instinctive understanding of her separation from her mother as well as from China contributes to her desire to bond with her daughter (Heung 603). Now her daughter must recognize her mothers' past struggles and her hopes for her in order to understand her own position. Through shared talk, stories about their diasporic selves, the mother and daughter may be able to find common ground: "So now I think. What did I lose? What did I get back in return? I will ask my daughter what she thinks" (Tan, *Joy* 305).

In the case of Jing-mei, the intertwining of mother-daughter life stories is perhaps most evident in her attempt to locate and visit her long-lost half-sisters. Finding them reflects not only her mother's own preoccupation to recover this essential part of her past, but also the symbolic effort of connecting with her dead mother and her Chinese heritage: Upon her reunion with her two sisters, June immediately notices the family resemblance and knows that her acknowledgement of her Chinese heritage will finally release her as an individuated self within the mother's first family: "Together we look like our mother. Her same eyes, her same mouth, open in surprise to see, at last, her long-cherished wish" (Tan, *Joy* 332). The family widens into a community of women connected by familial and experiential bonds.

"A Mother is Always the Beginning" (Tan, *The Bonesetter's Daughter* 228)

In other works, Amy Tan has dealt, in one way or another, with the connections between bicultural generations, most clearly expressed through her emphasis on mother-daughter relationships that play themselves out as the struggle between young Chinese American women and their China-born mothers. In *Bonesetter's Daughter*, for example, Tan emphasizes her characters' female lineage; therefore, it is only after working "to preserve the past" (264), by deciphering and giving voice to her mother's and her grandmother's narratives that the protagonist Ruth is able to envision a "New Destiny" (281) for herself, fraught with problems, of course, but leaving room nonetheless for her personal happiness. *Bonesetter's Daughter* is about silences and finding a voice and a memory by carefully listening to one's mother's story. This really means that Tan's daughters have finally arrived at the same point that Maxine reached in *The Woman Warrior*.

Kingston and Tan place readers in the same position as the fictional daughters as we attempt to fathom elaborate designs in which autobiography, history, and fiction intertwine. With Maxine and Jing-mei, we piece together their mothers' lives and the making of the daughters' stories. In their quest to establish modern identities, independent of their more traditional Chinese mothers, the daughters rebel, yet often end up unwittingly reliving their mothers' lives. Mothers and daughters here are bonded by linguistic and textual forces different and stronger than those described by Chodorow, Hirsch, and other cultural and literary critics.

As their narrative designs suggest, stories and lives are interwoven to such an extent that maternal and filial voices become almost interchangeable. By steering the plot away from the traditional Western patriarchal family romance, Kingston and Tan create a new appreciation of the Chinese American mother-daughter plot. When framed as talk-story, the mother-daughter plot does not hinge on the daughter's individuation, for the daughter can come into her own without committing "matricide" and can remain rooted in her culture, history, and community, while letting the mother's story also be heard on its own terms.

Unlike psychoanalytical theorist Jacques Lacan, who describes the "Name of the Father" as the originator of Law and individuation, Kingston and Tan trace the formation of language and thought to the "Name of the Mother." In their imaginative works, the fathers' conspicuous weakness or absence marks, not a search for the father, but a narrative constructed by and through mothers. Thus, Kingston's and Tan's writing successfully revises and rewrites Roland Barthes' assumption that all stories derive from a "search for the father." Instead, the diasporic immigrant experience becomes a metaphor for mother-daughter relationships. Daughters move into the new culture, which gives them new opportunities, but the distance from their mothers this move necessitates is as painful as a separation from the mother. Wholeness requires a building of bridges between cultures as well as between mother and daughter. In this cultural contact zone, the result is a hybrid existence that incorporates both elements into something new. That is Kingston's translation, a new song that uses old elements but whose notes are understood by both worlds.

Works Cited

Bloom, Harold, ed. *Amy Tan: Modern Critical Views*. Philadelphia: Chelsea House, 2000. Print.

Barthes, Roland. The *Pleasure of the Text*. Trans. Richard Miller. New York: Hill and Wang, 1975. Print.

Chin, Frank et al., eds. *Aiiieeee/An Anthology of Asian American Writers*. 1974. Washington, D.C.: Howard UP, 1983. Print.

Chodorow, Nancy. *The Reproduction of Mothering: Psychoanalysis and the Sociology of Gender*. Berkeley: U of California P, 1978. Print.

Cutter, Martha J. *Lost and Found in Translation*. Chapel Hill: U of North Carolina P, 2005. *ProQuest*. Web. 16 Mar. 2016.

Gilligan, Carol. *In a Different Voice: Psychological Theory and Women's Development*. Cambridge, MA: Harvard UP, 1982. Print.

Grice, Helena. *Contemporary World Writers: Maxine Hong Kingston*. Manchester, GBR: Manchester UP, 2006. *ProQuest*. Web. 15 Feb. 2016.

Heung, Marina. "Daughter-Text/Mother-Text: Matrilineage in Amy Tan's *The Joy Luck Club*." *Feminist Studies 19.3* (Fall 93). 597-616. Print.

Hirsch, Marianne. "Mothering and Mother-Daughter Relationships: A Selected Bibliography." *Women's Studies Quarterly* 11.4 (Winter 1983): 38-43. *JSTOR* 19 Feb. 2016.

_____. *The Mother/Daughter Plot: Narrative, Psychoanalysis, Feminism*. Bloomington: Indiana UP, 1989. Print.

Ho, Wendy. In Her Mother's House: The Politics of Asian American Mother-Daughter Writing Walnut Creek, CA: AltaMira P, 2000. Critical Perspectives on Asian Pacific Americans Ser. Print.

Kingston, Maxine Hong. *The Woman Warrior: Memoirs of Girlhood Among Ghosts*. 1976. New York: Vintage, 1989. Print.

Ling, Amy. *Between Worlds: Woman Writers of Chinese Ancestry*. New York: Pergamon, 1990. Print.

Rich, Adrienne. *Of Woman Born: Motherhood as Experience and Institution*. New York: Norton, 1976. Print.

Smith, Jeanne Rosier. "Monkey Business: Maxine Hong Kingston's Transformational Trickster Texts." *Modern Critical Views: Asian American Writers*. Ed. Harold Bloom. Philadelphia: Chelsea House, 1999. 201-216. Print.

Tan, Amy. *The Bonesetter's Daughter*. New York: Putnam, 2001.Print.

_____. *The Joy Luck Club*. New York: Ballantine,1989. Print.

_____. "Mother Tongue." *Dreams and Inward Journeys: A Rhetoric and Reader for Writers*. Ed. Marjorie Ford and Jon Ford. 7th Ed. New York: Longman-Pearson, 2010. 34-44. Print.

Tobin, Patricia. *Time and the Novel: The Genealogical Imperative*. Princeton: Princeton UP, 1978. Print.

Wu, Pei-Ju. "Translating Mother's Tongue(s) and Traveling Bodies: Palimpsest and Diaspora in Maxine Kingston's *The Woman Warrior*." Ed. Lan Dong. *Transnationalism and the Asian American Heroine: Essays on Literature, Film, Myth and Media*. Jefferson, NC: McFarland, 2010. *ProQuest*.Web. 14 Mar. 2016.

Yu, Yi-Ling. *Mother, She Wrote: Matrilineal Narratives in Contemporary Women's Writing*. NY: Lang, 2005. Print.

Yuan, Yuan. "The Semiotics of China Narratives in the Con/texts of Kingston and Tan." *Critique* 40.3 (Spring 99): 292-104. *MasterFilePremier*. Web.18 Feb. 2002.

Diaspora and its Others: *The Woman Warrior* and Southeast Asian Diasporic Literature_____

Christopher B. Patterson

In the last few decades, the term "diaspora" has been used across disciplines to join an ever-growing body of transnational studies in the humanities and to consolidate relationships among seemingly separate migrant experiences: immigration, establishing an ethnic community, expatriatism, exile, refugee and border experiences, and overseas nationalism. Since the early 1990s, with the publication of the first issue of the journal *Diaspora*, scholars have attempted to tame the concept of diaspora by creating definitive checklists (Tölölyan), by defining the concept through its limits (Clifford), and by noting how each diasporic group remains exceptional (Cohen). These gestures have been useful in placing diaspora studies as a model meant to understand a more globalized age, but the discussions over whether or not to name a group "diasporic," or how to best analyze a diasporic group as an object of inquiry, can sometimes take precedence over the political and social gestures that "diaspora" allows in the present, and enables for the future.

This chapter treats Maxine Hong Kingston's *The Woman Warrior* as a gateway to understanding how diaspora has emerged from discourses of postcolonialism, multiculturalism, and Pan-Africanism. *The Woman Warrior* can be considered a diasporic novel in that it responds to these discourses and also produces a particularly Asian American form of diaspora that has challenged previous conceptions. I compare Kingston's novel to Lan Cao's *Monkey Bridge*, the first novel published by a Vietnamese American, in the hopes of demonstrating, as James Clifford writes, "the problems of defining a traveling term, in changing global conditions" (302). Chief among these "global conditions" is how Asian migrant groups respond to American overseas intervention and their unique modes of diasporic communities within contexts of economic duress, as in the case with Chinese migrants, and within contexts of state violence, as in the case of Vietnamese refugees. Rather than read *The Woman Warrior* as an authentic portrayal of Chinese American subjectivity, diaspora allows us to see the novel within a larger Cold War context that traces the flexibility of cultural change.

Diaspora as Critique

The concept of diaspora first entered American public discourse in the 1930s through Jewish American academics, who sought to understand the historical "scattering" of Jews from Israel. Though Jewish diasporas have been the paradigmatic example of diaspora, they have, by no means, been homogenous or easy to define. In the first issue of *Diaspora*, William Safran developed the term by tracing diaspora as a community form beyond the limits of the nation. He came up with a definitive checklist for diaspora studies, focusing on "expatriate minority communities" (1) that are dispersed from an original "center" to at least two "peripheral" places; (2) that maintain a "memory, vision, or myth about their original homeland"; (3) that "believe they are not—and perhaps cannot be—fully accepted by their host country"; (4) that see the ancestral home as a place of eventual return, when the time is right; (5) that are committed to the maintenance or restoration of this homeland; and (6) of which the groups' consciousness and solidarity are "importantly defined" by this continuing relationship with the homeland (Safran 83-84, qtd. by Clifford 304-5).

Safran's list has been broadened out further by other scholars, but the core six elements remain in the background of diaspora studies today and serve as a concrete rubric. Safran's list, however, spotlights Jewish diasporas with the Zionist politics that sought to eventually return to the homeland and to renew it as a Jewish state. As James Clifford points out, "large segments of Jewish historical experience do not meet the test of Safran's last three criteria" (307). The presence of both "Zionist" and "anti-Zioinist" diasporas have problematized Jewish people's relationship to the homeland, and this has led scholars to separate these groups as "religions of the land" and "religions of the book" (Clifford 308). Ideas of a single Jewish diaspora seem to hold ground only on Safran's first three points of "dispersal," "historical memory," and refusal (or inability) to assimilate. In other words, Safran's definitions rely on a homogenous conception of the homeland, as one with a particular shared "historical memory," as an agreed-upon "center," and as a place that must be reclaimed from a foreign people.

The conception of a homeland as "center" and place of "historical memory" becomes more of an issue when black diasporas are considered. After the 1950s, the term "diaspora" became more political and fragmented in the work of black diasporic writers like George Shepperson, Paul Gilroy, and Brent Hayes Edwards. In the 2001 essay "The Uses of *Diaspora*," Edwards conceives of black diaspora as a concept "first developed . . . specifically around the issue of African resistance to colonialism" (49). Edwards presents an intellectual history of diaspora that emerges from Negritude and Pan-Africanism, but unlike Safran's view of Jewish diasporas, he finds that black diasporas did not share the same political gesture of homogenizing the homeland as a colonized nation capable of resistance. Instead, Edwards' history traces black diaspora as emerging from postcolonial paradigms towards conceptions that allow further complexity and ideological diversity. George Shepperson's 1962 article, which Edwards quotes extensively, contains this very move from postcolonial critique by suggesting that "the evolution of all-African ideology is more complicated than commonly imagined" (348). He describes Pan-Africanism as "not a clearly recognizable movement, with a single nucleus. . . . It is rather a group of movements, many very ephemeral" (346). Shepperson's 1962 work, which comes just after Algeria's decolonization but also before Kenya's, Malawi's, or Zimbabwe's, insists on a "very ephemeral" Pan-African movement and allows us to conceive of multiple diasporas with various ideological positions emerging from a single space of dispersal.

In 1991, the term diaspora became solidified into diaspora studies, and over time, the term has been broadened further to encompass Asian diasporas from China, India, and Vietnam. In 2007, *Diaspora* founder and editor Khachig Tölölyan redefined the term to account for the critiques of diaspora as a discourse that homogenizes the homeland and essentializes the groups dispersed from it. He names four characteristics: (1) a community experiencing collective trauma and commemoration or mourning, (2) a preserved cultural identity, (3) "a rhetoric of restoration or return," and (4) "a process of collective identification and form of identity" (Tölölyan 650). In this definition, adherence to the homeland appears only through the vague language of "restoration," "return," "mourning," and "preservation." Tölölyan here replaces the political importance of the homeland with an emotional and psychosocial focus, seeing diasporic peoples as hopelessly (and unconsciously) entangled with the homeland. By erasing the homeland politically, Tölölyan allows it to haunt these diasporic understandings as a lost object that must be restored, mourned for, preserved, or returned to. Furthermore, Tölölyan offers the notion that a diaspora can be characterized along "a" (single) "preserved cultural identity" while simultaneously being a part of a cultural "process." Perhaps unintentionally, Tölölyan's definitions reveal the very point of anxiety that makes "diaspora" significant: the attempt to preserve an imagined, homogenous cultural identity while, at the same time, belonging to a community where cultural identity is de-territorialized and in constant flux. The efforts to define diaspora through a homeland have thus far been an attempt to assuage this anxiety, when in fact it is this anxiety itself that makes "diaspora" a useful and productive term.

The preceding exploration of these various definitions of diaspora illustrate how diasporic discourse has emerged from postcolonial binaries between the colonizer and the colonized and show how these categories have carried over into diasporic discourse through emotional and political alliances with the homeland as a recurring specter "haunting" the diasporic subject. In the next section, I consider how *The Woman Warrior* reframes these questions into an Asian Cold War context, when the homeland of China was seemingly "lost" to Maoist Communism. Kingston wrote *The Woman Warrior* as the ten-year Maoist Cultural Revolution remained headline news for its witch hunting of "Westernized" Chinese and its destruction of traditional cultural institutions and religions. Published in 1976, the year that the Cultural Revolution ended, *The Woman Warrior* questions the notion of "homeland" as a space of political and emotional alliance, and instead attempts to reimagine the homeland in a way that serves the ideological warfare of Kingston's present.

The Woman Warrior as Diaspora Critique

The most well-known Asian American novel, Kingston's *The Woman Warrior*, has often been read within the framework of diaspora studies, as the Chinese American narrator must imagine herself confronted with ghosts once forgotten by the patriarchal Chinese homeland. In the beginning of its first and most widely-read story, "No Name Woman," the violence of the homeland is already cast as a lost object under erasure: "'You must not tell anyone,' my mother said, 'what I am about to tell you. In China your father had a sister who killed herself'" (3). The homeland here is casually homogenized ("in China"), though China itself contains a multitude of provinces, each with unique accents, languages, cultures, and religions, while the aunt herself is placed as a distant object who is radically free of this homogenization. She is not an aunt, but "the sister of the father"—not even the "father's" sister, but merely a sister that the father *had*. All of this is told to Kingston's narrator under the instruction that she "must not tell anyone." In these first lines, we see the radical division from the homeland that this narrator captures in "No Name Woman" as a past that must be forgotten if she is to live as an American. To deal with these ghosts, and with other struggles in her life, the narrator summons Chinese myths that parallel her actions as a part of the diaspora. Most famously, she invokes Fa Mu Lan to give her the courage to speak against her racist boss (63). The homeland in this text is placed into a narrative that deprecates its patriarchal and despotic history, while, at the same time, finds solace and identity within its myths. If previous definitions of diaspora have explored the relation to the homeland as political and psychological, in Kingston's text, we have an evolution of the concept catered to Cold War positions with regard to Asia. The homeland is neither a place to return to nor a space of (real) memory, but an imaginary space consistently deployed for the survival of the diaspora. Rather than ask what a Chinese diaspora is, Kingston's text asks the following: what is *the function* or the *practical use* of the homeland (China) for those who have been dispersed from it, and for their offspring, in a time of ideological warfare, when China (and thus Chinese Americans) were being vilified?

Kingston's efforts to reimagine China have been challenged by many Asian American writers, most notably the satirist Frank Chin, a contemporary of Kingston. The debate between Kingston and Chin over the representation of China in *The Woman Warrior* is perhaps the most well-known internal dispute within Asian American studies, as it emphasizes a shift in racial politics from one of Chin's cultural nationalism and anti-colonialism, to a diasporic view of empowerment through imagined homelands and collective memory. Chin's vociferous criticism of *The Woman Warrior* questions the author's misrepresentation of Chinese myths. Chin repeats this criticism in his 1991 article, "Come All Ye Asian American Writers of the Real and the Fake":

> With Kingston's autobiographical *Woman Warrior*, we have given up even the pretense of reporting from the real world. Chinese culture is so cruel and she is so helpless against its overwhelming cruelty that she lives entirely in her imagination. It is an imagination informed only by the stereotype communicated to her through the Christian Chinese American autobiography. (26)

In Chin's view, Kingston has chosen to side with American power rather than the homeland, which had faced decades of scorn and disrepute in American media. His aggravation articulates a postcolonial critique that places Kingston's work as complicit with a Christian colonizing power. The privilege Kingston gains, for Chin, reproduces the stereotype of China as backwards and patriarchal, and has convinced Asian American writers to join in confessing their ethnicity through autobiography. In 1993, the Asian American scholar King-Kok Cheung mounted a defense of Kingston's work, calling Kingston's mode of story-telling "talk-story," which "blurs the distinction between straight facts and pure fiction" in order to "reclaim a past and, more decisively, to envision a different future" (121). If Chin's critique performs a postcolonial reading of *The Woman Warrior*, Cheung's provides a reading more akin to a diasporic critique in Tölölyan's sense of diaspora as "restoration," "return," "mourning," and "preservation." The diasporic subject in this case is not merely entangled with a lost homeland, but works to reimagine the homeland in order to fit her own circumstances.

Chin's critique parallels some of the criteria Safran identified, as he holds a political alliance to his "authentic" vision of the homeland and finds other representations of it a threat to his own historical memory. His reliance on cultural nationalism and a strict singular notion of identity allows Chin to promote an alternative to mainstream Chinese American identity during and after the Cold War, but leaves little room for reinvention. Much of his critique came when Kingston's text was first published under the category of nonfiction autobiography with the implication that it was an objective and factual account of China. Today, scholarly interpretations and new editions have done away with this label and present the work instead as an attempt to reimagine and recreate Chinese history and myth. Chin's main flaw is that he sees any deviation from his vision of the homeland as performing Chinese-ness for white Americans, what Regina Lee calls "diaspora as boutique multiculturalism." Lee defines this conception of diaspora as that of "exotic, Other communities, whose value for the hostland lies in the fact of their being different" (54). The diaspora, in this case, highlights how the "dominant community has already 'read' diaspora in their hegemonic terms," and, as a response, *the diaspora recognizes and returns* the ethnic stereotype (55). This is undoubtedly a consumerist-based model of diaspora, where the diasporic subject self-consciously reenacts her own ethnicity for the dominant community.

The Woman Warrior, however, does not provide an easily consumable version of Chinese diaspora. Indeed, any adequate reading of "No Name Woman" will understand that the narrator is candidly critical of her own invented history. The narrator must recall the violence of the homeland, but within an imaginative ideal that fits her own circumstances and goals. First, she imagines her aunt as sexually free, but "imagining her free with sex doesn't fit, though. I don't know any women like that, or men either. Unless I see her life branching into mine, she gives me no ancestral help" (8). The narrator seeks to reimagine the past as a reservoir of myth, cultural values, and identity, and "real history" need not intervene. When read as a "talk-story," we see Kingston not merely recalling the homeland, but creating it through her own story. In this sense, she reclaims Chinese American diasporic consciousness from the hands of the "authentic homeland" of Chin, as well as from the American conceptions of Chinese America as a boutique multiculturalism. Kingston not only rejects this form, but replaces the patriarchal violence of an imagined China with the threat of sexual assault in the present, keeping the narrative from ever becoming an easily digestible tale of Chinese American gratitude and success.

The Woman Warrior's focus on patriarchy in multiple forms provides a vision of diaspora more critical than that of Pan-Africanism, Jewish dispersal, or others previously discussed. James Clifford, in a very brief reflection on *The Woman Warrior*, notes that the book articulates a feminist critique of the homeland and shows that "women sustaining and reconnecting diaspora ties do so critically, as strategies for survival in a new context" (314). King-Kok Cheung's association of *The Woman Warrior* with talk-story shows the form of this critical engagement, as it dismantles binaries inherent in Chin's analysis (between masculine/feminine, authentic/fake) to focus instead on how the homeland functions in various diasporic struggles: minority politics, Cold War politics, and gender politics. Kingston's *The Woman Warrior* constructs an imagined homeland that has its own unique productive value for these political ends and allows us to rethink postcolonial critiques, which simply point out complicity with the colonial culture. Cheung makes clear that the effort to reimagine the homeland is a political and social gesture of taking control of one's own future and of discovering a fitting identity when all other forces that portray history—the school, media, etc.—have failed. By labeling such history "talk-story," we emerge into a community of our own making. The reimagined homeland allows the diasporic subject a significant level of participation within the host society and creates a common ground of cultural belonging through which both the host country and the diaspora can understand each other. As the popularity of Kingston's novel suggests, this particular diasporic critique of an "imagined homeland" has become the vanguard of a multicultural society.

Viet Nguyen has used the debate between Chin and Kingston to make an altogether different critique, one that illustrates a "crisis of the 'real,'" as he calls it, "a crisis of the material in addition to the essential" (104). Nguyen names Chin a "historical fundamentalist," for whom "[h]istory is real . . . in the sense that it is absolute," and "[t]he dispute over history is a war-like dispute" (104). Nguyen sees Asian American literature as invoking flexible strategies that are often read as either resistant or accommodating, but he points out that these meanings are imposed by critics and audiences through their own political positions. Chin's politics thus inform his reading of *The Woman Warrior* as conveying an Orientalist view of China during the Cold War, but these politics also limit how the text can be read. Here we can understand *The Woman Warrior* as neither "resistant" nor "accommodating," but as akin to Rachel Lee's diasporic "transitional consciousness," which she defines as "a transitional or transformational state, representing diasporas as integrating in an informed (if not ambivalent) way with their host societies" (55).

Chin's disagreements, however limited, highlight questions of accommodation, not the accommodations *within* Kingston's *The Woman Warrior*, but the accommodations of the work made by mainstream American society. Indeed, literary scholarship on *The Woman Warrior* must take into account the work's unprecedented popularity within the academy, as it has become one of the most taught literary texts in the United States and, in effect, has heralded discourses of tolerance and multiculturalism in a way that seems easy for students (and more traditional faculty) to absorb. Meanwhile, Asian American educators have focused less on the book's depictions of China and more on its ability to destabilize Chinese American identity through its attempts to think through the function of imaginary homelands, its refusals to realistically depict segments of China, and its often meandering prose that reveals the imaginative (as opposed to objective) reality of its own narrative.

Southeast Asian Diaspora Critique in Lan Cao's *Monkey Bridge*

Since *The Woman Warrior* was published, writers from Southeast Asia have added to conceptions of diaspora, while picking up on Kingston's narrative style and use of the homeland. Southeast Asian diasporas, as opposed to Chinese American, African American, or Indian American diasporas, find themselves in the West with very little cultural content to perform. While Chinese, Japanese, and South Asian cultures have been fetishized to no end in the West, few Western societies have conception enough of Vietnamese, Filipino, Singaporean, Taiwanese, Hong Kong, or Malaysian cultural forms to demand its constant performance within a realm of "boutique multiculturalism." Likewise, Filipino migrants are often confused with Latinos, and their homelands—alongside Vietnamese, Cambodians, and Laotians—have been erased by American imperialism across the Pacific. Thus, Southeast Asian diasporas are not as subject to regimes of multicultural new racism, as Paul Gilroy defines it, a racism that "align[s] 'race' closely with the idea of national belonging" (*Black Atlantic* 10). Whereas debates over Kingston's work circulate around cultural difference and multicultural performance, these concepts of diaspora reach their limits with Southeast Asian diasporas. Their "racial mark" is often not one of containment or trademark, but of enigmatic bodies—symptoms of their erased heritages, racial mixing, and histories of continuous migration.

In Southeast Asian diasporic narratives, the homeland is often intentionally forgotten as a place of catastrophic violence, of shame, or of inferiority. Reflections on the homeland often result in guilt and anxiety over being complicit in imperial power for having "escaped" to the West. Rather than appear homogenized, the homeland is depicted as fragmented and forgotten, and narratives often focus less on the homeland and more on the continuous process of migration as it relates to labor; war; or, in the case of Filipinos, colonization. As many Southeast Asian migrants were already a part of a diaspora before coming to the West, they depict the homeland less as an origin point and more as "the last stop" along the way of a long historical past full of movement.

Lan Cao's 1997 work *Monkey Bridge* directly satirizes Kingston's "No Name Woman" to make an aggressive statement about how Vietnamese refugees must also reinvent their relationship with the homeland, not to find empowerment or one's true identity, but to survive the racism of the United States. The protagonist, Mai Nguyen, is a teenage Vietnamese immigrant who fled to America on the day Saigon fell in 1975. Like Kingston's narrator, Mai constructs an imaginary homeland based on the gossip and "talk-story" of her mother, who speaks to her in vignettes as a "traditional Vietnamese woman" with stories of rural Vietnam, traditional rites of marriage, and "rice fields," all of which are described with a type of cultural access exhibited in sayings such as: *"to know a rice field is to know the soul of Vietnam"* (172). The metonymic use of "rice field" as a way to access the homeland makes the turbulent history of its people easily consumable through a particular exotic metaphor. Such easy metaphors work on Mai through an internalized multiculturalism, a myth-making that becomes so intense that Mai cannot even imagine crossing the Canadian border without conjuring the Vietnamese myth of the Trung sisters (Trung Trac and Trung Nhi) who protected the border against the Chinese. Rather than give her daughter a history rooted in Vietnam's colonial and imperial histories, Mai's mother presents a history where her greatest problems were keeping track of *"where the canned milk was kept, where the salted duck eggs were stored,* [and] *how to please my father-in-law"* (191). The trick that Lan Cao performs in this narrative is to let the reader assume that this is the mother's voice, when it is never quite clear whether it is the mother's voice or merely the daughter's *speculation* of the mother's voice, invoked by the desire to know the Vietnamese "essence" as something as concrete as a rice field. In other words, the talk-story of the homeland speaks only to a fragmentation and forgetting that has made it possible for Mai to survive after the war. At the novel's end, the mother's suicide note reveals that this entire history has been fabricated, and she debunks all of the ethnic myths that Mai had connected with her cultural heritage. Instead, the note gives Mai a history of struggles with debt and landlords, efforts to gain capital through exploitation and prostitution, and French and American imperial violence.

Lan Cao's novel responds to and builds upon *The Woman Warrior* in three significant ways. First, as one of the first published Vietnamese American novels, *Monkey Bridge* depicts the racial formation of a group marked by a history of American imperialism and whose very presence conjures this imperial violence. Second, Cao shows that simply relying on imagined histories and homelands is often complicit with a policy of multicultural "containment," one that elides histories of imperialism and debt by emphasizing a mythical past that sees the homeland as a place of patriarchy and violence. As shown in Cao's novel, such a history produces subjects who may be "empowered," but who are also expected to show gratitude toward the host country.

Michele Janette emphasizes the irony of Cao's narrative history as one that is continually disrupted by other imagined histories. For Janette, this formal technique is meant to teach the audience "guerilla tactics" for surviving within a multicultural society: "by teaching us the very codes that allow us to decipher ironic elisions, gaps, and contradictions throughout the novel, Cao provides us grounds for entering the narrative dialogically, neither relying on prior experience nor assuming universal similarity" (74). Cao's novel thus puts the reader in a place of uncertainty by refusing an "appropriative gaze" and invites them into an alliance in "the sense of understanding, but not of possession" (74). Cao then presents us with a version of ethnic history that resists multicultural performance. In her suicide note, Mai's mother speaks of her efforts to contain Mai's past as an "act of sacrifice" that will give her "a new beginning" (253). By the novel's end, it is clear to Mai that she cannot perform her "Vietnamese-ness" within a "boutique multiculturalism," even though her mother's revealed history is filled with uncertainty and ambiguity. It is this uncertainty in historical narrative that is the novel's third useful insight, as it begins to construct "a new beginning" by expanding Kingston's vision of diaspora from one of self-creation and imagination, into the guerilla tactics of survival that emphasizes understanding not the homeland, but the process of migration within its political and historical context.

Cao's novel gives us a mode of transitive diasporic consciousness, one built from "real history," in the sense of a history of such complexity, ideological diversity, and intra-cultural as well as imperial violence that it cannot be confused for a homogenizing conception of the homeland. Her guerilla tactics take on the project of appearing non-diasporic, of forgetting the homeland in order to convey peace rather than war. As Mai thinks, "Not only could we become anything we wanted to be in America, we could change what we had once been in Vietnam" (40-41). As Vietnamese are taught to forget their homeland, they are less burdened by homogenous conceptions of it and can envision it as a complex political space without the risk of accommodating orientalist stereotypes. Cao's consistent uncovering of these guerilla tactics shows that the real attachment to the homeland is not integral to diaspora, but can be seen as a tool—like identity itself—shaped by "common histories" still in process, and undergoing revision by the diaspora. As she writes, "shape-shifting had been so important even by ordinary standards. America had rendered us invisible and at the same time awfully conspicuous" (42). In its acceptance of shape-shifting and reconstructing historical memory, Cao's novel allows a way of seeing both the "homeland" and the "host country" within a narrative of continuous scattering.

Southeast Asian diasporic narratives like Lan Cao's *Monkey Bridge* express a vision of diaspora more akin to Stuart Hall's conception of diasporas as "constantly producing and reproducing themselves anew, through transformation and difference" (235). Hall's definition comes from a Caribbean context that demonstrates hybridity, transition, and cultural, rather than political or psychological, ties to the homeland, where diaspora is defined "not by essence or purity, but by the recognition of a necessary heterogeneity and diversity." For social scientist Robin Cohen, Hall's definition is an attempt to formulate the Caribbean as diasporic even though "they are not native to the area," and they are also already parts of other diasporic groups—Indians, Europeans, Africans, Chinese. This panoply of diasporic groups in the Caribbean is also clearly present in Southeast Asia, where diasporic peoples have already been "hybridized" through migratory histories of Chinese, Tamil, Chinese, Malay, European, and Filipino peoples. Indeed, Southeast Asian diasporic groups are "Othered" in more than cultural difference, and in fact, such difference can function as a restraining device to cater cultures towards particular forms of labor, as we see affective and service-oriented migrations of Filipina and Indonesian domestic servants. Such diasporic groups then offer a view of diaspora that includes the myriad forms of precarious labor propelled by free market capitalism and emphasizes the acceptance of ethnic identities as a means of imperial incorporation. Read as diasporic narratives, Kingston's *The Woman Warrior* and Cao's *Monkey Bridge* both offer ways of conceiving diasporic relationships to the homeland not as "backwards-looking" or as politically or psychologically aligned, but as ways of consciously engaging with political and social issues in the present and for surviving well into the future.

Works Cited

Cao, Lan. *Monkey Bridge.* New York: Viking, 1997. Print.

Cheung, King-Kok. *Articulate Silences: Hisaye Yamamoto, Maxine Hong Kingston, Joy Kogawa.* Ithaca: Cornell UP, 1993. Print.

Chin, Frank. "Come all ye Asian American Writers of the Real and the Fake." *The Big Aiiieeeee! An Anthology of Chinese American and Japanese American Literature.* Ed. Jeffery Paul Chan, Frank Chin, Lawson Fusao Inada, & Shawn Wong. New York: Meridian, 1991: 1-92. Print.

Clifford, James. "Diasporas." *Cultural Anthropology* 9.3 (1994): 302-38. Print.

Cohen, Robin. *Global Diasporas: An Introduction.* Seattle: U of Washington P, 1997. Global Diasporas Ser. Print.

Edwards, Brent H. "The Uses of Diaspora." *Social Text* 19.1 (2001): 45-73. Print.

Gilroy, Paul. *The Black Atlantic: Modernity and Double Consciousness.* London and New York: Verso, 1993. Print.

_____. *'there Ain't No Black in the Union Jack': The Cultural Politics of Race and Nation.* Chicago, IL: U of Chicago P, 1991. Black Literature and Culture Ser. Print.

Hall, Stuart. "Cultural Identity and Diaspora." *Identity, Community, Culture, Difference.* Ed. Jonathan Rutherford. London: Lawrence and Wishart, 1990: 235. Print.

Janette, Michele. "Guerrilla Irony in Lan Cao's *Monkey Bridge.*" *Contemporary Literature.* 42.1 (2001): 50-77. Print.

Kingston, Maxine Hong. *The Woman Warrior: Memoirs of a Girlhood Among Ghosts.* New York: Vintage/Random, 1976. Print.

Lee, Regina. "Theorizing Diasporas: Three Types of Consciousness." *Asian Diasporas: Cultures, Identities, Representations.* Ed. Robbie B. H. Goh & Shawn Wong. Hong Kong: Hong Kong UP, 2004. 53-76. Print.

Nguyen, Viet Thanh. *Race and Resistance: Literature and Politics in Asian America.* Oxford and New York: Oxford UP, 2002. Print.

Safran, William. "Diasporas in Modern Societies: Myths of Homeland and Return." *Diaspora* 1.1 (1991): 83-99. Print.

Shepperson, George. "Pan-africanism and 'Pan-Africanism': Some Historical Notes." *Phylon* 23.4 (1962): 346-358. Print.

Tölölyan, Khachig. "The Contemporary Discourse of Diaspora Studies." *Comparative Studies of South Asia, Africa and the Middle East* 27.3 (2007): 647-655. Print.

Creating Meaning and Self-Affirmation through Stories: Existentialism and *The Woman Warrior*

Alex Pinnon

In *The Woman Warrior*, Maxine Hong Kingston presents a series of narratives describing a complicated negotiation between cultural identity, social norms, and the desire for self-affirmation and individual agency. Kingston, the daughter of Chinese immigrants, must try to make sense of the complicated nature of individual identity and how it relates to social rules related to gender and race, as well as to the cultural expectations associated with China and the US. Guiding the narrator are "talk-stories" associated with her mother, Brave Orchid, as well as a myriad of messages from the larger Chinese immigrant and mainstream American communities. Rather than clear-cut guidelines, the stories and messages prove to be confusing, contradictory, and worse, often denigrating to the narrator's identity. To counteract the negative messages, the narrator struggles to create new meanings through stories. In her efforts toward self-determination and agency, Kingston's narrator demonstrates the concerns of existentialism. Rather than focusing on the actions (or non-actions) of a protagonist in the pursuit of meaning, Kingston highlights the construction and telling of stories as an act of agency and self-affirmation.

The term "existentialism" refers to a philosophical approach developed in the late nineteenth and early twentieth century. Writers and theorists described as existentialist do not espouse a systematic or cohesive philosophy, which has resulted in multiple versions of existentialism. All of them, however, emphasize individual free will and choice and are concerned with the problem of finding meaning in existence. *Søren* Kierkegaard (1813–1855) and Friedrich Nietzsche (1844–1900) introduced foundational existentialist ideas in Europe that were later expanded upon and made popular by twentieth century French intellectuals Jean-Paul Sartre (1905–1980), Simone de Beauvoir (1908–1986), and Albert Camus (1913–1916). Fundamental works such as Sartre's play, *No Exit* (in French, *Huis Clos*, 1944), Beauvoir's study, *The Second Sex* (*Le Deuxiéme Sexe*, 1949), and Camus's essay,"The Myth of Sisyphus" ("Le Mythe de Sisyphe," 1942) explain the relationship between humanity and an objectively meaningless existence. In their respective works, this group of writers expresses a central claim in existential thought: "existence precedes essence." In other words, it is not enough merely to be alive. The qualities associated with being human ("essence") are not determined by existence. Humans are "condemned to be free" ("Being and Nothingness," Sartre), confined by social attitudes related to gender (Beauvoir), and responsible for deciding whether life is worth living and how to live it ("Myth of Sisyphus," Camus). For existentialists, the individual must determine meaning and create their own values. Reading *The Woman Warrior* through the lens of existentialism highlights the narrator's journey towards self-affirmation, which she accomplishes through talk-story, a type of narrative inspired by Chinese oral tradition at which her mother is particularly adept. Kingston's particular approach to self-affirmation and agency comes into focus through "a narrative conception of subjectivity" with which she is able "to improvise, to innovate, to re-invent, the stories into which she has been thrown" (Gatens 48). As the narrator adapts and expands upon stories she has heard from others, she creates new narrative forms and meanings that allow her to escape messages that belittle her sense of self.

Existentialism has been described as pessimistic, even nihilistic, especially with regard to its disavowal of the notion of an ultimate authority or objective meaning. It would be unfair and too simplistic, however, to portray this mode of thinking as merely negative. While existentialists place the responsibility (some would say, burden) for creating meaning on individuals, they also suggest the capacity for humanity to affect positive change in the world. Sartre, for example, argued that the lack of an ultimate authority made it imperative for humans to act responsibly and ethically. Paul Tillich, in *The Courage to Be* (1952), also describes a positive outcome emerging from the "anxiety" and "fear" that accompanies an awareness of the loss of meaning. Courage for Tillich is a remedy for meaninglessness; it is "the ethical act in which man affirms his own being in spite of those elements of his existence which conflict with his essential self-affirmation" (3). Kingston's narrator undergoes a process similar to the one described by Tillich; she acknowledges and confronts her anxiety about her identity and what it means to be a Chinese American woman.

For the narrator, the path to self-affirmation is influenced by socio-culturally embedded ideas about gender. In the stories she recounts, the narrator reveals "[t]here simply is no [gender] neutral position from which to judge" (Gatens 41). Individuals are subject to "the contingency of temporal being, the fact that [they] exist in this and no other period of time, beginning in a contingent moment, ending in a contingent moment, filled with experiences that are contingent themselves with respect to quantity and quality" (Tillich 44). Tillich uses variations of the word "contingent" to suggest the range of possibilities for and intersections of factors that govern an individual's sense of self and situation in life. For example, while the narrator, her mother, and her aunts share the same gender, their lives and choices differ depending upon where and when they live. Where the absence of a husband may lead to suicide (No Name Woman) or insanity (Moon Orchid), with a different set of contingencies, it could lead to adaptation, survival, and resistance to practices that denigrate women (Brave Orchid). Numerous times the narrator reflects on the constraints and contingencies of being female and Chinese American. She reflects on the negative comparisons of girls to boys ("Better to raise geese than girls" [46]); the Chinese practice of foot-binding and pressure in the US to be "American-feminine" (46); the heroic tradition of Fa Mu Lan, a warrior woman; and her mother's ability to gain social authority as a medical practitioner in China. Because of the ambiguous, even contradictory, meaning of these stories, every potential action carried out by the narrator contributes to her "anxiety of guilt," to borrow from Tillich, over failing to make the right choices and become the "correct" type of woman. In the context of existentialism, the recognition of our own freedom is a challenging and sometimes disturbing thought; as

Sartre put it: "Man is condemned to be free." By actively engaging in storytelling and interpretation, the narrator begins to cognitively recognize her anxieties, which in turn may lead her to participate in being (Tillich 179).

Kingston begins *The Woman Warrior* by recounting the narrator's story about "No Name Woman." The narrator explicitly points to this story as the driving force behind her work, revealing: "My aunt haunts me—her ghost drawn to me because now, after fifty years of neglect, I alone devote pages of paper to her" (16). Kingston is troubled by this story, because she can see the devastating effects of gender bias. The story also encapsulates the anxiety of becoming a no name woman, one who no longer participates in the active stories or creations being passed down. "It is as if she had never been born" (1), her mother tells her, reflecting the overarching context of nihility. The no name woman seems to have lacked agency. Her entire life, identity, and story are controlled by the rules that dictate a woman's behavior. The woman follows social convention when she becomes a wife; however, her husband leaves for opportunities in the US and does not return. During his absence, she engages in extramarital sex, quite possibly against her will, becomes pregnant, and faces the condemnation of her family and community. The man, however, goes unpunished. Feeling herself to be "without home, without a companion, in eternal cold and silence" and envisioning only an existence where "there would be no end of fear" (14), she drowns her newborn infant and herself. Her death, however, does not absolve her of the social condemnation, and it endures in those who will not speak of or acknowledge her; "there would be no marker for her anywhere, neither in the earth nor the family hall" (15).

The narrator, however, provides her paternal aunt with an imaginative marker by repeating her story. Her version highlights sexism and the double standard that punishes women, but not men, for sex outside marriage. Teasing out details elaborated from her knowledge of other family stories and traditional Chinese customs, she makes room in her version for alternative interpretations. Although "[t]radition dictates that "[d]aughters-in-law lived with their husbands' parents, not their own" (10), her aunt lives in her family compound. The narrator imagines opposing reasons for this; it either "hint[s] at disgraces not told [the narrator]" or "[s]he may have been unusually beloved, the precious only daughter" in a family with four sons" (10). Both could be true. In addition, infanticide becomes "a last act of responsibility: she would protect this child" (15). In this act, the narrator also finds "loving. Otherwise abandon it. Turn its face into the mud. Mothers who love their children take them along" (15). Reading against the meaning implied by her family's silence and social attitudes, the narrator breathes new life and meaning into the forgotten aunt's life. In the narrator's new version, she also restores the aunt's agency as she examines her ability to endure and ultimately decide her own fate. As a "spite suicide," who "drown[s] herself in the drinking water," her aunt avenges herself and her newborn child. In this way, the narrator can "see her life branching into mine" (8); she becomes a role model of free will and agency despite the constraints imposed on her by society.

The narrator also lives with the contingency of being female. She cannot change the fact that gender defines an aspect of her identity. Her mother tells her, "Now that you have started to menstruate, what happened to her could happen to you" (5). Although her mother points to a biological marker of gender, the aunt's story highlights the ways "[o]ne is not born, but rather becomes, a woman" (Beauvoir 301). Combined with the social construction of gender, the narrator must also contend with the contingencies of location and culture. She must "figure out how the invisible world the emigrants built around [her] childhood fits in solid America" (5). We see the intersection of these contingencies in the narrator's internal struggle to establish an identity. She admits, "I have tried to turn myself American-feminine" (11) and refers to attempts to "ma[k]e myself American-pretty" (12). For the narrator, "race, ethnicity, class, and so on, are made socially visible in the immigrant's case because of her non-normative status" (Gatens 47). The contingencies of her particular existence could lead her to a similar fate as that of her aunt. In the narrator's mind, she might be more vulnerable to this condemnation. While her aunt only had one culture to navigate, she has two.

The narrator continues to actively create meaning in her reconstruction of the legend of Fa Mu Lan in "White Tigers," the second section of *The Woman Warrior*. The original legend of the female warrior is believed to have been composed by a northern Chinese writer during the Tang dynasty, a detail scholars Ivy Hseih and Marylou Matoush find significant. Noting that Northern Chinese "were considered not to represent mainstream culture, being under the influence of foreign barbarians" (215), they argue that Kingston uses the story, learned from her mother, to suggest the theme of multicultural plurality and fusion. While the original version from the Tang dynasty illustrates filial piety (duty to family and/or elders), the narrator adapts and highlights details to convey her particular concerns about gender (Hsieh & Matoush 216). The story of the brave and heroic female warrior contrasts with other messages from the immigrant community: "we [Chinese girls] failed if we grew up to be but wives or slaves" (19). She pairs this reflection by speculating that a practice associated with female passivity is actually a sign of power: "women were once so dangerous that they had to have their feet bound" (19). Envisioning the possibility that women could again be dangerous, the legend becomes an inspirational guide. Like Fa Mu Lan, the narrator can become a woman warrior by seeking self-affirmation in the face of societal constraints.

An existential approach to "White Tigers" also highlights the multiple contingencies the narrator must navigate in order to make her own choices and define herself by her own terms and not those imposed upon her by society. After telling her mother that she "got straight A's" (45), which accentuates individual effort, her mother counters with a story that stresses community. "Let me tell you a true story about a girl who saved her village," she begins (45). This story that follows accentuates a couple of anxieties. The narrator must learn who her village is, and then she must discover how she is supposed to create meaning and identity from her relationship to it. The narrator's Chinese American identity has forced a complicated set of "villages" upon her. Is she in the village of the Chinese culture? Is she in the village of the American culture? In defining herself, the narrator seeks allegiance to multiple "villages"; however, each requires a different set of strategies to generate a positive sense of self. For example, she asserts her agency and independence in her refusal to be financially dependent on a man: "Nobody supports me at the expense of his own adventure" (48). And yet as a product of an era where "women loved enough to be supported," she feels "bitter" (48) when she finds herself without support. In her journey toward self-affirmation, the narrator must contend with her own internal bias.

The exploration of models of female agency and self-affirmation continues with Brave Orchid's recollection of her experiences in "Shaman," the third section. The use of the term "ghost" surfaces in a variety of ways. Brave Orchid uses "ghost" to refer to spirits of those who have died and to supernatural beings that represent malevolent qualities. She also applies the term to non-Chinese individuals whom she encounters in her day-to-day life in the US: "Taxi Ghosts, Bus Ghosts, Police Ghosts, Fire Ghosts, Meter Reader Ghosts, Tree Trimming Ghosts, Five-and Dime Ghosts" (97). Regardless of her usage, Brave Orchid's ghost references share a common theme: the loss of individuality and personhood. The talk-story about her encounter with a ghost underscores her refusal to cave into imposed gender roles. After the departure of her husband from their village in China, she resists the conventional role assigned to a "Gold Mountain widow," thus refusing to become a ghost, or at least ghost-like. Although her actions, thoughts, and purposes are circumscribed by the circumstances into which she was arbitrarily born; Brave Orchid works hard not to ever relinquish control of her future.

The sitting ghost described by Brave Orchid corresponds to a figure which appears throughout history and across a spectrum of cultures. In Western cultures, this figure is commonly known as a "night hag," or a "seated" or "sitting demon." Medical experts ascribe these descriptions to sleep paralysis, a phenomenon in which an individual experiences, just before falling asleep or upon awakening, the inability to move. This is accompanied by the sense that a "malevolent agent" is present (Green 588). Brave Orchid's demon has few physically definable features. It has "no true head, no eyes, no face, so low in its level of incarnation it did not have the shape of the recognizable animal" (72); its most notable feature is that it renders its victims physically immobile. The sitting ghost serves as a metaphor for the social constraints that are imposed on Brave Orchid. Much like the paralysis of the dream, social roles and designations can appear to paralyze our ability to make choices. Brave Orchid's winning strategy consists of talking to and insulting the ghost.

In describing her battle with the sitting ghost, Brave Orchid says that she lost her way, and summarizes her life up to that point as "so much work leading to other work" (71). Later in her story, Brave Orchid employs similar language when she describes life in America as a place "where a human being works her life away" (105). Both Brave Orchid and her narrator-daughter understand that their lives are not necessarily being guided solely by their own agency. Instead, their identities seem in some ways assigned to them; their next assignment may not necessarily come as a result of their own choice. This is a point often highlighted in existentialist writing. Individuals can lose their subjectivity in society and become objects; however, once a person recognizes their objectification, they may seek to rebel. The sitting ghost reenacts those moments when Brave Orchid lacked control of her own fate and thus put her existential meaning into question. In her recognition of her vulnerability, Brave Orchid rebels against traditional female roles by becoming another type of woman warrior, one whose identity will not be completely dictated by gender expectations. During her medical training, she took on other responsibilities, moving out of the domestic realm where she was primarily concerned with children, a husband, and following the commands of her mother-in-law. While Brave Orchid is often a source of anxiety and ambiguity for her daughter, she is also a positive source of inspiration. Much like Brave Orchid, the narrator rebels against a domestic role by pursuing her own individual desires in work and family.

Brave Orchid's story of the sitting ghost encounter also models the importance of community and recognizes the affirming aspects of different cultural practices. Brave Orchid's fight against the oppressive forces also represents the danger of alienation, a theme common to existential literature. Existentialism's focus on individuality derives from the idea that each person is essentially alone; this is what necessitates individual responsibility. The solitude Brave Orchid experiences, however, is only temporary. Her community performs a chant to "bring her home" to them and the story Brave Orchid recounts for them further reinforces their connection to one another. The importance of community in *The Woman Warrior* signals an expansion of existential thinking that accounts for Kingston's awareness of the ways racism and sexism affect individual identity. In response to prejudice against women and against racial minorities in both the US and China, forging an identity based on the sharing of mutual goals, cooperation, and a shared culture can be a strategy of resistance. This identity may not be dictated by a higher being or reflect a "universal" truth applicable to any situation (values rejected by many existentialists), but it can lead to self-affirmation. As a medical student, Brave Orchid embraces the anxiety symbolized by the sitting ghost to create something new. She and her classmates use creativity to improvise a community that embraces traditional spiritual elements and the new empirical elements of medicine. The future female healers "would have to back their science with magical spells" (74). They "changed the rituals" (75) by being "new women" (75).

The second phase of "Shaman" stands in direct contrast to the uplifting tale of community and self-affirmation. It illustrates the continuing challenges to self-affirmation and agency imposed by society. As in the previous talk-stories, this one is coupled with existential anxiety triggered by war. While the early descriptions of Brave Orchid as a doctor demonstrate an ability to establish a positive identity, her account of a "village crazy lady" she encounters at a clinic she founded in a mountain village during war years is a reminder of the contingencies of existence. War and the continual air raids visited upon the villagers reinforce their sense of futility and meaninglessness: "The bombing drove people insane. They rolled on the ground, pushed themselves against it, as if the earth could open a door for them" (94). Mirroring Brave Orchid's strategy against the "sitting ghost," the villagers create an object onto which they project their fears as a way to control them. Their actions are like those of Brave Orchid's classmates who bond and forge a community against a symbol of their fears; however, the villagers choose for their scapegoat a woman who is mentally ill, although generally thought to be harmless. She wears a headdress of small mirrors and performs a dance, "fanning circles, now flying the sleeves in the air, not trailing them on the grass, dancing in the middle of the light" (95) while airplanes pass overhead. Brave Orchid recognizes the artistry of the woman's dance, comparing it to something she might glimpse while "peering into Li T'ieh-kual's magic gourd to check the fate of an impish mortal" (95). The villagers, however, turn this display and the woman into an object of fear claiming, "She's signaling the planes" and "She's a spy. A spy for the Japanese" (95). The villagers take up stones and hurl them at the woman. Not only do they end this woman's life, but they continue to brutalize her by remaining with her after death and beating her until she is a singular "mass of flesh and rocks" (96). All of Brave Orchid's training could not prevent this event, and in the face of the woman's violent and senseless death, her earlier decision to build a hospital to help the villagers seems empty. The same day the woman is murdered, "the planes came again" and "the villagers buried the crazy lady along with the rest of the dead" (96). The profession she put meaning into and received meaning from becomes empty of meaning; Brave Orchid could not save, heal, or remedy.

In the following chapter, the narrator relates another talk-story concerning the existential struggles of another female family member. "At the Western Palace" recounts another challenge faced by Brave Orchid in her plan to reunite her sister and brother-in-law, who have been separated by an ocean for thirty years, she in Hong Kong, he in California. Moon Orchid's story shows similarities and connections to earlier accounts of the no name woman, Fa Mu Lan, and the "village crazy lady." Moon Orchid has been content living in Hong Kong without a spouse, but determined to have Moon Orchid confront her estranged husband. Moon Orchid's story highlights the importance of creating meaning in the process toward self-affirmation. It serves as a cautionary tale of what happens when individuals lose that ability.

Moon Orchid's marriage reveals vitally different expectations for men and women. It also highlights the contingencies of place as an influence on identity. Moon Orchid's husband left for America decades prior, like many of the narrator's elder male relatives, with the promise to send for her when he became financially established. As the years go by, he supports her by regularly sending money, but never actually sends for her. Moon Orchid is forced to "live like a widow" (153) while her husband goes to medical school, becomes a doctor, and marries an ethnic Chinese woman who is American. After moving to the US, Moon Orchid lacks the skills and aptitude to gain a job to support herself, and as a senior citizen, she lacks the physical stamina for the demanding low-wage jobs most often available to unskilled immigrants (136). Unlike her husband, she is unable to adapt and assimilate to American culture.

Brave Orchid's intentions are good. She wants her sister to affirm herself by demanding her rights as wife from her estranged husband; however, Brave Orchid does not urge her sister to employ the same strategy she had employed for herself. While Brave Orchid challenges social norms related to gender to affirm herself (while also resisting negative attitudes toward Asian immigrants), she encourages Moon Orchid to align and create meaning from socially prescribed roles as wife and mother. Moon Orchid never really wants to follow through with Brave Orchid's plan, and when she finally reunites with her husband, he explicitly rejects her, even passing her off as an elderly stranger in front of his younger wife. Moon Orchid is understandably devastated. Her identity, wrapped around the concept of being a wife, mother, and Chinese, is now threatened. When her husband points out that she is unable to fit the role of "wife" in an American context, she becomes "so ashamed, she held her hands over her face. They had . . . entered the land of ghosts" (153) where she is unable to adapt and create new meaning. Without the ability to adapt and forge another role in the US, Moon Orchid remains dependent upon other people in the midst of a foreign culture where few people, including her family, can understand her.

Unable to "construct a viable narrative out of these multiple and contradictory normative demands" (Gatens 48), she is consumed by emptiness and meaninglessness and eventually spirals into insanity (the medication she is prescribed, thorazine, suggests schizophrenia). Much like the "village crazy lady" Moon Orchid demonstrates how vulnerable people are to the arbitrary contingencies of fate.

Despite Moon Orchid's failed attempt to reunite with her husband in the US, the narrator finds a way to create a nearly "happy" ending (160). Just as she had done for her paternal "no name" aunt, the narrator teases out evidence of Moon Orchid's agency, albeit a limited version. Brave Orchid equates her sister's madness to a singular story, observing that, "sane people have variety when they talk-story. Mad people have only one story that they talk over and over" (159). After being committed to a mental health facility, Moon Orchid creates a new meaning for herself by "mak[ing] up a new story" (160) that imagines a familial relationship among the other female residents. Moon Orchid reclaims an identity based on a traditional female role—as a mother whose daughters are the other "inmates in the ward" (160).

The final section, "A Song for a Barbarian Reed Pipe," combines the narrator's mother's voice with her own. The story takes its beginning from Brave Orchid and its ending from the narrator. In her contribution, Brave Orchid recalls her grandmother whose predilection for live performances leads to the latter's conclusion "that our family was immune to harm as long as they went to plays" (207). This is a surprising interpretation of events that include robbery and a near-kidnapping during a family outing to the theatre. The narrator enters the mother's narrative by imagining a story that features actors entertaining her ancestors with a performance based on a historical figure, the famous poet, Ts'ai Yen, who was "born in A.D. 175" (207). After being captured by a roaming barbarian war tribe, Ts'ai Yen is taken as a wife by a chieftain and has two children.

Implicit in the narrator's rendition of Ts'ai Yen's life story are themes of captivity and female servitude. The brief description of her rescue, rendered in passive voice, suggests female passivity. She is not an actor and instead, acts are done to her and not by her;

she "was ransomed and married to Tung Ssu" (208). The reason behind her rescue further paints her as an object rather than subject; it is motivated not by an acknowledgment of her wishes but by her father's desire to "have Han descendants" (208). In recounting the poet's story, the narrator recognizes bias in traditional accounts. Following her mother's (and grandmother's) lead, however, she reads against typical interpretations by elaborating and accentuating aspects suggestive of female agency, thus providing an alternative meaning. Rather than building her story on female captivity and passivity, the narrator focuses on Ts'ai Yen's agency, particularly the power to create. While exiled with the barbarians, she sings "as if to her babies, a song so high and clear, it matched the [barbarian] flutes. Ts'ai Yen sang about China and her family there" (209). Through art, the poet refuses objectification by expressing her "sadness and anger" (209).

Not surprisingly, the narrator's skillful storytelling transforms the poet Ts'ai Yen into a warrior woman; she is "[l]ike other captive soldiers" (208). Her goal throughout *The Woman Warrior* has been to create stories that transform marginalized and objectified women into agents of social change. In this way, they become positive role models. Mirroring the central concern of existentialism, the narrator has struggled to find meaning within existence. In doing so, she grapples with sexist messages and racial slurs ("'chink' words and 'gook' words too" [53]), that permeate the cultural, historical, national, and social contexts she inhabits and is affected by. Through storytelling, the narrator, as female warrior, becomes an existential hero. While she cannot completely escape the stories and messages society imposes on women and racial Others, she can expose, resist, transform, and impart her own meaning onto them. Her stories not only "translat[e] well," they convey a positive Chinese American and female identity.

Works Cited

DeSazher, Mary K. "'Sisters in Arms': The Warrior Construct in Writings by Contemporary U.S. Women of Color." *NWSA Journal* 2.3 (1990): 349. *Academic Search Complete*. Web. 25 May 2016.

Gatens, Moira. "Let's Talk Story." *Critical Horizons* 15.1 (2014): 40-51. *Academic Search Complete*. Web. 25 May 2016.

Green, Thomas, ed. "Night Hag." *Folklore: An Encyclopedia of Beliefs, Customs, Tales, Music, and Art*. Vol. 1. Santa Barbara: ABC-CLIO, 1997. 588-589.

Hsieh, Ivy & Marylou Matoush. "Filial Daughter, Woman Warrior, or Identity-Seeking Fairytale Princess: Fostering Critical Awareness through Mulan." *Children's Literature in Education* 43.3 (2012): 213-222. *Academic Search Complete*. Web. 25 May 2016.

Kingston, Maxine Hong. *The Woman Warrior: Memoirs of a Girlhood among Ghosts*. 1976. New York: Vintage-Random, 1989.

Paradis, Cheryl, et al. "The Assessment of the Phenomenology of Sleep Paralysis: The Unusual Sleep Experiences Questionnaire (USEQ)." *CNS Neuroscience & Therapeutics* 15.3 (2009): 220-226. *Academic Search Complete*. Web. 25 May 2016.

Tillich, Paul & Peter J. Gomes. *The Courage to Be*. 1952. New Haven: Yale UP, 2000.

Mythopoesis and Cultural Hybridity in Maxine Hong Kingston's *The Woman Warrior*_____

Nelly Mok

> Chinese-Americans, when you try to understand what things in you are Chinese, how do you separate what is peculiar to childhood, to poverty, insanities, one family, your mother who marked your growing with stories, from what is Chinese? What is Chinese tradition and what is the movies?
>
> (Maxine Hong Kingston)

In *The Woman Warrior*, Kingston's narrator-protagonist addresses the Chinese American community while pondering her own relationship to Chinese tradition as an American-born Chinese. In doing so, she formulates the central questions to *The Woman Warrior*: What is Chinese culture? Does it contain an essential core to be uncovered under layers of personal and familial idiosyncrasies and stories? Where to draw the line between Chinese folklore and its multifarious variants? Kingston's choice *not* to draw such a line informs the parallel stories of the narrator who grows up in Stockton's Chinatown and of her Chinese-born avatar, Kingston's own version of the Chinese folkloric heroine, Fa Mu Lan. As this essay means to demonstrate, the writer's creative dialogue with Chinese cultural tradition is indeed what beautifully characterizes her memoir, permeating her writing and giving birth to a unique poetics of cultural hybridity.

Cultural Hybridity and "Revisionist Mythmaking"

In *Beyond Literary Chinatown*, Jeffrey Partridge endorses the notion that cultural hybridity names the condition of the subject who engages in "continuous negotiation between the foreign and the familiar" (166). One's self-(re)definition and perception of the world hinge on a complex processing of the cultural differences that compose one's education and structure one's social environment.

Cultural hybridity therefore implies the subject's active role in his/ her relationship to the Other's culture—the one of the dominant group and/or that of ancestors—stressing its creative potential as it is likely to give birth to a new, multivalent identity, which, far from being fixed, is continuously redefined, engaged in constant "hybridization." Cultural hybridity depends on the perception of culture as a sphere—instead of an invariable entity—which necessarily undergoes continuous mutations, a space for creative negotiation and contestation wherein cultural traditions and folklore can be reinterpreted, retold, and rewritten through the prism of the individual's life experiences and journey.

Cultural hybridity imbues Kingston's narrative, which sheds light on the transformations Chinese culture is subjected to both within her family stories—mostly told by her mother—and her own perception, shaped by her imagination and growing up in America. As Kingston insists, "The myths and the lives in *The Woman Warrior* are integrated in the women's and girls' stories so that we cannot find the seams where a myth leaves off and a life and imagination begin" ("Personal Statement" 24). Kingston's version of Chinese myths and legends results from her necessarily subjective, doubly mediated reception of Chinese folklore whose unfixed, variable nature makes it prone to distortions and additions both in the stories passed on by the immigrant generation and in her own American-shaped gaze and interpretation.

What drives Kingston's rewriting of the Chinese cultural tradition is her urge to provide a version of the myths and legends that resonates with the stories of the immigrant women in her family and with her own story as an American-born Chinese woman growing up and living in the United States. "I take the power I need from whatever myth," the writer explains, stressing the potential of mythopoesis—from the Greek noun "*mūthos*" (tale, story) and verb "*poiein*" (make)—or mythmaking to shed light on the ideological and ontological meaning of her American-based, American-shaped reality ("Personal Statement" 24). Only through a subjective interpretation and retelling of Chinese myths and legends can the narrator hope to reach her cultural and existential truth. Kingston resorts to what Alicia Ostriker calls "revisionist mythmaking," thereby contributing, like most women poets, to cultural revitalization/rejuvenation.

> Whenever a poet employs a figure or story previously accepted and defined by a culture, the poet is using myth, and the potential is always present that the use will be revisionist: that is, the figure or tale will be appropriated for altered ends, the old vessel filled with new wine, initially satisfying the thirst of the individual poet, but ultimately making cultural change possible. (Ostriker 317)

Kingston's mythopoeic rewriting of Chinese cultural tradition puts forward her notion of culture as a continuously fluctuating, mutating sphere and her fundamentally creative and integrative relationship to Otherness. What makes *The Woman Warrior* a groundbreaking life-writing narrative is Kingston's artistic contestation of a monocultural paradigm of self-representation through her aesthetic claim of cultural hybridity.

Kingston's Fa Mu Lan as Intercultural Heroine
Kingston's version of the story of Fa Mu Lan is striking for its various influences from the Chinese literary canon, as emphasized by critic Sau-ling Cynthia Wong in her essential analysis of traditional Chinese sources in *The Woman Warrior*. Such rich intertextuality suggests the preeminently intracultural dynamics of Kingston's mythopoeic work, particularly in her rewriting of the legend of Fa Mu Lan as part of the narrator's fantasy in the "White Tigers" chapter. Because Fa Mu Lan is not a historical figure but a folk heroine whose story has bred multiple versions in different literary genres ever since the Tang dynasty (618–907 C.E.) (Wong 29)—a parallel is commonly drawn between the "Ballad of Mulan" and the warrior song of Lady Mu in the *Book of Songs* (1122–600 B.C.E.), traditionally attributed to Confucius (VanSpanckeren 44)—she has stood out as malleable folk material prone to myriad alterations depending on Chinese authors' ideological purposes. Wong notes, for instance, that propaganda plays staged the Mulan story during China's war against Japanese invaders from 1937 to 1945 (29). Consequently, Kingston's bold,

syncretic retelling of the Mulan story partakes of the Chinese artistic tradition's mythopoeic relationship to one of its most prominent folk heroines. Among the various influences nurturing Kingston's version of the Chinese legend, Wong notes that a key feature of the young woman's apprenticeship is the evocation of "popular *wuxia xiaoshuo*, or martial-arts novels and their modern incarnations in the cinema" (30) in scenes depicting the would-be warrior's learning of meditation, self-defense, and asceticism as well as her journey in the mountains of the white tigers. The archetypal good-versus-evil plot of Chinese martial art novels underpins the story of Kingston's woman warrior who, through several trials meant to test her resistance and self-discipline, learns to master extraordinary strength and abilities that ultimately enable her to fight and defeat the evil enemy, thereby righting the wrongs caused to her family and to the oppressed (Wong 30).

Kingston ascribes new ideological meaning to the material she draws from Chinese cultural tradition: "The myths I write are new, American" ("Personal Statement" 24). In this way, she reveals the concurrently intracultural and intercultural dimension of her mythopoeic revision of the Fa Mu Lan legend. Cultural hybridization necessarily informs the narrator, as exemplified by her Americanized retelling of the Fa Mu Lan story. Kingston's version of the Chinese legend provides the narrator with a space for cultural negotiation wherein her ambivalence towards the Confucian tenets of Chinese culture can be thematized—most likely fueled by the 1960s–1970s American zeitgeist of ethnic-conscious and second-wave feminist movements shaping the sociocultural and political background of her youth and adulthood.

The beginning of the "White Tigers" chapter opens in the narrator's imagined China, the setting of her avatar's training and life as a Chinese warrior, daughter, wife, and mother. It then materializes into her American reality as a teenage girl growing up in Stockton's Chinatown and appears again when the adult narrator faces sexist and racist slurs in a white male-dominated society. Cheng Lok Chua interestingly points out the cultural "interpenetration" between the Chinese legend and the narrator's American experience: "Fa Mu

Lan's education into heroism starts at the age of seven (about the age at which many Americans enter grade school) and ends at age twenty-two (when many Americans graduate from college)" (149). Kingston's juxtaposition of the warrior-narrator's territories and journeys signals the culturally hybrid nature of her education and experience wherein her two cultural spheres constantly overlap.

Correspondingly, Kingston exploits the ambiguous ideological resonance of the "Ballad of Mulan." Some Chinese scholars claim a Confucian reading of the poem, while others stress its antipatriarchal stance, questioning the Han origins of the heroine (Wong 29). Kinsgton's choice to retell such a controversial ballad brings to the fore her fundamental ambivalence towards Chinese culture and Confucian beliefs, stemming from her culturally hybrid perception of herself and the world. By amplifying the subversive potential of the Fa Mu Lan story while ultimately asserting its filial exemplarity, Kingston's version of the Chinese legend both discusses the relevance of Chinese patriarchal education in her American reality and also escapes a narrow assimilationist reading.

Kingston chooses to amplify the subversive potential of the Mu Lan ballad by drawing on other Chinese sources to shed light on the woman warrior's mission. The scene in which the woman warrior's parents carve her people's oaths of vengeance on her back is inspired by the story of "Ngak Fei (Yue Fei), a historical hero whose mother is said to have carved four characters on his back" to ensure his patriotic loyalty (Wong 30-31). Kingston's choice to transform the four characters into an endless "list of grievances" (*Woman Warrior* 35) signals the juxtaposition of her familial and personal stories within her culturally hybrid perception. The words of anger and revenge, lining up on the woman warrior's back like soldiers, "words in red and black files, like an army, like [her] army" (35), abound since they name the myriad grievances of the oppressed—those of China's peasants, whom the warrior is to free from rich barons, and the narrator's family, who was chased from their homeland to the land of "ghosts" by Communists and who slave away for a decent life in America, but also of the narrator herself, who, as a Chinese American woman, has faced racist and sexist slurs from abusive employers. Drawing a parallel between her warlike Chinese avatar and herself, the American-born Chinese narrator formulates their common motives and mission:

> It's not just the stupid racists that I have to do something about, but the tyrants who for whatever reason can deny my family food and work.... Nobody in history has conquered and united both North America and Asia. A descendant of eighty pole fighters, I ought to be able to set out confidently, march straight down our street, get going right now. There's work to do, ground to cover. (49)

> The swordswoman and I are not so dissimilar. [...] What we have in common are the words at our backs. The idioms for *revenge* [italics in the original] are "report a crime" and "report to five families." ... And I have so many words—"chink" words and "gook" words too— that they do not fit on my skin. (53)

Commenting on that scene, Kingston emphasizes the empowering role of revisionist mythopoesis: "I mean to take [Ngak Fei the Patriot's] power for women" ("Personal Statement" 24). The author ascribes new ideological meaning to Ngak Fei's parable, moving the cursor away from its original patriotic moral to its potential for political—in particular, feminist—subversion. Indeed, what spurs the battles of the woman warrior—and of all the women warriors in the book—is her need to right the wrongs caused both by American and Chinese patriarchal tyrants. She has to face American enemies, "business-suited in their American executive guise, each boss two feet taller than [she is] and impossible to meet eye to eye" (*Woman Warrior* 48). In addition, she also has to stand up to the cruel baron, the emigrant villagers in Stockton and her sexist uncle—namely, all the Chinese purveyors of the Confucian sayings she heard as she grew up: "Girls are maggots in the rice"; "It is more profitable to raise geese than daughters" (43); and "Feeding girls is feeding cowbirds" (46).

The woman warrior stresses feminist claims in her confrontation with the baron. "I am a female avenger," she declares before beheading him and freeing his concubines who then become a "band of swordswomen," "a mercenary army" of "witch amazons" (44-45). Yet, her story paradoxically ends in a scene where she asserts her filial piety and her respect for Confucian patriarchal traditions. Definitively shedding her armor and putting on a wedding garment, the woman warrior readily vows to devote her life to her duties as a wife, a mother, and a daughter-in-law: "I knelt at my parents-in-law's feet, as I would have done as a bride. 'Now my public duties are finished,' I said. 'I will stay with you, doing farmwork and housework, and giving you more sons'" (45). As the woman warrior yields to the roles assigned to women in Chinese Confucian society, the model of "perfect filiality" (45) merges with the feminist icon. Such a conclusion offers the American-born Chinese narrator a symbolical space for cultural negotiation and compromise, which her mother has similarly called for: "[My mother] said I would grow up a wife and a slave, but she taught me the song of the warrior woman, Fa Mu Lan" (20).

The power of revisionist mythmaking, Kingston contends, is to shape and alter the lives that it inspires: "The myths transform lives and are themselves changed" ("Personal Statement" 24). As the narrator is told and retells the story of Fa Mu Lan, she grasps the telos of her life: "I would have to grow up a warrior woman" (20). Nevertheless, the warrior she has grown into is one who wields words, "reports" the harm done to her and her family, who "tell[s] on" her aunt, No Name Woman (6), and denounces the shame she was made to endure: "The reporting is the vengeance—not the beheading, not the gutting, but the words" (53).

"The artist . . . is her icon" (Wong 35)

Significantly, Kingston chooses to conclude her memoir with the story of Ts'ai Yen, the first acclaimed Chinese female poet whose existence, unlike Fa Mu Lan's, is historically evidenced (see Wong 32 and VanSpanckeren for more on Ts'ai Yen sources and biography). The title of the last chapter explicitly refers to a poem written by the Chinese poet, "Eighteen Stanzas for a Barbarian Reed Pipe," one of the three poems attributed to her. Comparing Kingston's version to the original "Eighteen Stanzas," Wong notes that Kingston's version is based on the main facts of Ts'ai Yen's life; however, it does not mention the poet's pain of leaving her children behind when she returns to the Han people, a feeling that pervades the three poems attributed to her (Wong 32). Rather, Kingston insists on Ts'ai Yen's feeling of estrangement as she is forced to adjust to her life among "the barbarians" and face the cultural and linguistic barriers separating her from her own children: "Her children did not speak Chinese. She spoke it to them when their father was out of the tent, but they imitated her with senseless singsong words and laughed" (*Woman Warrior* 208). In highlighting Ts'ai Yen's experience of uprooting and self-silencing in the face of her offspring's disregard for her native language, Kingston casts an American light on the Chinese poetess's story. Thus, she makes her both the "alter ego of the American-born daughter" (Wong 34) who tries to find her voice in a country where Chinese language is contemptuously mocked as "chingchong ugly" (*Woman Warrior* 171) and the representative of the generation of Chinese immigrants who strive to live among "ghosts," "barbarians." Ts'ai Yen is both the narrator and her mother.

Consequently, Kingston's version emphasizes the "communicative power of art" (Wong 34) through the song that the Chinese musician sings to the tune of the barbarians' instruments, her words imbued with homesickness echoing the stories of homelessness conjured by the Hsiung-nus' music: "Ts'ai Yen sang about China and her family there. Her words seemed Chinese, but the barbarians understood their sadness and anger. Sometimes they thought they could catch barbarian phrases about forever wandering" (*Woman Warrior* 209). Ts'ai Yen's song ultimately enables her to engage in a cross-cultural dialogue with her abductors and her children: "Her children did not laugh, but eventually sang along when she left her tent to sit by the winter campfires, ringed by barbarians" (209). Unlike Liu Shang, whose "imitation" of "Eighteen Stanzas" stresses Ts'ai Yen's welcome respite from cultural estrangement and asserts her allegiance to Han customs (Wong 35), Kingston endows Ts'ai Yen's final return to the Han people with transcultural resonance. Scaring silence away—that is, all the self-imposed/collectively-inflicted silences that knot tongues, mute female voices—with her sword-song, the poetess stands out as an intercultural icon, thereby shedding light on the American-born Chinese writer-artist's role: to give birth to a cross-cultural and cross-generational art, an art that "translated well" (*Woman Warrior* 209).

Kingston's final emphasis on the translatability of Ts'ai Yen's songs reveals her perception of culture as intrinsically evolving, prone to taking in and appropriating life experiences, familial and communal stories, and folklore, through translation, revision, and imagination. In the last pages of *The Woman Warrior*, the narrator insists "I continue to sort out what's just my childhood, just my imagination, just my family, just the village, just movies, just living," hence pointing to the rhetorical nature of her earlier question, "What is Chinese tradition and what is the movies?" (6). The version of Ts'ai Yen's story that culminates the mother-daughter story brings to light the fundamentally dynamic relationship of both immigrant and American-born Chinese to Chinese cultural tradition. Like Brave Orchid who, far from passing on a fixed collective folkloric knowledge to her daughter, lets family stories and Chinese legends twist, bend, grow, and expand in her practice of "talk-story," Kingston lets her imagination and American life experiences reshape Chinese myths in an ongoing, rejuvenating process of cultural appropriation and adaptation.

Therefore, Kingston dismisses the representation of the Chinese/Asian American writer as the purveyor of a dusty, static cultural stock allegedly endowed with an "authentic" core, a mere "cultural bridge" (Kim, *Charlie Chan is Dead* xvii) meant to promote his/her culture and help Western readers decipher Chinese people's supposedly inscrutable customs and mores. By retelling Chinese myths, she signals her refusal to be confined to the role of "ambassador of goodwill," traditionally assigned to Asian American writers in mainstream literary America ever since the end of the nineteenth century (Kim, *Asian American Literature* 24). To Kingston, culture's vitality and potential for self-renewal and rejuvenation lie in its very resistance to a fixed definition: "We have to do more than record myth. . . . That's just more ancestor worship. The way I keep the old Chinese myths alive is by telling them in a new American way," she insists in an interview (Pfaff 26, qtd. in Wong 31).

Kingston's Aesthetics of Mobility and Hybridity: Constructing a Multicultural, Pluralistic Self-Perception

Kingston, as Chinese American mythmaker, envisages *The Woman Warrior* as a space wherein cultural antagonisms are dismantled and her fundamentally dynamic, transcultural self-perception can emerge, both through the polyvocal composition of her narrative and through her poetics of fluidity. By blending her own story—which she concurrently recalls and imagines, weaving her version of Chinese folklore into it—with the stories of her Chinese female ancestors and relatives, Kingston prompts a broader communal resonance in a dialogic reading of her memoir in a way described by Wolfgang Iser, who defines reading as a "dynamic happening," the product of a "dyadic interaction" between the text and the reader. The Chinese American narrator-protagonist therefore stands out as a multivoiced, multifaceted woman warrior who necessarily thrives beyond cultural dichotomy.

A close reading of the key scene where the narrator, imagining herself as a fourteen-year-old novice warrior, experiences an epiphany at the end of her survival test in the mountains of the white tigers brings to light Kingston's poetics of cultural and ontological relationality. As she is about to engage in the second and last phase of her training and to start learning "dragon ways," the narrator acquires a new, enlightened perception of the world and of existence wherein cultures, living creatures and natural elements complement and "transmigrate" (28) into each other.

> I saw two people made of gold dancing the earth's dances. They turned so perfectly that together they were the axis of the earth's turning. They were light; they were molten, changing gold—Chinese lion dancers, African lion dancers in midstep. I heard high Javanese bells deepen in midring to Indian bells, Hindu Indian, American Indian. Before my eyes, gold bells shredded into gold tassles [*sic*] that fanned into two royal capes that softened into lions' fur. Manes grew tall into feathers that shone—became light

rays. Then the dancers danced the future—a machine-future—in clothes I had never seen before. I am watching the centuries pass in moments because suddenly I understand time, which is spinning and fixed like the North Star. And I understand how working and hoeing are dancing; how peasant clothes are golden, as king's clothes are golden; how one of the dancers is always a man and the other a woman. (27)

Beautifully highlighted in this passage, Kingston's writing is characteristically propelled by her philosophical and artistic commitment not only to relationality but also to translationality. Evidence of this appeared earlier in the "White Tigers" section when the narrator follows the bird-ideograph into the ink-washed mist of charcoal-rubbed mountains to start her training as a warrior (20-21). Echoes abound in the passage, flowering within and between the sentences composing the paragraph. In the first two sentences, the writer plays with words' ability to shift from one grammatical function to another: the word "dance" assumes the double function of a verb and a noun—"I saw two people made of gold *dancing* the earth's *dances*" (emphasis mine)—both calling for and complementing itself within the same syntactic unit. Similarly, in the next sentence, the word "turn" shifts from verb to gerund—"They *turned* so perfectly that together they were the axis of the earth's *turning*" (emphasis mine)—naming both the source of the earth's rotation and its dance-induced spinning. The key words "gold" and "dance," which are introduced in the very first sentence, visually and semantically pervade the passage—as enhanced by the subsequent occurrences of "golden," "dancer(s)," "danced," and "dancing"— illustrating how movement and light harmoniously cohere into the narrator's epiphanic vision.

Each sentence echoes the others thanks to lexical repetitions and thematic connections: as the first two sentences evoke the couple's and the earth's movements merging into one continuously whirling dance, the dancers' sensation of "light[ness]" and the bright "light" emanating from them spread into the next two sentences: "They were light; they were molten, changing gold." The shifting nature of the "gold" the dancers are made of playfully mirrors the lexical ambiguity of the adjective "light." Within the narrator's newly gained perception, gestures and sounds never die, the former expanding in kinetic suspension, the latter reverberating and amplifying: "Chinese lion dancers, African lion dancers *in midstep*. I heard high Javanese bells deepen *in midring* to Indian bells, Hindu Indian, American Indian" (emphasis mine). Cultures literally engage in a waltz as the dancers' ethnic origins and species vary and the plural referentiality of the word "Indian" whirls from one lexical partner to another. The bells soon dissolve, giving way to successive mutations: "gold bells shredded into gold tassles [*sic*] that fanned into two royal capes that softened into lions' fur. Manes grew tall into feathers that shone—became *light rays*" (emphasis mine). Central to such a seemingly illogical yet smooth series of transformations, stand—or rather, turn—the dancers, as suggested by the "light rays" shining from them and concluding the mutating process. The rich interplay of visual and sound echoes that abound in the passage characterizes the enlightened perception of the narrator, who has ultimately become blind and deaf to category boundaries.

Equally striking is the atemporal dimension of the scene wherein the past, present, and future merge before the narrator's eyes. Her "vision of existence as an alchemic cosmic dance" (Chua 149) culminates in the oxymoronic truths she asserts at the end of the passage, thereby invalidating boundaries in time ("Then the dancers danc*ed* the *future*"); dismissing social classes ("And I understand [. . .] how *peasant* clothes are golden, as *king*'s clothes are golden"); and deconstructing aporia ("I understand time, which *is spinning and fixed* like the North Star" [emphasis mine in preceding quotations]). The passage reveals the influence of Taoist philosophy on Kingston's writing, as emphasized by the dancing couple—the avatars of the immortals mentoring the would-be warrior—who embodies the primeval complementarity of all elements: "I understand how one of the dancers is always a man and the other a woman." After returning from the mountains and undergoing another eight years of training, the narrator attains a new "cosmogonic" consciousness (Chua 150): "I learned to make my mind large, as the universe is large, so that there is room for paradoxes" (29). The woman warrior's ultimate power henceforth lies in her ability to perceive the primeval impetus of the universe, namely the interaction of the vital breaths of Yin (essentially feminine) described as "receptive softness" and Yang (essentially masculine) described as "active force" that were engendered by the Tao or "supreme Void" (Cheng 59).

Transmigration permeates Kingston's writing, as in the lesson demonstrated by a self-immolating rabbit—reminiscent of the selfless Boddhisattva Rabbit, one of the virtuous animals embodied by Siddartha Gautama before he became the Buddha, and a symbol of Buddhist reincarnation: "I had met a rabbit who taught me about self-immolation and how to speed up transmigration: one does not have to become worms first but can change directly into a human being—as in our own humaneness we had just changed bowls of vegetable soup into people too" (28). Her writing thus metaphorizes the continuous process of cultural hybridization that is central to Kingston's aesthetics and the narrator's self-construction. Through her artistic commitment to deconstructing hermetic categories and to questioning cultural delineations, the narrator expresses her mistrust of self-binding allegiances and lays claim to all living creatures' primitive, ecological sense of belonging: "We belong to the planet now," she tells her mother, "Does it make sense to you that we're no longer attached to one piece of land, we belong to the planet? Wherever we happen to be standing, why, that spot belongs to us as much as any other spot" (107). Although the transnational turn of Asian American critique was not formally acknowledged until the 1990s, the narrator's statement here suggests the relevance of a transnational approach to Kingston's poetics of cultural identity in *The Woman Warrior*, a reading to which the author herself readily agreed at a 2011 international conference on her work in Mulhouse, France.

Kingston's mythopoeic rewriting of Chinese literary and folkloric sources partakes in the process of cultural hybridization that characterizes her life journey and shapes her identity as a Chinese woman growing up and living in the United States. In the face of critics denouncing what they consider to be irresponsible manipulation of Chinese culture and accusations of "fakeness" and inauthenticity (most notably Frank Chin), Kingston claims a personal, subjective, necessarily Americanized—albeit no less truthful—relationship to Chinese culture. By making her memoir an imaginative site wherein her culturally hybrid, even pluralistic and transnational self-perception can emerge, the Chinese American artist innovatively outgrows the accoutrements of the cultural ambassador icon assigned to ethnic writers within mainstream literary America.

Works Cited

Cheng, François. *Empty and Full: The Language of Chinese Painting.* Trans. Michael H.Kohn. Boston: Shambala, 1994. Print.

Chua, Cheng Lok. "Mythopoesis East and West in *The Woman Warrior.*" *Approaches to Teaching Kingston's* The Woman Warrior. Ed. Sau-ling Cynthia Wong. New York: MLA, 1991. 146–150.

Iser, Wolfgang. *The Act of Reading: A Theory of Aesthetic Response.* Baltimore, MD: The Johns Hopkins UP, 1978.

Kim, Elaine. *Asian American Literature: An Introduction to the Writings and Their Social Context.* Philadelphia: Temple UP. 1982.

Kingston, Maxine Hong. "Personal Statement." *Approaches to Teaching Kingston's* The Woman Warrior. Ed. Sau-ling Cynthia Wong. New York: MLA, 1991. 23–25.

_____. *The Woman Warrior: Memoirs of a Girlhood Among Ghosts.* 1976. New York: Vintage International, 1989.

Ostriker, Alicia. "The Thieves of Language: Women Poets and Revisionist Mythmaking." *The New Feminist Criticism: Essays on Women, Literature, Theory.* Ed. Elaine Showalter. New York: Pantheon, 1985. 314–338.

Partridge, Jeffrey F. L. *Beyond Literary Chinatown.* Seattle, WA: U of Washington P, 2007.

VanSpanckeren, Kathryn. "The Asian Literary Background in *The Woman Warrior.*" *Approaches to Teaching Kingston's* The Woman Warrior. Ed. Sau-ling Cynthia Wong. New York: MLA, 1991. 44–51.

Wong, Sau-ling Cynthia. "Kingston's Handling of Traditional Chinese Sources." *Approaches to Teaching Kingston's* The Woman Warrior. Ed. Sau-ling Cynthia Wong. New York: MLA, 1991. 26–36.

Truths and Tellings: *The Woman Warrior* and Kingston's Transformational Genres of the Real_____

Elizabeth Rodrigues

The question of the real has been central to critical considerations of Maxine Hong Kingston's *The Woman Warrior* since its publication. With "real" and "reality" in these debates variously used to refer to the reality of second-generation Chinese American experience, the historical facts of Kingston's biography, authentic Chinese cultural traditions, and global-political material histories, representing some form of the real is a task Asian American writers are frequently expected to undertake. Instead of adhering to a single definition of the real, however, *The Woman Warrior* instead launches Kingston's career of experimentation with the boundaries between fictional and autobiographical genres. Famously, in this work, Kingston does not distinguish between episodes drawn from her own memory, those that her family's collective memory may have passed on to her through oral storytelling, or those that blend traditional Chinese myth with personal imagination. She collates each of these sources of knowledge within the generic rubric of the life story. Kingston's sustained questioning of the presumed separation between story and truth, narrative and reality, requires her readers to reconsider the role of rigidly defined constructs of "reality" and "authenticity" in light of the cognitive and spiritual demands of a world globalized by both commerce and violence. While there have been numerous studies of the generic innovations of *The Woman Warrior*, there has been little work done to contextualize the question of the real in the longer arc of her career. This essay examines the genre experimentation of *The Woman Warrior*, alongside Kingston's later works *Tripmaster Monkey: His Fake Book* (1989) and *The Fifth Book of Peace* (2003). Together, these works constitute Kingston's persistent critique of narrative forms that constrain the representation and imagination of difference. By refusing and re-forming the boundaries of the real in autobiographical and fictional genres, Kingston interrogates and revises crucial underlying assumptions and overarching trajectories of Western and US narratives of Self, such as: that gender and ethnicity are identities achieved rather than Selves assembled, that peace is not a viable possibility and that war is an eventuality, and that creative practice is obsolete in an era of capitalist production.

Representation of the real is a burden frequently placed on *The Woman Warrior* and Asian American literatures in general, and it is also a shifting one. For the purposes of establishing a basic outline, we might say there are three distinct demands for the real placed upon these works: the desire of many mainstream audiences to gain knowledge of minority experience by reading Asian American texts; the political imperative to challenge stereotypes and Orientalizing discourse through the substitution of authentic history and culture for exoticized tropes; and, most recently, the challenge proposed by Asian American critique to refuse the formal panacea of multicultural pluralism and address longer histories and transnational frames of US empire as it has played out in Asian migration.

These demands can be seen throughout the history of *The Woman Warrior*'s reception. The desire to represent the reality of Chinese American life may even have begun to shape the text before its publication. Publisher Knopf's judgment that "it would sell better as nonfiction" (Outka 447) reflects a perception that mainstream audiences' hunger for knowledge about the Other and comfort with the narrative of the US as a haven from Chinese patriarchy was best satisfied by proffering the text as factual. Initial reviews were generally positive, but reviewers' comments, whether positive or negative, seemed to hinge upon the judgment of whether Kingston's was a typical story, sufficient to educate mainstream readers about Chinese American culture. A reviewer for the *School Library Journal*, for example, writes approvingly: "Kingston reveals to readers the very different world inhabited by her immigrant parents—the world of legends, folklore, customs, and manners of China" (Greenspan 108). Here, *The Woman Warrior* is valued for its (presumably) accurate revelation of a world deemed wholly Other. Other reviewers criticize the work for its departure from this pedagogical goal. Kingston, in her essay "Cultural Mis-Reading by American Reviewers," catalogs several examples. One reviewer complains, "Her autobiographical story (in my opinion) is atypical of the relationship between Chinese parents and their American Chinese children whom I have known" (58), implying this atypicality is a flaw and that Asian American literature should strive to represent the experiences of an entire group rather than those of an individual. Another reviewer writes with derision: "The background is exotic, but the book is in the mainstream of American feminist literature" (58). Kingston unpacks the double-edged dismissal of these words: "He disliked the book *because* it is part of the mainstream. He is saying, then, that I am not to step out of the 'exotic' role, not to enter the mainstream" (58). Whether being praised for seeming to represent the reality of Chinese and Chinese American life or condemned for not doing so, Kingston is circumscribed to dutiful reportage.

Reviewers within the Asian American literary community also criticize Kingston for failing to portray Chinese culture in ways they consider accurate. They fault, in particular, her departure from canonical versions of Chinese literary texts in her re-casting of the story of Fa Mu Lan. In their introduction to *The Big Aiiieeeee!: An Anthology of Chinese American and Japanese American Literature,* editors Jeffrey Paul Chan, Frank Chin, Lawson Fusao Inada, and Shawn Wong group Kingston with writers of "the fake," drawing, in their view "from sources in Christian dogma and in Western philosophy, history and literature" rather than focusing on "the real, from its sources in the Asian fairy tale and the Confucian heroic tradition" (xv). In his essay "Come All Ye Asian American Writers of the Real and the Fake," Frank Chin continues to develop "the real" and "the fake" as the essential criteria of Asian American literatures and argues that Kingston fails at the task of building real Chinese American culture. Chin accuses Kingston of taking a classic childhood rhyme, "The Ballad of Fa Mu Lan," and rewriting it "to the specs of the stereotype of the Chinese woman as a pathological white supremacist victimized and trapped in a hideous

Chinese civilization" (3). He sees Kingston and writers Amy Tan and David Henry Hwang as faking Asian American history and literature through their retellings of traditional tales in ways that, he argues, confirm rather than challenge mainstream American stereotypes of Asians. Chin's primary critique of Kingston is that she has substituted something fake—her own experiences and ideas in place of long tradition—for a real that would enable, in his view, more robust resistance to white supremacy.

More recently, critics including Lisa Lowe, Jodi Kim, and Kandice Chuh have argued that Asian American literary studies must develop a mode of Asian American critique, moving away from readings for and celebrations of individuals' representation of ethnic identity in a multicultural United States and toward attention to the material and historical conditions that give rise to discourses of ethnic identity. As Lowe influentially articulates in *Immigrant Acts*, the designation "Asian American" reflects not a pre-existing cultural identity or innate difference between people but instead arises from the historical need for capitalist formations to create divisions among the labor force through discourses that enable certain populations' exclusion from citizenship and labor rights. The question of the real here hinges not on the preservation of cultural authenticity but on representation of "the linked contexts of the migrations and displacements precipitated by the Cold War in Asia and domestic and global gendered racial formations" and on the "transpacific and transnational scope and imaginary that refract narrow national(ist) schemas" (Kim 5) that Asian American cultural products bring to the fore. Kingston's *China Men*, with its overt emphasis on global migration and economics, has been considered through this lens. In contrast, *The Woman Warrior* has not often featured as a primary object of inquiry in studies that pursue this project, perhaps in part because of its long-standing association with multiculturalist pedagogy or its seemingly domestic focus on Selfhood and mother-daughter relationships. Yet, its thematic grappling with the real, especially when contextualized in Kingston's larger body of work, is relevant to the concerns of Asian American critique in ways that have not yet been discussed. By examining Kingston's formulations of and challenges to ideas of the real in *The Woman Warrior*, *Tripmaster Monkey*, and *The Fifth Book of Peace*, we gain not only a sense of the vitality of Kingston's creative practice but also tap into a powerful vein of resistance to ossified narrative forms that underlie racism, militarism, and empire.

The Woman Warrior's relationship to the real is initiated by its subtitle, "Memoirs of a Girlhood Among Ghosts," which triggers its reading as autobiographical narrative. Kingston's use of "memoir" as opposed to "autobiography" as a subtitle positions the work as a "mode of life narrative that situate[s] the subject in a social environment, as either observer or participant" and "directs attention more toward the lives and actions of others than to the narrator" (Smith & Watson 274). The substantive generic claim is that the historical lives of individuals are being narrated. As Michael M. J. Fischer suggests, autobiographical writing is defined by a "commitment to the actual" (198) on the part of the author. In linking the work to a genre of the real, the labeling establishes a set of resonances, specifying a range of narrative strategies that the book will work within and against. Read as an autobiographical genre, the five sections that make up the book form both a challenge to and expansion of the boundaries of literary autobiography. Although critics have come to recognize autobiography as a form that can embrace complexity and "allow the autobiographer to see the discontinuities in 'identity'" (Gilmore 16), as a genre, it is historically thought of in a much more restrictive and reductive fashion. It is more often associated with "master narratives of conflict resolution and development, whose hero—the overrepresented Western white male—identifies his perspective with a God's-eye view and, from that divine height, sums up his life" (17). As Christi Rishoi observes, *The Woman Warrior* is instead a "radical departure from the familiar linear narrative of the autobiography" that uses "five separate narratives, only one of which focuses directly on her own experiences, to define the contours of [Kingston's] identity" (148). While it is no longer seriously assumed by critics that autobiographies contain nothing but empirical truth, the designation of an autobiographical genre prompts readers to see its words as referential in some way and, in some way making, through its representation, an argument about the real. By not only including but focusing almost exclusively on its narrator's extended imaginings' of others' lives, *The Woman Warrior* makes a case that fantasy and imagined worlds have a claim on the "actual" as well, and the truths she offers readers do not align with verifiable historical facticity or fall within the bounds of individual subjectivity as traditionally conceived. In addition to this epistemological challenge, her formations of truth highlight the inaccessibility and perniciousness of single, unrevisable stories leveraged as definitive truth.

Perhaps the most blatant challenge to a strict definition of autobiographical truth comes in the fourth section of the book, "At the Western Palace." This section imagines the narrator's aunt, Moon Orchid, visiting Los Angeles to confront her absent husband in the company of her sister, Brave Orchid, the narrator's mother. It challenges the expectations associated with autobiography almost as much as the mythical reverie of "White Tigers." The story of Moon Orchid's visit is pure fabrication, which Kingston confesses only at the beginning of the chapter that comes after it. As Sidonie Smith describes, "Out of a single factual sentence, Kingston creates a complex story of the two sisters" (164). Kingston's subtle but explicit designation of this episode as fiction, however, marks it not as deception but as an enactment of the lesson that the episode teaches the young Kingston. By clinging to one narrative and refusing to accept revisions or imagine alternate endings, Moon Orchid loses more than a marriage when she learns that her husband has taken a younger wife in his long absence. She loses her identity and her ability to function in the world. She has no other story to live by and refuses to create one. Brave Orchid explains to the narrator, "Mad people have only one story that they talk over and over" (160). A single story is a sign of insanity and fragility, while a resilient narrative of the Self is a history of revision and alteration.

Revision and alteration are not only a necessary response to personal trauma but also a survival strategy in the complicated legal and historical contexts of Chinese immigration to the US. In the final section of *The Woman Warrior*, "Song for a Barbarian Reed

Pipe," Kingston sums up the advice that her mother has given her about forming life stories:

> Lie to Americans. Tell them you were born during the San Francisco earthquake. Tell them your birth certificate and your parents were burned up in the fire. Don't report crimes; tell them we have no crimes and no poverty. Give a new name every time you get arrested; the ghosts won't recognize you then. (184)

Her mother's message, in essence, is that she should keep her true identity a formless secret so that she will always have the ability to recreate herself out of trouble. Owning up to a single life story could open her up to being punished for it. The perpetual recreation of Self has been a survival technique of Chinese immigrants, Kingston's parents included, and so often called upon that they claim no longer to know even their true ages (*Woman Warrior* 104). The empirical truth of their lives has never been as important as telling the right story to get immigration papers, legal passage for spouse and family, or a job. Kingston has no need to gain citizenship, but she does need strategies to create discursive and cultural space for the facets of her identity to coexist. She must preempt stereotyped readings, and she draws upon her parents' tradition of identity-shifting to do so. Even though her autobiography breaks with the cultural traditions of her parents, it retains their narrative strategies as its birthright.

Constructing a Self on shifting stories is not always a comfortable position for the narrator, however, just as it often proves frustrating to readers of *The Woman Warrior*. At times, her mother's insistence that "[w]e like to say opposite" (204) frustrates a daughter who longs for direct praise and honest appraisal. As she tries to sort through the mixed messages of the two cultures that compete to define her, she finds no stable history in the constantly reinvented stories of the family's past that her mother offers. Even as Kingston, the author, denies the reader any certainty as to the details of her autobiography, Kingston the narrator protests to her mother, "I don't want to listen to any more of your stories; they have no logic. They scramble me up. You lie with stories. You won't tell me a story and then say, 'This is a true story,' or, 'This is just a story.' I can't tell the difference"

(202). Maturity for Kingston, as indicated by the shared creation of the story of Ts'ai Yen that closes the book, is the slowly accepted knowledge that her truest inheritance may be the imperative to craft her own story of the real. It is an inheritance that will take her a lifetime to receive. In the voice of an adult, she writes, "I continue to sort out what's just my childhood, just my imagination, just my family, just the village, just movies, just living" (206). These multiple sources of the real, rather than cohering in a single version of what it means to be Chinese, American, Chinese American, or her individual Self, demand narration, the choice-driven weaving of multiple sources of truth, rather than enabling factual recitation that reveals a consumable autobiographical reality for readers to master.

From Memoir to Novel: *Tripmaster Monkey*

Kingston's first novel, *Tripmaster Monkey: His Fake Book* (1989), again reveals and defies generic boundaries between fiction and the real. Jeanne Rosier Smith describes it as a "boundary-breaking work that revises and reinvents cultural myths, resists conventional plotting, and unsettles the reader's comfortable assumptions" (49). Weaving together foundational texts of Chinese and American culture and bringing as much reality into her fiction as she was once wont to bring fiction into reality, Kingston creates a fictional world intimately connected to the real world and one that again challenges the idea that fiction and reality are distinct epistemological categories.

Despite being a novel drenched in myth, *Tripmaster Monkey* builds an elaborate architecture of the actual. The novel begins by locating its protagonist Wittman Ah Sing culturally, politically, and physically in the San Francisco of the early 1960s, an epicenter of counterculture as well as a locus of violence and exploitation due to the omnipresence of the Vietnam War and racism aimed at Asian immigrants on the western coast of the United States. In this context, Wittman is both one of the most recognizably American characters possible, a bohemian hippie "imbued with the 1960s challenge to corporate and military authority" (Simmons 143) and a minority figure pushed, economically and culturally, to the margins of American society. The novel opens with a meticulously charted trip from Golden Gate Park to Chinatown. Witmann waits for the bus specifically at the "corner of Arguello and Fulton" (7), passing by an encyclopedia of distinct locations before he walks "through the Stockton Street tunnel . . . and emerge[s] in Chinatown" (10). Kingston places equally concerted emphasis on concrete specificity about the materiality of Wittman's world. There is no activity too mundane to be recorded as a part of his life. The narrator is sure to specify, for example, that when "[a]t noon, Wittman got up and walked his bathroom gear" to the shared toilet where he lives, he also carries "his private roll of toilet paper" (43). Wittman's visit to the unemployment office in the chapter "A Song for Occupations" records, over the space of twenty pages, the entirety of his visit, as he waits in multiple lines and fills out multiple forms. Certainly, an emphasis on material reality is not foreign to the genre of the novel, but its inclusion alongside goddess-narrated instances of fantasy, myth, and a kind of magic realism is unexpected and jars the reader out of categorizing *Tripmaster Monkey* by any single style. It also challenges the reader's instinct to separate the world of the novel from his or her own world. Just when the reader might be tempted to disconnect Wittman from reality in order to understand his wild journeys—for surely no true reality could contain a character with as much energy, freedom, and creativity as Wittman—Kingston re-grounds her protagonist in a recognizable world and rhythm of embodiment. Kingston's insistence on precise detail roots Wittman in a way that forces us to imagine him as real, despite the fantastic plot of itinerancy and creativity.

The dense intertextuality of *Tripmaster Monkey* forms another grid of external reference upon which Wittman's story is built. Continuing and expanding upon a practice begun in *The Woman Warrior*, Kingston uses Wittman to retell foundational myths of China and the United States. Wittman Ah Sing is named after Walt Whitman, another American poet who "is concerned with the construction of the two entities, the self and the community" (Tanner 64). Wittman's character is also based upon the character, Sun Wu Kong, the Monkey King of the Chinese epic *Journey to the West*, who defends the monk Tripitaka on his journey back to

China with the Buddhist scriptures. Although neither Whitman's imagined community nor Sun Wu Kong are real in the literal sense, they link Wittman to a history of creative practice that seeks to re-shape the world. In American tradition, his namesake Walt Whitman is identified with the search for an American community that embraces expansive diversity, and in the Chinese tradition, Monkey is the guardian of the texts that will build a religious community of practice centered on meditation and interconnectedness. Wittman's literary ancestors present an interwoven lineage of those whose stories create communities.

Like *The Woman Warrior, Tripmaster Monkey* also utilizes a subtitle that makes a claim on the real. The subtitle, *His Fake Book*, refers to a practical "guide book of basic melodies that jazz musicians use when improvising" (Grice 87). Given the centrality of the terms "real" and "fake" to the reception of *The Woman Warrior*, though, the subtitle can also be seen as a bold claim for fakeness as a valid method of constituting community. This fakeness, though, is a specific and deliberately employed kind. A fake book, as devised by Kingston, challenges Chin's argument that Chinese myths must offer a single, fixed narrative. Instead, it holds a collection of starting points for the creation of other narratives. With its reference to jazz practice, it also turns away from single-author narration toward communal performance, as Wittman does. Ultimately, he finds that the poetry and fiction he initially uses to express Self and community are inadequate means of creating a shared cultural reality. He turns away from these forms and implicitly away from the genre of the novel and toward the stage play as a means of creating community and artistically representing "the life of the human soul receiving its birth through art" (276). Kingston and Wittman seek to use narrative to transform American society, but both find that in order to be effective, narrative must become public and shared, an "inventive, renewing, participatory text" (J. Smith 69). Wittman's theatrical production is defined by "[a]udience participation—they eat and they're sworn in in this blood ceremony" (145). He turns readers and watchers into actors and creators as he learns, "Community is not built once-and-for-all; people have to imagine practice, and recreate it" (306). Wittman must go beyond the static, private genres of the written into the improvisatory and public forms of theatre and music in order to turn a reading audience into a creating audience, just as Kingston uses the fictional genre of the novel to represent art touching the world. Her emphasis on geographical and quotidian detail, here, serves a vital purpose in rooting the utopian vision of Wittman's theatrical performances. By being asked to imagine all of the logistical details, physical burdens, and mishaps of such performances, the reader is asked to imagine Wittman's work as real and really changing the lives of its participants. Yet, just as reality frustrates narrative in its continual unfolding, the end of *Tripmaster Monkey* is anything but an ending; rather, the text opens into an extravagant and uncertain future. The narrator-goddess sends Wittman forward as a recombination of cultures, artistries, and philosophies, exclaiming in the final sentences, "Studying the mightiest war epic of all time, Wittman changed—beeen!—into a pacifist. Dear American monkey, don't be afraid" (340). As a pacifist, Wittman is something neither traditionally Chinese nor American. How he will continue to live this identity is a mystery launched into with only the admonition not to fear its unfolding.

Kingston's dense interweavings of world and story work toward the unified end of creating a character and a community empowered to recreate the real with their stories. *Tripmaster Monkey*'s relationship to genre mirrors Wittman's relationship to identity. As Royal observes: "Just as [Kingston's] maniacally heteroglossic protagonist opens up the stage to a dramatic redefinition of what it means to be a Chinese American, Kingston manipulates genre expectations in order to open up Chinese American representations as well as the very act of representing itself" (143). Just as *Tripmaster Monkey* reiterates *The Woman Warrior*'s critique of strict division of reality and story, it also transforms this critique into a mode of political action, one that is specifically anti-war and anti-racist.

A Bit of Both Memoir and Novel: *The Fifth Book of Peace*

The Fifth Book of Peace (2003) develops Kingston's purposeful confusion of the boundaries between novel and autobiography into a profound attempt to challenge American narratives of military violence and empire as she retells her self-story after suffering several losses. In sections side by side, the book recounts her own life in the 1990s and continues the story of Wittman's life. As Kingston describes it in an interview with Neila Seshachari, "this book enters a real nonfiction place, then flies to a fiction place, and then it grounds us again in a nonfiction place" (qtd. in Grice 116). It is, she acknowledges during the interview, a genre unto itself in its radical simultaneous inclusion of genres of fact and fiction: "I haven't seen another book like it, nor, once again, do I know how people will categorize it. Are they going to call it fiction or nonfiction?" (Grice 116). Again foregrounding identity and creation of community as process rather than as finished product, she continues to posit a vital connection between storytelling and real world-making.

The Fifth Book of Peace grew out of Kingston's intention to write a sequel to Tripmaster Monkey, in which Wittman would grow out of his Peter Pan phase and become a mature adult, a story she knew would once again require a reformulation of genre. In 1990, more than a decade before the publication of Fifth Book, she told Marilyn Chin: "There are books now . . . about grown men and grown women, but quite often they are tragedies. . . . People keep writing these tragedies, the tragedy of when you grow up. I would have to change the whole novel form to write it" (73). In this interview, she also hints that she herself may not be wise enough to tell this story: "This glimmering that I have of the grown-up novel—I don't understand it yet. I'm not sure that I'm wise enough myself to understand how to make him mature like that" (73). More than she knew, Kingston would indeed gain painful wisdom and maturity before the story of Wittman's adulthood could be written. Fifth Book begins with Kingston's house burning down during the October 1991 Berkeley Hills fire (known officially as the Tunnel Fire), which took place on the day of her father's memorial service. The fire also claimed the sequel to Tripmaster Monkey that was in progress; all of her printed pages as well as her computer were destroyed in the fire.

In this dramatic opening, so improbable that one might question its believability in the context of a novel, one day and three devastating losses thrust Kingston into vulnerability—which is to say, into an awareness of her inextricable relationship with the world beyond herself. This is apparent in her connection of the landscape before her with landscapes from the history of US military action. As she narrates traveling on obstructed roads through neighborhoods rendered unnavigable, Kingston splices together descriptions of Berkeley Hills with descriptions of Cold War zones and zones of the protracted Cold War, in which a good versus evil, us versus them logic continues to underwrite imperialist aggression long after the initial conflict for which these rhetorics and tactics were developed has seemingly ended (Kim 3-4). She describes "firewinds [that] blow over the top of the earth. You can see why people lived in tunnels in Viet Nam and Okinawa. (But months ago we bulldozed the desert sand into the trenches, and buried Iraqi soldiers alive)" (*Fifth Book* 14). She looks around, translating a landscape that used to be recognizable as her home into a view of Vietnam and Iraq, two proxy battlegrounds of US wars to secure economic and political dominance. The text's careful piecing of historical references, autobiographical experience, and fiction writing continues. The fusion of genre that *Fifth Book* employs is a product of trauma and reflects the slow process by which Kingston develops a mode of writing that reflects her new sense of worldedness. She now lives with a constant awareness of the multiple local, global, and historical frameworks of vulnerability, responsibility, and agency within which she moves. The first two sections of the book, "Fire" and "Paper," narrate the loss of her father, her manuscript, and her realization that she cannot simply re-write the material. She writes, "After the fire, I could not re-enter fiction" (61).

After a third section entitled "Water," which is the newly conceived version of the lost sequel to *Tripmaster Monkey*, Kingston enters the fourth and final section of the book, "Earth," in which she returns to the mode of autobiography to record how the process of coming to write fiction again has brought her into a new form of relationship with a community of veterans. Though she stated at the end of the second section that writing had become "selfish" (62), her re-engagement with Wittman's need to create community leads her to direct her writing outward again. She begins holding writing workshops for Vietnam veterans, and the final section of the book relates their incremental and halting progress toward the "happy ending" (241) that she sought for the war in the sequel to *Tripmaster Monkey* but did not find. While the past cannot be erased, it can be re-seen, and at the close of the book Kingston re-envisions her own past and revises the narrative of *The Woman Warrior* by retelling the myth of Fa Mook Lan (transcribed as Fa Mu Lan in the earlier work) as "a peace story, of homecoming" (Grice 124). Kingston writes, "I have told her story as a women's liberation story, and as a war story. But I now understand, it is a homecoming story. Fa Mook Lan leads her army home from war" (390). Revising the key assertion of what remains her most celebrated book, she writes "Oh no, I'm not a warrior" (256). Like Wittman, she has grown up. There is no return to former selves or former homes. What is possible is a new homecoming, and this is what she coaxes the veterans to find by constructing narratives of their lives that preserve pain and joy, restoring a fullness to their identities rather than erasing the past.

Tripmaster Monkey and *The Fifth Book of Peace* not only continue but extend a key claim of *The Woman Warrior*: "Be careful what you say. It comes true. It comes true" (204). As if to prove this assertion, she finds that one of the veterans who attends her workshop is a living version of Wittman Ah Sing. In *Fifth Book*, she writes, "Wittman Ah Sing has arrived. I made him up, and he exists" (290). The scope of narrative defines the scope of perception; expanding narrative possibilities expands the realities that one is prepared to recognize. Combining autobiography and the novel, this work can be seen as a culmination of an overarching narrative project. For Kingston, the stories we tell of the realities we live can form the path to peace and community, and she uses both the fiction and the nonfiction of these books to show how.

Works Cited

Chin, Frank. "Come All Ye Asian American Writers of the Real and the Fake." *The Big Aiiieeeee! An Anthology of Chinese American and Japanese American Literature*. Ed. Jeffery Paul Chan, et al. New York: Meridan, 1991. 1-93. Print.

Chin, Marilyn. "A *MELUS* Interview: Maxine Hong Kingston." *MELUS* 16.4 (1989–1990): 57-74. Print.

Chuh, Kandice. *Imagine Otherwise: On Asian Americanist Critique*. Durham, NC: Duke UP, 2003. Print.

Fischer, Michael M. J. "Ethnicity and the Post-Modern Arts of Memory." *Writing Culture*. Edited by James Clifford and George Marcus. Berkeley: U of California P, 1986. 194-233. Print.

Gilmore, Leigh. *Autobiographics: A Feminist Theory of Women's Self-Representation*. Ithaca, NY: Cornell UP, 1994. Print.

Greenspan, Miriam. Rev. of *The Woman Warrior*, by Maxine Hong Kingston. *School Library Journal* (January 1977): 108. Web. 4 March 2016.

Grice, Helena. *Maxine Hong Kingston*. Manchester, UK: Manchester UP, 2006. Print.

Kim, Jodi. *Ends of Empire: Asian American Critique and the Cold War*. Minneapolis: U of Minnesota P, 2010. Print.

Kingston, Maxine Hong. "Cultural Mis-Reading by American Reviewers." *Asian and Western Writers in Dialogue: New Cultural Identities*. Ed. Guy Amirthanayagam. London: Macmillan, 1982. 55-65. Print.

_____. *The Fifth Book of Peace*. New York: Knopf, 2003. Print.

_____. *The Woman Warrior, China Men*. New York: Everyman's Library, 2005. Print.

_____. *Tripmaster Monkey: His Fake Book*. New York: Knopf, 1989. Print.

Lowe, Lisa. *Immigrant Acts: On Asian American Cultural Politics*. Durham: Duke UP, 1996. Print.

Nishime, LeiLani. "Engendering Genre: Gender and Nationalism in *China Men* and *The Woman Warrior*." *MELUS* 20.1 (1995): 67-82. Print.

Outka, Paul. "Publish or Perish: Food, Hunger, and Self-Construction in Maxine Hong Kingston's *The Woman Warrior*." *Contemporary Literature* 38.3 (1997): 447-482. Print.

Rishoi, Christy. *From Girl to Woman: American Women's Coming-of-Age Narratives*. New York: SUNY, 2003. Print.

Royal, Derek. "Literary Genre as Ethnic Resistance in Maxine Hong Kingston's *Tripmaster Monkey: His Fake Book*." *MELUS* 29.2 (2004): 141-156. Print.

Simmons, Diane. *Maxine Hong Kingston*. New York: Twayne, 1999. Print.

Smith, Jeanne Rosier. *Writing Tricksters: Mythic Gambols in American Ethnic Literature*. Berkeley: U of California P, 1997. Print.

Smith, Sidonie. *A Poetics of Women's Autobiography: Marginality and the Fictions of Self-Representation*. Bloomington, IN: Indiana UP, 1987. Print.

_____., and Julia Watson. *Reading Autobiography: A Guide for Interpreting Life Narratives*. Minneapolis: Minnesota UP, 2010. Print.

Tanner, James T. F. "Walt Whitman's Presence in *Maxine Hong Kingston's Tripmaster Monkey: His Fake Book*." *MELUS* 20:4 (1995): 61-74. Print.

RESOURCES

Chronology of Maxine Hong Kingston's Life_____

1924	Tom Hong emigrates from China to New York City. After first seeking work as a poet or a calligrapher, he takes employment in a laundry.
1939	Ying Lan Hong immigrates through Angel Island to join her husband; their two children, born in China, had already died.
1940	October 27, in Stockton, California, Maxine Ting Ting Hong (湯婷婷; Tāng Tíngtíng) is born, the eldest of six American-born children. The Hongs support their family with a laundry business, but Kingston's father also sometimes ran a gambling operation, while her mother, who had practiced medicine in China, found seasonal work as a field hand.
1954-1958	Maxine attends Edison High School in Stockton, California.
1955	Publishes an essay, "I am an American," in *American Girl*, the official magazine of the Girls Scouts. She receives five dollars for the essay.
1958	Maxine receives eleven scholarships to attend the University of California, Berkeley (UCB). She enters as an engineering major due to her facility with math, but later switches to English. While at UCB, she works on the staff of *The Daily Californian* and participates in the Free Speech Movement (FSM) and the anti-war movement.
1962	November, Maxine Hong marries Earll Kingston, an actor.

1964	Joseph Lawrence Chung Mei Kingston is born, the Kingston's only child.
1965	Maxine earns a teaching certificate from Berkeley.
1966	Kingston begins teaching English and math at Sunset High School in Hayward, California.
1967	On their way to Japan, Kingston and her family stop in Hawai'i and decide to relocate there. She teaches English and writing at several schools, including Mid-Pacific Institute and the University of Hawai'i, over the next few years.
1976	*The Woman Warrior: Memoirs of a Girlhood Among Ghosts* is published by Knopf. It receives the National Book Critics Circle Award for Nonfiction.
1977	Kingston publishes the short story "Duck Boy" in the June 12 issue of the *New York Times Magazine*. She receives the *Mademoiselle* Magazine Award.
1977-1981	Kingston is visiting professor of English at the University of Hawai'i in Honolulu.
1978	Kingston receives the Anisfield-Wolf Race Relations Award.
1980	Kingston publishes *China Men*. It is named to the American Library Association Notable Books List. Kingston is honored as a "Living Treasure of Hawai'i" and receives a National Endowment for the Arts writing fellowship.
1980	*China Men* receives the National Book Award for Nonfiction. It is a finalist for a

Pulitzer Prize in nonfiction. Also in 1981, the Bancroft Library (UCLA) begins a collection of Kingston's papers.

1982	Kingston receives a Guggenheim Fellowship.
1984	With fellow acclaimed American authors Allen Ginsberg, Toni Morrison, Leslie Marmon Silko, and Gary Snyder, through the sponsorship of UCLA and the Chinese Writers' Association, Kingston visits China.
1984	Maxine and Earll Kingston relocate to Los Angeles, California; son Joseph remains in Hawai'i.
1987	Her *Hawai'i One Summer*, a collection of twelve essays, is published; the family moves to Oakland, California.
1989	Kingston's novel, *Tripmaster Monkey: His Fake Book*, is published. It receives the PEN/USA West Award in Fiction.
1990	Kingston is appointed Chancellor's Distinguished Professor of English at University of California, Berkeley. KQED in San Francisco produces a television program, *Maxine Hong Kingston: Talking Story.*
1991	October, the Oakland Hills firestorm, officially known as the "Tunnel Fire," destroys Kingston's home and personal belongings, including a book manuscript for a sequel to *Tripmaster Monkey*. She discovers the fire while driving back from a memorial service for her father, Tom Hong, who had passed away a month before.
1992	Kingston is inducted into the American Academy of Arts and Sciences.

1993	With money from a Lila Wallace Reader's Digest Fund fellowship, Kingston begins offering writing workshops for Vietnam veterans; the workshops eventually expand to include veterans of all wars.
1994	The Berkeley Repertory Theatre presents a dramatized version of *The Woman Warrior*; later in the year, the Huntington Theatre Company at Boston University performs it.
1995	The Center Theatre Group of Los Angeles produces the stage adaptation of *The Woman Warrior.*
1997	Kingston is awarded the National Humanities Medal by President Bill Clinton. She returns to teaching at the University of California, Berkeley. Her mother, Ying Lan (Brave Orchid in *The Woman Warrior*), passes away.
1998	*Tripmaster Monkey* receives the John Dos Passos Prize in Literature.
2000	Kingston delivers the William E. Massey Sr. Lectures in History of American Civilization at Harvard University.
2001	With Jack Hicks, James D. Houston, and Al Young, Kingston edits *The Literature of California*, Volume I, a highly praised anthology that begins with works by indigenous peoples and comes forward to literature between the world wars.
2002	*To Be the Poet,* based on her Massey lectures, is published.
2003	Kingston publishes *The Fifth Book of Peace*, in part a reconstruction of the manuscript lost in the 1991 fire.

2003	March, Kingston is arrested on International Women's Day in Washington, DC, for participating in an anti-War demonstration. Writers Terry Tempest Williams and Alice Walker are among her cell mates.
2006	Kingston edits *Veterans of War, Veterans of Peace*, a compilation of works growing out of her writing workshops. The Asian American Writer's Workshop awards her their Lifetime Achievement Award.
2008	Kingston receives the Medal for Distinguished Contribution to American Letters from the National Book Foundation, recognizing lifetime achievement.
2011	Kingston publishes *I Love a Broad Margin to My Life*.
2013	Kingston is awarded the National Medal of Arts for her accomplishments; awarded by the sitting President (in this case, President Barack Obama), it is the highest award given for achievement in the arts by the US.
2016	Kingston receives the Distinguished Achievement Award from the Western Literature Association.

Works by Maxine Hong Kingston_____

Prose:

China Men. New York: Random House, 1989.

The Fifth Book of Peace. New York: Knopf, 2003.

Hawai'i One Summer. San Francisco: Meadow, 1987.

Tripmaster Monkey: His Fake Book. New York: Knopf, 1989.

The Woman Warrior: Memoirs of a Girlhood Among Ghosts. 1976. New York: Vintage-Random, 1989.

Mixed Genre: Prose and Poetry:

I Love a Broad Margin to My Life. New York: Vintage/Random, 2011.

To Be the Poet. The William E. Massey Sr. Lectures in the History of American Civilization. Cambridge, MA: Harvard UP, 2002.

Essays, Short Fiction, and Poems:

"Absorption of Rock." *Iowa Review* 12.2-3 (1981): 207-208.

"A Chinese Garland." *North American Review* 273.3 (1988): 38-42.

"Bones and Jones." *Conjunctions* 13 (1989): 7-21.

"The Coming Book." *The Writer on Her Work*. Ed. Janet Sternburg. New York: Norton, 1980. 181-85.

"Cultural Mis-readings by American Reviewers." *Asian and Western Writers in Dialogue: New Cultural Identities*. Ed. Guy Amirthanayagam. London: MacMillan, 1982. 55-65.

"Duck Boy." *New York Times Magazine* (12 June 1977): 55+.

"Literature for a Scientific Age: Lorenz's King Solomon's Ring." *English Journal* 62 (January 1973): 30-32.

"El Lobo." *World Literature Today* 84.6 (2010): 17-19.

"Finding A Voice." *Language: Readings in Language and Culture*. New York: St. Martin's, 1998. 13-18.

"Imagined Life." *Michigan Quarterly Review* 22.4 (1983): 561-571.

"Kingston on Ethnic Theatre" in Letters. *Nation* (23 October 1982): 386.

"A Letter in Response to Lara Narcisi." *Connotations: A Journal for Critical Debate* 13.1-2 (2003): 179.

"A Letter to Garret Hongo Upon the Publication of *The Open Boat*." *Amerasia Journal* 20.3 (1994): 25.

"Lew Welch: An Appreciation." *Manoa* 25.1 (2013): 183-185.

"The Making of More Americans." *New Yorker* (11 February 1980): 34+.

"Maxine Hong Kingston: Exploring Old Myths in a Contemporary American Voice." *Humanities Discourse* 2.6 (1988): 3-5.

"The Novel's Next Step: From the Novel of the Americas to the Global Novel." *Mother Jones* (December 1989): 37-41. Rpt. in *The Novel in the Americas*. Niwot: UP of Colorado, 1992. 13-18.

"On 'China Journal' and Traveling with Charles Wright to Tu Fu's Cottage." *Northwest Review* 49.2 (2011): 96-97.

"Opening Speech." *The Legacy of Maxine Hong Kingston: The Mulhouse Book*. Zurich, CH: LIT Verlag, 2014. 21-29.

"Personal Statement." *Approaches to Teaching Kingston's* The Woman Warrior. Ed. Shirley Geok-lin Lim. New York: Modern Language Association, 1991. 23-25.

"Reservations About China." *Ms*. (October 1978): 67-68.

"Restaurant." *Iowa Review* 12.2-3 (1981): 206.

"Rupert Garcia: Dancing Between Realms." *Mother Jones* (October 1988): 32-35.

"San Francisco's Chinatown: A View from the Other Side of Arnold Genthe's Camera." *American Heritage* 30 (December 1978): 36-47.

"War And Love." *Living with Shakespeare: Essays by Writers, Actors, and Directors*. Ed. Susannah Carson. New York: Vintage, 2013. 433-439.

"A Writer's Notebook from the Far East." *Ms*. (January 1983): 85-86.

"Violence And Non-Violence In China, 1989." *Michigan Quarterly Review* 29.1 (1990): 62-67.

Interviews:

Skenazy, Paul & Tera Martin, eds. *Conversations with Maxine Hong Kingston.* Jackson: UP of Mississippi, 1998.

Work as Editor:

Veterans of War, Veterans of Peace. Kihei, Hawai'i: Koa, 2006.

Bibliography

Baker, Houston A., ed. *Three American Literatures: Essays in Chicano, Native American, and Asian-American Literature for Teachers of American Literature.* New York: Modern Language Association of America, 1982.

"Bill Moyers Interview." *Bill Moyers Journal.* Public Affairs Television, 25 May 2007. Web. 11 Sept. 2016. <http://www.pbs.org/moyers/journal/05252007/transcript1.html>.

Cheung, King-Kok. *Articulate Silences: Hisaye Yamamoto, Maxine Hong Kingston, Joy Kogawa.* Ithaca, NY: Cornell UP, 1993.

_____. "Self-fulfilling Visions in *The Woman Warrior* and *Thousand Pieces of Gold.*" *Biography* 13.2 (1990): 143-53.

Chin, Frank. "Come All Ye Asian American Writers of the Real and the Fake." *The Big Aiiieeeee! An Anthology of Chinese American and Japanese American Writers.* Ed. Jeffrey Paul Chan, Frank Chin, Lawson Fusao Inada, & Shawn Wong. New York: Meridian, 1991. 1-93.

Chu, Patricia. "'The Invisible World the Immigrants Build': Cultural Self-Inscription and the Anti-Romantic Plots of *The Woman Warrior.*" *Diaspora: A Journal of Transnational Studies* 2.1 (Spring 1992): 85-94.

Dong, Lan. "Writing Chinese America Into Words and Images: Storytelling and Retelling of the Song of Mu Lan." *The Lion and the Unicorn* 30.2 (April 2006): 218-233.

Grice, Helena. *Maxine Hong Kingston.* Manchester, UK: Manchester UP, 2006.

Ho, Wendy. *In Her Mother's House: The Politics of Asian American Mother-Daughter Writing.* Walnut Creek and Oxford: AltaMira-Rowman & Littlefield, 1999. Critical Perspectives on Asian Pacific Americans Ser.

Huntley, E. D. *Maxine Hong Kingston: A Critical Companion.* Westport, CT: Greenwood, 2001.

Kingston, Maxine Hong. "Reading Back, Looking Forward: A Retrospective Interview with Maxine Hong Kingston." Interview by Shirley Geok-lin Lim. *MELUS* 33.1 (2008): 157-170.

Lan, Feng. "The Female Individual and the Empire: A Historicist Approach to Mulan and Kingston's Woman Warrior." *Comparative Literature* 55.3 (2003): 229-45.

Lappas, Catherine. "'The Way I Heard It Was. . .': Myth, Memory, and Autobiography in 'Storyteller' and *The Woman Warrior*." *CEA Critic* 57.1 (Fall 1994): 57-67.

Lei, Daphne. "The Blood-Stained Text in Translation: Tattooing, Bodily Writing, and Performance of Chinese Virtue." *Anthropological Quarterly* 82.1 (Winter, 2009): 99-127.

Li, David Leiwei. *Imagining the Nation: Asian American Literature and Cultural Consent*. Stanford: Stanford UP, 1998.

Lim, Jeehyun. "Cutting the Tongue: Language and the Body in Kingston's *The Woman Warrior*." *MELUS* 31.3 (Fall 2006): 49-65.

Lim, Shirley Geok-lin, ed. *Approaches to Teaching Kingston's* The Woman Warrior. New York: Modern Language Association, 1991. 26-36.

_____. "Chinese American Women's Life Stories: Thematics of Race and Gender in Jade Snow Wong's *Fifth Chinese Daughter* and Maxine Hong Kingston's *The Woman Warrior*." *American Women's Autobiography: Fea(s)ts of Memory*. Ed. Margo Culley. Madison: U of Wisconsin P, 1992. 252-267.

Ling, Amy. *Between Worlds: Woman Writers of Chinese Ancestry*. New York: Pergamon, 1990.

_____. "Thematic Threads in Maxine Hong Kingston's *The Woman Warrior*." *Tamkang Review* 14.1-4 (Autumn/Summer 1983–1984): 155-64.

Madsen, Deborah L. "Chinese American Writers of the Real and the Fake: Authenticity and the Twin Traditions of Life Writing." *Canadian Review of American Studies* 36.3 (2006): 257-271.

Martin, Holly E. *Writing Between Cultures: A Study of Hybrid Narratives in Ethnic Literature of the United States*. Jefferson, NC: McFarland, 2011.

Nishime, LeiLani. "Engendering Genre: Gender and Nationalism in *China Men* and *The Woman Warrior*." *MELUS* 20.1 (1995): 67-82.

Outka, Paul. "Publish or Perish: Food, Hunger, and Self-Construction in Maxine Hong Kingston's *The Woman Warrior*." *Contemporary Literature* 38.3 (1997): 447-482.

Parrott, Jill M. "Power and Discourse: Silence as Rhetorical Choice in Maxine Hong Kingston's *The Woman Warrior*." *Rhetorica: A Journal of the History of Rhetoric* 30.4 (2012): 375-391.

Petit, Angela. "Words So Strong: Maxine Hong Kingston's 'No Name Woman' Introduces Students to the Power of Words." *Journal of Adolescent and Adult Literacy* 46 (March 2003): 482-493.

Rabine, Leslie W. "No Lost Paradise: Social Gender and Symbolic Gender in the Writings of Maxine Hong Kingston." *Signs* 12.3 (Spring, 1987): 471-492.

Reesman, Jeanne Campbell, ed. *Trickster Lives: Culture and Myth in American Fiction.* Athens: U of Georgia P, 2001.

Sabine, Maureen. *Maxine Hong Kingston's Broken Book of Life: An Intertextual Study of* The Woman Warrior *and* China Men. Honolulu; U of Hawai'i P, 2004.

Shu, Yuan. "Cultural Politics and Chinese-American Female Subjectivity: Rethinking Kingston's 'Woman Warrior.'" *MELUS* 26.2 (2001): 199-223.

Simmons, Diane. *Maxine Hong Kingston.* New York: Twayne, 1999.

Skenazy, Paul & Tera Martin, eds. *Conversations with Maxine Hong Kingston.* Jackson: UP of Mississippi, 1998. Print.

Smith, Jeanne Rosier. *Writing Tricksters: Mythic Gambols in American Ethnic Literature.* Berkeley: U of California P, 1997.

Stanley, Sandra Kumamoto. *Other Sisterhoods: Literary Theory and U.S. Women of Color.* Urbana and Chicago: U of Illinois P, 1998.

Takaki, Ronald. *A Different Mirror: A History of Multicultural America.* Boston: Little, Brown, 1993.

_____. *A Larger Memory: A History of Our Diversity, with Voices.* New York: Little, Brown, 1998.

TuSmith, Bonnie. "Literary Tricksterism: Maxine Hong Kingston's *The Woman Warrior: Memoirs of a Girlhood Among Ghosts*." *Anxious Power: Reading, Writing, and Ambivalence in by Women.* Ed. Carol J. Singly & Susan Elizabeth Sweeney. Albany, NY: SUNY, 1993. 279-294.

Winsbro, Bonnie C. *Supernatural Forces: Belief, Difference, and Power in Contemporary Works by Ethnic Women.* Amherst: U of Massachusetts P, 1993.

Wong, Sau-ling Cynthia. *Maxine Hong Kingston's* The Woman Warrior: *A Casebook*. New York and Oxford: Oxford UP, 1999.

_____. "Necessity and Extravagance in Maxine Hong Kingston's *Woman Warrior*: Art and the Ethnic Experience." *MELUS* 15.1 (1988): 3-26.

About the Editors

Linda Trinh Moser teaches and writes about multicultural American and world literature and women's literature at Missouri State University where she is professor and Assistant Head of the English Department. Her work has appeared in *Critical Insights: American Multicultural Identity*, coedited with Kathryn West, for which she contributed an essay on Sui Sin Far (Edith Eaton). She has published essays on "Feminism and Women's Writing," "Literature and the Environment," "Multiculturalism and Globalization," and "Vietnam War (And Anti-war) Literature" for *Contemporary Literature, 1970 to Present* (Facts on File, 2011), also coedited with Dr. West. Dr. Moser has edited and introduced the work of Onoto Watanna in *Me: A Book of Remembrance* (UP of Mississippi, 1997) and *"A Half Caste" and Other Writings* (U of Illinois P, 2003) and has been recognized with an Outstanding Faculty Advisor Award by the National Academic Advising Association.

Kathryn West is professor and chair of the Department of English at Bellarmine University in Louisville, Kentucky. She teaches primarily twentieth- and twenty-first-century American literature, women's literature, and women's and gender studies. With Linda Trinh Moser, Dr. West edited *Contemporary Literature, 1970 to Present*, part of the Research Guides to American Literature series. To that volume, she contributed entries on "African American Literature," "The Native American Renaissance," and "Postmodernism," as well as essays on a number of contemporary writers. Also with Dr. Moser, she edited *Critical Insights: American Multicultural Identity*, for which she contributed an essay on Sherman Alexie's *The Absolutely True Diary of a Part-Time Indian*. She is coauthor of *Women Writers in the United States: A Timeline of Literary, Cultural, and Social History* (Oxford, 1994), and she has published articles on contemporary American literature and women's literature.

Contributors

David Borman teaches for the Department of English at Bellarmine University. His essay, "Philip Roth, *The Human Stain*," was included in *Contemporary Literature, 1970–Present*. Other work has been published in *Research in African Literatures*, *ARIEL: A Review of International English Literature*, and *The South Carolina Review*.

Susanna Hoeness-Krupsaw is Associate Professor of English at the University of Southern Indiana in Evansville. She teaches all levels of modern American literature, modern Canadian literature, as well as humanities and composition courses. Her research interests include the family theme in the novels of E. L. Doctorow, fiction by Margaret Atwood and other women writers, graphic narratives, and the pedagogy of online instruction. Her recent publications focus on Marguerite Abouet's *Aya*, Mary Gordon's novels, and Amy Tan's *Saving Fish From Drowning*. Her interest in the role of family themes in American literature also informs her examination of the mother-daughter plot in the works of Kingston and Tan.

Rickie-Ann Legleitner is an Assistant Professor of English at the University of Wisconsin-Stout. Her research interests include American women writers, multicultural literature, disability studies, the artist figure, and coming-of-age literature. She previously contributed a chapter entitled "Four American Poets Explore Hybrid Identity Formation and Familial Relationships" to the Critical Insights volume *American Multicultural Identity*.

Lorna Martens is Professor of German and Comparative Literature at the University of Virginia. She is the author of *The Diary Novel* (1985); *Shadow Lines: Austrian Literature from Freud to Kafka* (1996); *The Promised Land? Feminist Writings in the German Democratic Republic* (2001); and *The Promise of Memory: Childhood Recollection and its Objects in Literary Modernism* (2011). She has published on authors including Butor, Freud, Musil, Kafka, Rilke, Hofmannsthal, Schnitzler, Valéry, Proust, and Benjamin, and on topics such as memory, poetic style, narrative theory and technique, psychoanalysis, and aesthetics. She is currently writing a book on women's childhood autobiographies worldwide.

Nelly Mok is Associate Professor in the Department of English at Université Paul Valéry in Montpellier, France. She is a member of the research unit EMMA (English-speaking World Studies of Montpellier) and of the French Association for American Studies (AFEA). In 2011, she received a PhD from Université Michel de Montaigne, Bordeaux, France; her dissertation title is *Writing of or From the Margin in Twentieth-Century Autobiographical Narratives by Chinese American Women Writers*. Her research interests include the issues of exile, diaspora, transnationalism, trauma, and memory in Asian American literature, particularly in Chinese and Cambodian American autobiographies and testimonies. She has given presentations and published articles on Gish Jen, Shirley Geok-lin Lim, Maxine Hong Kingston, and more recently on Cambodian American writer and activist Loung Ung. Her current project is a collection of essays on the notion of Otherness in twentieth- and twenty-first-century ethnic American autobiographies.

Christopher B. Patterson is Post-Doctoral Research Fellow at the Centre for Cultural Studies, Chinese University of Hong Kong. He received his PhD in English from the University of Washington and is Assistant Professor at the New York Institute of Technology in Nanjing, China. His articles have appeared or are forthcoming in *American Quarterly*, *Games and Culture*, *MELUS*, and the anthologies *Global Asian American Popular Cultures* (NYU Press, 2016) and *Queer Sex Work* (Routledge, 2015). He writes book reviews for *Asiatic*, hosts the podcast "New Books in Asian American Studies," and spent two years as a program director for the Seattle Asian American Film Festival.

Alex Pinnon is Director of the Darr Honors Program and Department Head of the Philosophy Department at Missouri State University-West Plains, where he has taught composition, literature, and philosophy since 2011. In his research and in the classroom, he focuses on multiculturalism, utopian studies, and neo-Existentialism. When not teaching or writing, Alex spends time with his family of four or traveling the globe with his students. He is currently developing a community activism program at his institution.

Elizabeth Rodrigues is Assistant Professor and Humanities and Digital Scholarship Librarian at Grinnell College. She received her PhD from the University of Michigan in 2015 and specializes in multiethnic US modernisms, autobiography, and critical data studies. Her work on immigrant and postcolonial autobiography has appeared in the journal *Biography*.

Anne Rüggemeier is Junior Research Group Leader at the Heidelberg School of Education (University of Heidelberg/University of Education Heidelberg, Germany). She has published a monograph on relational autobiographies in contemporary literature in English that focuses on texts by Hanif Kureishi, Alison Bechdel, Nancy. K. Miller, Rudy Wiebe, Pat Mora, and John M. Coetzee (*Die relationale Autobiographie.* Wissenschaftlicher Verlag Trier, 2014). She has also published various articles on life writing and medialization, multimodality, and self-narratives and autobiographers as family archivists. Her research interests include teaching multimodal literacies, narratology, illness narratives, and the field of literature and knowledge.

Jeffrey Westover is Associate Professor of English at Boise State University. His research focuses on American literature, especially poetry, and he has contributed review articles for the section on American poetry from 1900 to 1950 in *American Literary Scholarship* (2013, 2014). In 2004, he published *The Colonial Moment: Discoveries and Settlements in Modern American Poetry* (Northern Illinois University Press), which analyzes colonization and nationhood in the work of Marianne Moore, Robert Frost, William Carlos Williams, Langston Hughes, and Hart Crane. He has published articles in *The William Carlos Williams Review* (2014), the *Wallace Stevens Journal* (2009), and *Critical Essays on James Merrill's Poetry (1996)*, while his chapter on African American sonnets appears in *A Companion to Poetic Genre* (Blackwell, 2012). He has also published on Lorine Niedecker (*Paideuma*, 2010), James Merrill (*Classical and Modern Literature*, 1998), Herman Melville (*The Massachusetts Review, 1998*), and Henry James (*Style, 1994*).

Index